RE-EXAMINING PEDAGOGICAL CONTENT KNOWLEDGE IN SCIENCE EDUCATION

"This book provides a state-of-the-art overview of the most recent developments in PCK research in the world and identifies common themes and perspectives for future research. A distinct feature is the proposal of a consensus model of teacher professional knowledge including PCK. As such, this is a must-read for every researcher working in the field of science teacher education as well as science teacher educators who want to learn more about what to teach and how to teach it to their students."

Knut Neumann, Leibniz Institute for Science and Mathematics Education, Germany

"This book can offer guidance and direction for other science education researchers in pursuing the impact of PCK on teaching and learning in science. It is timely, and it is needed. It is an important resource for all PCK researchers."

William R. Veal, College of Charleston, USA

Pedagogical content knowledge (PCK) has been adapted, adopted, and taken up in a diversity of ways in science education since the concept was introduced in the mid-1980s. Now that it is so well embedded within the language of teaching and learning, research and knowledge about the construct needs to be more useable and applicable to the work of science teachers, especially so in these times when standards and other measures are being used to define their knowledge, skills, and abilities.

Featuring the most up-to-date work from leading PCK scholars in science education across the globe, this volume maps where PCK has been, where it is going, and how it now informs and enhances knowledge of science teachers' professional knowledge. It illustrates how the PCK research agenda has developed and can make a difference to teachers' practice and students' learning of science.

Amanda Berry is Associate Professor, ICLON, Leiden University, the Netherlands.

Patricia Friedrichsen is Associate Professor, University of Missouri, USA.

John Loughran is Dean, Faculty of Education, Monash University, Australia.

Teaching and Learning in Science Series
Norman G. Lederman, Series Editor

Re-examining Pedagogical Content Knowledge in Science Education
Berry/Friedrichsen/Loughran

Student Thinking and Learning in Science: Perspectives on the Nature and Development of Learners' Ideas
Taber

Integrating Science, Technology, Engineering, and Mathematics: Issues, Reflections, and Ways Forward
Rennie/Venville/Wallace (Eds.)

Rethinking the Way We Teach Science: The Interplay of Content, Pedagogy, and the Nature of Science
Rosenblatt

Exploring the Landscape of Scientific Literacy
Linder/Östman/Roberts/Wickman/Erickson/MacKinnon (Eds.)

Designing and Teaching the Elementary Science Methods Course
Abell/Appleton/Hanuscin

Interdisciplinary Language Arts and Science Instruction in Elementary Classrooms: Applying Research to Practice
Akerson (Ed.)

Aesthetic Experience in Science Education: Learning and Meaning-Making as Situated Talk and Action
Wickman

Visit **www.routledge.com/education** for additional information on titles in the Teaching and Learning in Science Series

RE-EXAMINING PEDAGOGICAL CONTENT KNOWLEDGE IN SCIENCE EDUCATION

Edited by
Amanda Berry
Patricia Friedrichsen
John Loughran

NEW YORK AND LONDON

First published 2015
by Routledge
711 Third Avenue, New York, NY 10017

and by Routledge
2 Park Square, Milton Park, Abingdon, Oxon OX14 4RN

Routledge is an imprint of the Taylor & Francis Group, an informa business

© 2015 Taylor & Francis

The right of Amanda Berry, Patricia Friedrichsen, and John Loughran to be identified as authors of the editorial material, and of the authors for their individual chapters, has been asserted by them in accordance with sections 77 and 78 of the Copyright, Designs and Patents Act 1988.

All rights reserved. No part of this book may be reprinted or reproduced or utilised in any form or by any electronic, mechanical, or other means, now known or hereafter invented, including photocopying and recording, or in any information storage or retrieval system, without permission in writing from the publishers.

Trademark notice: Product or corporate names may be trademarks or registered trademarks, and are used only for identification and explanation without intent to infringe.

Library of Congress Cataloging-in-Publication Data
Re-examining pedagogical content knowledge in science education/
edited by Amanda Berry, Patricia Friedrichsen, John Loughran.
pages cm.—(Teaching and learning in science series)
Includes bibliographical references and index.
1. Pedagogical content knowledge—Congresses. 2. Science—Study and teaching—Congresses. 3. Science teachers—Training of—Congresses.
I. Berry, Amanda, 1960- II. Friedrichsen, Patrica J. III. Loughran, John, 1957-
Q181.R38 2015
507.1—dc23
2014036556

ISBN: 978-1-138-83299-2 (hbk)
ISBN: 978-1-138-83300-5 (pbk)
ISBN: 978-1-315-73566-5 (ebk)

Typeset in Bembo
by Swales and Willis Ltd, Exeter, Devon, UK

CONTENTS

Preface ix

PART I
Introducing PCK: Issues, ideas, and development 1

1 PCK: Its genesis and exodus 3
   Lee S. Shulman

2 The PCK Summit: A process and structure for challenging current ideas, provoking future work, and considering new directions 14
   Janet Carlson, Laura Stokes, Jenifer Helms, Julie Gess-Newsome, & April Gardner

3 A model of teacher professional knowledge and skill including PCK: Results of the thinking from the PCK Summit 28
   Julie Gess-Newsome

PART II
Research developments and trajectories 43

4 Supporting growth of pedagogical content knowledge in science 45
   Kirsten R. Daehler, Joan I. Heller, & Nicole Wong

5 Science teachers' PCK: Understanding sophisticated practice 60
Rebecca Cooper, John Loughran, & Amanda Berry

6 Tracing a research trajectory on PCK and chemistry university professors' beliefs 75
Kira Padilla & Andoni Garritz

7 Assessing PCK: A new application of the uncertainty principle 88
P. Sean Smith & Eric R. Banilower

8 From portraying toward assessing PCK: Drivers, dilemmas, and directions for future research 104
Soonhye Park & Jee Kyung Suh

9 Toward a more comprehensive way to capture PCK in its complexity 120
Ineke Henze & Jan H. Van Driel

10 The PCK Summit and its effect on work in South Africa 135
Marissa Rollnick & Elizabeth Mavhunga

11 My PCK research trajectory: A purple book prompts new questions 147
Patricia Friedrichsen

12 Pedagogical content knowledge reconsidered: A teacher educator's perspective 162
Rebecca M. Schneider

13 On the beauty of knowing then not knowing: Pinning down the elusive qualities of PCK 178
Vanessa Kind

PART III
Pedagogical content knowledge: Emerging themes 197

14 Examining PCK research in the context of current policy initiatives 199
Aaron J. Sickel, Eric R. Banilower, Janet Carlson, & Jan H. Van Driel

15 Science teacher PCK learning progressions: Promises and challenges 214
Patricia Friedrichsen & Amanda Berry

16 Gathering evidence for the validity of PCK measures: Connecting ideas to analytic approaches 229
Sophie Kirschner, Joseph Taylor, Marissa Rollnick, Andreas Borowski, & Elizabeth Mavhunga

PART IV
Provocations and closing thoughts 243

17 Re-examining PCK: A personal commentary 245
Richard F. Gunstone

About the contributors 256
Index 262

PREFACE

In October 2012, a group of 24 researchers from seven countries met in Colorado Springs, USA, for a five-day PCK Summit, a working conference designed to foster conversation, collaboration, and consensus around the PCK construct. During the conference we were challenged to move beyond our individual research agendas and to work together to better understand the issues and concerns of PCK research and its impact and value to science teaching and learning. As a group, we identified the need for common terminology and definitions, robust assessment tools, and a consensus model of PCK.

Throughout our time together, we spent our days discussing PCK during sessions, over meals, and around the evening fire on the patio. From the diversity of inputs, workshops, and productive ongoing discussions, persistent research challenges became increasingly evident as, through close examination of the situation, a sharper focus was achieved; common goals were envisioned, and new collaborations were formed. After the PCK Summit, many of the participants shared Summit outcomes with colleagues, and at national and international research conferences. An important purpose for these conference sessions was to extend the conversations initiated at the Summit with a wider audience of teacher educators, graduate students, and researchers engaged in PCK research.

Throughout our time together, participants continually talked about different approaches to documenting their work and one tangible form of that documentation was through writing a book. Once the decision was made to pursue that outcome, in less than six months, we found a publisher, solicited chapter proposals, wrote chapters, engaged in peer review, and compiled this book.

Working together on this book has re-ignited the collective energy so apparent at the Summit and helped to bring the ideas and thinking back to the front of our minds as the chapters have taken shape and collectively, created a new research agenda. As co-editors, we did not want the book to be *about* the PCK Summit, but rather an opportunity for us to reflect on our learning as PCK researchers before and beyond the Summit. Therefore, although the Summit was important, it is what has been developed as a consequence that matters most to us; this book is one such tangible product.

This book is organized in four parts. Part I situates our collective work. It begins with a reflective essay by Lee Shulman, the 'father' of PCK who offers the history and thinking that drove the early work around PCK. Janet Carlson's chapter provides an overview of the PCK Summit, including the goals and supporting structures and is followed by Julie Gess-Newsome's chapter that attempts to present a consensus PCK model developed as a consequence of continuing collaborations after the Summit.

Part II consists of chapters written by individuals and research teams who attended the Summit, and explores their research trajectories. In this set of chapters, the authors explore their starting point as PCK researchers, how their work progressed, the PCK model(s) guiding their work, insights gained and challenges encountered in their work, reflections on the influence of the Summit, and future research directions. We deliberately chose this chapter structure because one rarely sees a researcher's trajectory; rather, we read individual published studies, without gaining insight into how one study influences the next, or the difficulties encountered in developing a trajectory.

Part III explores emerging themes and collaborations, and includes chapters from authors who took up issues raised at the Summit on the role of PCK in policy-making, the promises and challenges of PCK learning progressions, and the measurement of PCK.

Part IV concludes the book with an invited chapter by Professor Richard Gunstone, a distinguished scholar in science education, in which he offers his views on the ideas developed through the book and, in his closing remarks, shares his insights and provocations based on his reading of the chapters.

The PCK Summit brought together a small group of PCK researchers and provided a structure for productive dialogue. This book gave us the opportunity to reflect on our research, explore the influence of the Summit, and envision new directions for our work. It has been more than 15 years since the publication of *Examining Pedagogical Content Knowledge: The construct and its implications for Science Education* (Gess-Newsome & Lederman, 1999), which both captured and stimulated rich and productive PCK research in science education. In subsequent years, through our involvement in PCK research and our participation in the PCK Summit, we have come to understand the construct in more complex ways. And yet, as these chapters reveal, while we know a great deal, there is still much to learn.

It has been our pleasure to co-edit this follow-up book, *Re-Examining Pedagogical Content Knowledge in Science Education*. It is our hope that this book engages you in the ongoing dialogue around a PCK research agenda for the future just as it has for all of those who have been a part of this particular project.

Amanda Berry
Patricia Friedrichsen
John Loughran

PART I
Introducing PCK
Issues, ideas, and development

1
PCK
Its genesis and exodus

Lee S. Shulman
STANFORD UNIVERSITY

Background

When the contributing authors of this book met together at what became known as the PCK Summit, the first session was a video conference with Lee Shulman who offered a personal glimpse into his thinking about the issues, times, and events that have shaped PCK. Shulman typically presented a coherent, thoughtful, and well-structured presentation and invited the audience into his thinking in ways that gave insights into the history of PCK; a history that is important in understanding why this seductive construct has attracted so much attention from researchers for so long.

The chapter that follows is an edited transcript of Shulman's presentation and, as quickly becomes apparent, brings the construct to life in ways that build a deep understanding of PCK, its value, and the place of sophisticated knowledge in teaching.

The birth of PCK

In some ways I feel a little uncomfortable talking authoritatively about pedagogical content knowledge now. I feel like the biological father of a baby that was raised in its infancy and then given away for adoption or foster care when it was about five years old. During the years that followed, the youngster was raised by many parents and played with many peers. Now that it has survived adolescence and reached emergent adulthood, most of you know far more about PCK than I possibly could because you have been living with, developing, elaborating, revising, and applying that set of ideas in serious research and pedagogical work.

I have been caught up in a number of other topics in the last 30 years. Therefore, the most appropriate thing for me to do on this occasion is to take us back and re-think with you where this idea came from and what I had in mind when it was first conceived. What was its provenance? What was my motivation? And now, looking back at PCK and its evolution, what do I see as its strengths, but also what do I see as its weaknesses? I think that any idea, however generative, is a product of its time and circumstance. Any idea must be understood as a contribution to the conversation of which it was a part, not as a universal truth or generalization. PCK certainly has weaknesses, and I trust that many of you are shoring up those deficiencies, elaborating and going beyond its initial formulation, as should be the fate of any reasonably good idea.

A discipline can be organized in different ways

I have tried to ask myself what were the very first roots of this idea that I can remember? And what I remember is sitting in an undergraduate classroom at the University of Chicago with Professor Joseph Schwab in 1957 or 1958. Schwab was either teaching a course in the biological sciences or a course in the history, philosophy, and methods of science—I don't recall which because I was blessed with the opportunity to be his student in both those year-long courses. Schwab was regularly talking about a painfully difficult idea—the structure of the subject matter. He was wrestling with concepts of the structure of subject matter, the organization of knowledge, and how disciplinary organization relates to how people come to a discipline. He would later refer to the distinction between the substantive and syntactic structures of subject matter, and I believe he was engaging with the precursors of those ideas as he taught.

The Summit at which we are now engaged has been organized by BSCS, the Biological Science Curriculum Study. As Schwab described it to me (we remained close until he died in 1988), the scientists who were trying to invent BSCS as a curriculum in the late fifties and early sixties had come to a stalemate. They were attempting to create the biological curricular equivalent of the 'new math' and the 'new physics.' But they seemed unable to make any progress. Instead, they were constantly arguing. As he described the situation, Schwab and a couple of others had this great insight. Their insight was that the reason they were arguing is that tacitly they had competing conceptions of what counted as biology. And if you can't agree on what a subject entails, it's rather difficult to design a curriculum to teach it. Schwab and his co-conspirators made the modest suggestion that they should divide biology into three variations, divide the developers into three compatible groups, who then create three parallel curricula rather than continue trying to develop an elusive consensus on just one. Thus three BSCS curricula emerged—cell biology, structure-function biology, and ecology (forgive me if I have these wrong)—each representing contrasting starting points and syntactic and substantive structures for the discipline. The notion that the content of a discipline was not a 'given' but was a decision, a construction, a matter of debate and deliberation, left an indelible impression upon me. A discipline did not necessarily have but one structure (contrary to those who insisted on discussing 'the' structure of a subject matter); its structures depended upon how one organized the discipline for both inquiry and for teaching.

Connecting subject matter to pedagogy

Five years after arriving at Michigan State for my first post-PhD academic appointment, during which time I was primarily engaged in studying the problem-solving processes of teachers (a continuation of my doctoral dissertation), I was invited to join the faculty of Michigan State's new medical school because I was doing research on complex problem-solving and because I understood some of the factors associated with developing new methods for teaching novices how to engage with medical problems. We were inventing a novel curriculum for this new school, in which medical problem-solving was one of the organizing principles of the entire school, along with the importance of doctor–patient interaction, empathy, and communication. I was able to take my extant research program on teacher thinking and I shifted it entirely to looking at how physicians think and how physicians solve problems in the processes of medical diagnosis. Among the findings of this body of research, which we pursued for almost ten years in collaboration with my close friend and colleague Professor Arthur Elstein (Elstein, Shulman, & Sprafka, 1978) was the domain-specificity of clinical diagnosis. It was quite striking that although medicine was traditionally taught as if there was some generic cognitive skill called Diagnostic Ability, there was no evidence of the presence of such a general cognitive skill. Indeed, what we discovered about the ability to think like a physician—as we studied outstanding specialists in general internal medicine and how they worked on complicated medical problems—the great surprise that we brought to the medical world was there wasn't such a thing as Diagnostic Ability, that diagnostic knowledge and competence was domain specific. Physicians didn't have generalized diagnostic knowledge. They had domain-specific knowledge. If your specialty was cardiovascular medicine, and you encountered a patient who presented with a case of neurological dysfunction or of renal dysfunction, we could not presume that you would be very good at diagnosing it. Here was perhaps the most important finding of our studies in medical problem-solving, a finding that influenced both assessment and teaching in medical education, and I didn't immediately see its relevance for my primary field, the study of teaching at the primary and secondary levels.

In the mid-1970s, my MSU colleagues and I took our general strategies and methods for studying medical thinking and applied them to the study of pedagogical reasoning and decision-making among teachers. We took a cognitive (though not yet a domain-specific) approach to the study of teaching, and using that model we received substantial government funding to create the Institute for Research on Teaching (IRT) at Michigan State. The big contribution of the IRT was to shift the focus of research on teaching, from the then-dominant behaviorist paradigm for research on teacher behavior that was called process–product research, to research on teacher thinking, teacher knowledge, teacher planning, teacher decision-making, and teachers' conceptions of their subject matter and how that related to how they performed. It was really quite a major shift, and it helped lead the field in quite new directions. What strikes me looking back on those years, for some of which we were doing the medical and pedagogical research concurrently, is we were so invested in looking at teacher knowledge and thinking that we never connected questions of subject matter content to that. We never examined how teacher thinking was domain specific. The work on teacher planning was work on teacher planning generically. It was not differentiated to look at the differences between planning in the teaching of mathematics and the teaching of history.

And so it was that in the early eighties, shortly after I moved to Stanford after two productive decades at Michigan State in the teacher education programs, the medical school and the IRT, the notion that there was a 'missing paradigm' in the study of teaching and teacher education hit me between the eyes. It was embodied in the title that Susan Stodolsky later gave to her important book *The Subject Matters* (Stodolsky, 1988). It really matters. The deep problem of process–product research was not simply that it ignored teacher thinking and only looked at teacher behavior; it treated the skills of teaching simply and generically. Indeed, even the cognitive approaches that we pioneered at the IRT could be indicted on those grounds. That's when we began the work that became the work on PCK. But where did this notion of PCK come from in more immediate terms?

Inferring the existence of PCK without actually locating it

I look back on the speculations regarding PCK as similar to the way in which astronomers discovered the planet Neptune. We were comfortable using the idea of teacher content knowledge; we knew that there was a category called content knowledge. There had been a lot of research on content knowledge and one of the striking things about the empirical relationship between content knowledge and the quality of teaching was that the coefficients and beta weights were far weaker than we thought they ought to be and there was a lot of variation in those values. By the same token we had several decades of experience measuring generic pedagogical skill and knowledge and those constructs appeared to have better correlations with teaching and a teaching practice than content knowledge alone. And yet pedagogical skill was relentlessly domain-independent and generic. I think it was only when we began to think that way that we were able to put together the much older findings from medicine and think, "You know what? If the work of a physician and the quality of a physician's diagnoses and treatment decisions are domain specific, isn't this the case with teaching as well? Isn't there a missing 'planet' between content and pedagogy that defines the essential missing aspect of teaching?" Thus did the work on PCK begin.

Evolution of PCK: Teacher knowledge is domain specific and contextualized

The research began with a multi-year study called *The Teacher Knowledge Project* supported by a grant from the Spencer Foundation. With the participation of several generations of remarkable graduate students, we studied how new secondary school teachers learn to teach within the content areas of science, math, English, and history. Slowly but surely the knowledge grew. Studies were conducted within disciplines as well as between them. Maher Hashweh studied how middle school teachers' instruction on topics in physical sciences and biological sciences (often taught together in the general science middle school curriculum) were taught quite differently depending on the depth and quality of a given teacher's grasp of both the content and associated pedagogy of those topics. Pam Grossman discovered how the same teacher's approach to teaching English literature changed when teaching the same students the rules of grammar. Bill Carlsen described how biology teachers' planning and teaching within a year-long biology course for the same class changed when they moved from aspects of biology whose content and pedagogy they knew well, for example ecology or the physiology of organ systems, to topics they found more difficult to teach, for example genetics.

As we were pursuing this research and moving ahead in articulating a conception of content knowledge, pedagogical knowledge, and PCK (Shulman, 1986), there arose a very critical challenge and opportunity. Gary Sykes (also among the cohort of graduate students) and I were invited by the Carnegie Corporation's Commission on the Future of the Teaching Profession to do a policy analysis of whether a medicine-like National Board would make the kind of sense in teaching as it did to define and govern standards of medical knowledge and practice.

In the policy paper we wrote, *A National Board for Teaching: In search of a Bold Standard*, (Shulman & Sykes, 1986), we came to three conclusions. One was that a National Board was a fine idea, well worth establishing and supporting. Teaching ought to have its own National Board with an associated program of quality assessment. The second conclusion was that it couldn't have just one board and a single assessment because teaching was not a singular practice. Really accomplished teaching had to be looked at contextually which meant it had to be content specific. So we proposed that there be different boards for different teachers who taught different subject matters at different age levels. The third thing we argued was if you try to measure accomplished teaching and the understandings and skills needed to engage in such teaching by using the kinds of assessment methods that were currently extant, more harm than good would be brought upon the teaching profession. Extant assessment methods tended to be some combination of multiple-choice tests of teaching and generic observation schedules used generally by principals who visited classrooms for thirty minutes at a time, and didn't need to know the subject matter being taught.

The challenge to develop a theoretical rationale for a National Board was turned on its head when I was given the challenge by the Carnegie Corporation to lead a research group to design this National Board assessment for teachers that Sykes and I had described in principle, primarily by calling attention to what it should avoid. When I accepted that challenge, it was clear that any assessments of teaching competence would have to be domain specific. A new assessment wasn't going to look like the one-size-fits-all National Teacher's Examination of the ETS (Educational Testing Service). The assessment system we created, designed, revised, field tested, and handed over to the newly organized National Board during that period reflected our research and thinking about PCK. It is domain specific. It is also development-level specific, vis-à-vis the students being taught. We initially devoted two years to developing very complex assessments that were simulations of the many facets of domain-specific teaching. Our cases-in-point were elementary-level mathematics and secondary history. When we appreciated the limitations of the simulation-based four-day assessment center (it was not an inexpensive endeavor), we turned to a portfolio-based system that was field tested in elementary language arts and secondary biology. Angelo Collins, who later led the science standards project for the National Academy of Sciences and was the founding executive director of the Knowles Science Teaching Foundation program, directed our work in secondary biology. In all this work, attention was carefully directed at the intersection of pedagogy and content, at what teachers needed to know and be able to do in order to teach the content and skills of the curriculum to students of different ages and backgrounds. It was applied PCK on steroids.

The reason we shifted from a simulation-based assessment system to a year-long portfolio-based assessment documenting in a structured fashion the teaching and learning that occurred in teachers' classrooms foreshadows the comments I shall soon make about some of the limitations of the original PCK idea. We moved to portfolios because we came to recognize that domain-specific teacher knowledge couldn't be rendered operational unless it is also contextualized. Paraphrasing Schwab's commonplaces, teachers teach what they teach to specific students in some setting. Unless you have a mode of assessment that can document the students they were teaching, the specific content, the instructional setting, and, in some manner, the 'historical' context in which they were teaching over a school year (early or late, during a heavy testing period or before the holidays), you would have a much impoverished measure of teaching competence. The subject mattered, but so did lots of other things.

Challenges of defining a domain

The claim of domain-specificity is very important and also highly elusive. What counts as a domain? Is it a discipline, specific topics or problems within a traditional discipline, a broad hybrid space that encompasses several disciplines, a field of practice or policy? It's different in different settings, in different kinds of schools and cultures and what functions as a domain will depend on the interaction of all those factors. I was stimulated by a note that Deborah Ball and Magdalene Lampert wrote to me many years ago from the perspective of teaching practice, that suggested that the 'strategic knowledge' I had posited as a critical feature of PCK was not to be construed as 'something' that teachers had in their heads but was a more dynamic construct that described the processes that teachers employed when confronted with the challenge of teaching particular subjects to particular learners in specific settings. It is a place in your thinking and acting as a teacher that you know you have to address every time you get to teach in these situations. There are indeed some kinds of knowledge such as powerful pedagogical representations (e.g., analogies, metaphors, narratives, physical models) that can be acquired and transformed by teachers when designing instruction in predictably difficult areas, for example, aspects of evolutionary biology and conceptions of chance, adaptation, and survival. But these forms of high-leverage knowledge and the teaching practices associated with them are a generative starting-point for teachers. They are not the sum of their pedagogical know-how.

Limitations of the original PCK formulation

What are some of the real weaknesses and limitations of the original formulations of what we now fondly know as PCK? Let us remember that the idea was put forward at a particular point in time, in the midst of a set of conversations and debates about education as theory, practice, policy, and moral action. The form that PCK took in those years was a function, in large measure, of the discourse that was ongoing at the time. It was a response to a set of prevailing views that treated teaching as process without content, and teachers as skilled actors without minds, emotions, and careers.

The first limitation is that PCK as I originally conceived it was devoid of emotion, affect, feelings, and motivation, all of the non-cognitive attributes. It also gave short shrift to the moral character of teaching, an aspect of my work that so annoyed one of my former teachers, Philip Jackson. I was so intent on combatting the missing paradigm of content that I did not devote attention to affect and motivation, nor to moral judgment and reasoning in teaching. This is such an important missing piece. The affective aspects of teacher understanding and action are important both because a lot of what teachers 'know and do' is connected to their own affective and motivation states, as well as their ability to influence the feelings, motives, persistence, and identity formation processes of their students. All of this is also related to their normative vision for the kind of world to which they aspire to contribute as professional educators and as citizens in democratic society. If you think about how important social justice perspectives have been in teacher education in the last 20 years, part of it is because the notion of a good society, of an equitable society, of a just society, and all of the feelings that go along with that should not be ignored. I did not pay attention to those issues in our original work, but anyone working in this area cannot afford, as I did thirty years ago, not to pay really close attention to the affective and moral dimensions of teaching.

Second, my conception of PCK was relentlessly intellectual; it was attentive to the life of the pedagogical mind, and it didn't attend sufficiently to pedagogical *action*. Nate Gage once accused me of leaving teachers "lost in thought." He was among the heroes of 'process–product' approaches, and the idea of process was a description of what teachers actively do. The idea of PCK needs to place much-needed emphasis on teacher thought and emotion, but not by ignoring the role of action in teaching practice. If you look at the work on PCK in the early days, it so emphasized teachers as thinkers, as problem solvers, as decision makers. It was almost as if they were sitting in some ivory tower. It wasn't sufficiently about "what am I going to do with all this thinking I am doing?" It's a flaw that a number of current teaching scholars are trying to repair now. It simply doesn't make much sense to be reflective about practices you're not skilled at performing, and teaching IS a form of skilled performance.

A third limitation was that PCK was insufficiently attentive to questions of the broader social and cultural context. Culture and context are huge envelopes within which we find many of the determinants of teaching and learning. PCK must be pedagogical content knowledge, but also pedagogical culture knowledge, and pedagogical context knowledge. It is also about language, religion, and identity as features of the lived settings in which teaching, learning, and development occur. I now understand that the big idea within PCK was that all teaching must be mindfully situated in the disciplinary, cultural, personal, and social settings in which it occurs. PCK is about the importance of situating teaching in all those 'cultures' in the sense of 'culture' that we use in science, as a medium within which things grow (or die).

Fourth, in the early work on PCK, there really wasn't enough about outcomes. When we threw out process–product research we replaced the behavioral processes with intellectual processes, but we managed to ignore questions of products or outcomes of instruction. We did not attend to the relationships between how teachers thought and evidence of learning in the students they instructed. The relationship between measured teaching and measured learning is not only an artifact of the accountability policies of government agencies; we have a moral obligation to ask how our teaching is affecting the minds and hearts of our students.

I'm sure I have not exhausted the litany of ways in which the original ideas of PCK had limitations. There are certainly more. Every theory is limited by the very need to set boundaries around the aspects of life that the theory aims to explain. So it is with PCK as well.

PCK as a policy claim about teachers as professionals

One of the motivations for inventing the notion of PCK was not only to do a better job of educating teachers, to have a better theory of teaching; it was a policy claim, an ideological claim. That's why it so rapidly led to a National Board for Teaching. That's why we took pride in the fact that only 35 percent of the candidates for the Board pass the assessment when they first take it, much less people who have never been trained nor taught. Teachers are professionals, who like other professionals, develop a body of understanding that is so special and so unique that they deserve to be treated as professionals by the society around them, with respect, with autonomy, and yes, with compensation. Teaching is demanding and difficult mental and physical work that only the most well-educated and mentored professionals can accomplish. PCK is an attribute that teachers develop, and it cannot be found among mere subject matter experts or among those who are "good with kids." It was really a policy claim about how special teachers were and how they ought to be regarded and respected.

Domain-specific pedagogies and a domain-specific identity

The last thing I will say is that a lot of what I did as president of *The Carnegie Foundation for the Advancement of Teaching* was to lead a twelve-year program of research on how people are educated across the professions. We conducted extensive multi-year studies that led to books on educating lawyers, engineers, clergy, physicians, nurses, and business leaders. We addressed the education of teachers and scholars in different ways. I urge you to look at some of those studies, because in many ways, teaching and the preparation of teachers shares many features with other learned professions. One of the things that stands out was that in every one of these professions we identified what we called *Signature Pedagogies* (Shulman, 2005). These are profession-specific modes of teaching that we associate with that profession, that seem to fit what it means to learn to be a member of that profession, to learn to think like a lawyer, to learn to act like a nurse, to learn what it means to think like an engineer who is a designer. One of the fascinating things that has emerged from that work on Signature Pedagogy, was that, on the one hand, these pedagogies of the professions are indeed domain specific. Educating physicians uses pedagogies distinctly different from educating lawyers, engineers, or ministers. Each field has developed its own PPK, a kind of pedagogical professional knowledge. The practices of medical and nursing teaching rounds are quite different from the case dialogues of law or the studio practices of design or architecture.

Even though the surface structures of professions are distinctive one from the other, I now think I understand that there are underlying *principles* of professional education that are the deep structure of all those pedagogies and are common across them. What's even more fascinating (and disturbing) for us as teacher educators is that most of those deep structure principles of the signature pedagogies of the professions are absent in most teacher education programs. One of the things I am concerned about now is why doesn't teacher education have a fully developed intentionally practiced powerful set of signature pedagogies like other professions? That, mercifully, is a topic for another essay.

One final observation was that in those other professions, what were especially important were the habits of mind, habits of heart, and habits of practice that a candidate learns to become a professional. All the habits of technical practice, ways of thinking, and professional values you learn come together in the formation of professional identity. An engineer learns how to mess with the world, but also that she is then responsible for the mess she has made. The responsibilities of a nurse are organized around his role as an advocate for patients, which serves as the central pivot for that profession's powerful sense of professional identity. I have a feeling that when the dust settles, and we think about what it means to truly learn to be a science teacher or a math teacher, we will recognize that to become a mature teacher of science, you don't only learn to think certain ways and practice certain ways, it also involves developing an identity, a sense of self, of personhood. I think the whole notion of what constitutes the professional identity of a superb teacher of science is not one to be ignored.

Concluding thoughts for the work of the Summit

I urge you to build on the tradition of BSCS, in the spirit of the story I told you about Schwab's contributions in recognizing that even though there was not one singular structure of biology that didn't mean that asking about structures of biology was a vain effort. It meant that if you looked for a single monolithic unifying effort then there will be very good reasons why you will argue endlessly and accomplish little. Similarly, there will be plural perspectives on PCK, more than one legitimate, exciting, and fruitful way of thinking about PCK. No one can think of everything simultaneously; we're just not constructed that way as human thinkers. Can we get two or three of these in balance, more or less? Which three do you want to give priority in a given situation? How do such competing conceptions relate to what the major challenge of educating teachers is in your country? Maybe if you're in Germany or the Netherlands, teacher content knowledge is not your primary concern; it's their ability to do pedagogical transformations and representations. In elementary math and science teaching in the US, the content knowledge of teachers is a serious challenge because so many of the people who decide to become elementary school teachers were not well prepared in math and science and may have acquired negative identities as learners in those areas. As you juggle with the many aspects of teaching and learning, keep all these balls in the air but recognize that as you contextualize things and link PCK to the normative needs of the society that you're working in and of the global society, different factors will come to the forefront and others will have to take a backseat.

Having given PCK up for adoption nearly a quarter century ago, I am deeply appreciative of the care with which you have raised the baby into adulthood. PCK is now a citizen of many nations, traveling the world with many passports. I have met PCK in China and in Germany, in Norway and the Netherlands, in Australia, Brazil and in Israel, as well as in California and Massachusetts. You have been very good foster parents. Your work is not yet complete.

References

Elstein, A. S., Shulman, L. S., & Sprafka, S. A. (1978). *Medical problem solving: An analysis of clinical reasoning*. Cambridge, MA: Harvard University Press.

Shulman, L. S. (1986). Those who understand: Knowledge growth in teaching. *Educational Researcher, 15*(2), 4–14.

Shulman, L. S. (1987). Knowledge and teaching: Foundations of the new reform. *Harvard Educational Review, 57*(1), 1–22.

Shulman, L. S. (2005). Signature pedagogies in the profession. *Daedalus, 134*(3), 52–59.

Shulman, L. S., & Sykes, G. (1986). *A National Board for Teaching? In search of a Bold Standard*. A paper prepared for the Task Force on Teaching as a Profession, Carnegie Forum on Education and the Economy.

Stodolsky, S. S. (1988). *The subject matters: Classroom activity in math and social studies*. Chicago, IL: University of Chicago Press.

2

THE PCK SUMMIT

A process and structure for challenging current ideas, provoking future work, and considering new directions

Janet Carlson
STANFORD UNIVERSITY

Laura Stokes & Jenifer Helms
INVERNESS RESEARCH

Julie Gess-Newsome
OREGON STATE UNIVERSITY-CASCADES

April Gardner
BSCS (BIOLOGICAL SCIENCES CURRICULUM STUDY)

Introduction

The PCK Summit took place from 20 to 25 October 2012 in Colorado Springs, Colorado, USA. This event was not a typical conference, but a small, international gathering of 22 science education researchers from multiple countries. These researchers had in common an interest in understanding the development and measurement of pedagogical content knowledge (PCK) in science teachers and a willingness to consider how to strengthen this field of research by examining our work collectively. We were convinced that for this field of study to advance, it was time for researchers to attend to the considerable divergences in the interpretation and understanding of PCK and clarify distinctions between different, viable models of PCK. The Summit participants came from seven different countries and all had a history of studying PCK within science education and a willingness to consider whether or not it was possible to agree to a consensus model for studying PCK.

This chapter combines the perspectives of the principal investigators for this project (Julie Gess-Newsome, Janet Carlson, and April Gardner) and the external evaluators for the project (Laura Stokes and Jenifer Helms). Collectively, we discuss the details of the processes and structures that made the Summit a unique professional event in which we challenged our current ideas and pushed our thinking in new directions for the future.

Why a summit? Why not a conference?

We were quite deliberate in our decision not to refer to this event as a conference. A conference is a familiar mode of work for academics. Conferences provide opportunities to bring together professionals with common interests to share and build knowledge; however, they are quite challenging to design in ways that truly succeed in galvanizing the attention of an academic community on a shared problem, in generating powerful new understandings, and in energizing and shaping an agenda for future research and development work that will move a field forward. Conferences may aspire to these ends but, as typically designed, they rarely achieve them.

In this chapter we present a case study of a conference-like event—called the PCK Summit—that provided an exceptionally powerful experience for the participants—both individually and as a professional community—and pushed forward important work in the field.

The PCK Summit was designed to accomplish two major outcomes:

- Formation of a professional learning community to explore the potential of a consensus model of PCK to guide science education research in this area through multiple research approaches.
- Identification of specific next steps that would move the field forward.

To understand how the design of the Summit worked to accomplish these outcomes, we discuss the key components that include the following:

- The rationale for and focus of the Summit
- The identification of participants
- The preparation tasks
- The selection of the setting
- The design and structure of the agenda
- The selection and role of the facilitators
- The plan for the future.

The rationale for and focus of the Summit

The construct of PCK was introduced by Shulman over 25 years ago and has been enthusiastically studied by many education researchers since then (Borko

& Livingston, 1989; Gess-Newsome, 1999; Grossman, 1990; Hashweh, 1987; Magnusson, et al., 1999). It has become clear, however, that there is now considerable divergence in the interpretation and understanding of PCK. In particular, we noticed that there were significant and troubling divergences in the key elements of science PCK that drive the research and make it meaningful, including definitions, conceptual frameworks, instruments, methods, and, subsequently, the findings.

The idea for a conference was born from the recognition of a weakness that limited the utility of PCK in the field both theoretically and practically. Key researchers working with the concept of pedagogical content knowledge saw that while PCK had been a useful construct, particularly for improving science teachers' preparation, research about and application of PCK had been suffering from a lack of shared definitions and conceptualizations of the construct in the field. The Summit was formed around the clear purpose of naming this weakness and working to strengthen the concept itself, as well as the research community, and thus increase the relevance and value of both to the field. As a result of our own work in PCK and our knowledge of others' research, we realized that in spite of the fact that research has been ongoing in science PCK since the late 1990s, researchers were not speaking the same language.

The utility of PCK in science education was limited by divergences present in several key aspects of PCK research. Key examples include the following:

- Appropriate level of focus for PCK's explanatory power (e.g., is PCK meaningfully linked to a specific area within a discipline (energy), to a discipline (physics), or to science overall?).
- The relationship of PCK to content knowledge and to pedagogical knowledge.
- The role of personal orientations or beliefs in PCK.
- The means of assessing PCK.

We felt that these divergences diminished the power and value of the PCK construct to contribute effectively to the improvement of science teaching and learning.

We used the areas of divergence in the field that we identified and translated them into the organizing structure for the meeting. These then drove our decisions about the presentation topics we asked the invited participants to prepare. The expressed purpose of the Summit was to bring together leaders in the field to share aspects of their research and to discuss issues related to research on PCK that would address and 'solve' the problem of divergence. We stated this objective from the beginning, so everyone invited to attend could decide if this was a challenge of attempting to create a unified vision of PCK *or* a challenge focused on identifying how explicitly recognized divergences could lead to productive lines of research was of interest. As Julie Gess-Newsome stated in her remarks to open the Summit:

There is something that is not playing right in the field. This seems like the right time to bring the field together and ask: Can we come up with either a unifying definition for pedagogical content knowledge or maybe even a theoretical grounding for it that will drive measurement and assessment techniques? If we are going to be divergent, can we be purposefully divergent so we have lines of research that we can determine which are going to be more fruitful or less fruitful in getting us the kind of answers that we seek.

We shared this focus and purpose early on in an email to the participants, stating:

As we all know, Pedagogical Content Knowledge (PCK) has generated a lot of interest in the research community. Unfortunately, few commonalities exist in the way we have conceptualized or operationalized the construct in science education. The PCK Summit is designed to allow an international group of experienced PCK researchers the time and space to delve into our collective efforts, uncover our assumptions, understand the divergences in our approaches, and perhaps agree upon the most fruitful tools that have been found to date in the exploration of teachers' professional knowledge, including PCK . . . We hope that all of us participating in the Summit, as a research community, will agree upon a few deliberate and purposeful paths on which to focus our individual and collective research in the future. The ultimate goal of the Summit is to catapult the research on teachers' professional knowledge on a productive trajectory.

(8 March 2012)

Our concerns resonated with the invited participants, which quickly validated our rationale for the Summit. In fact, a theme we heard during the discussion at the Summit was that a 'status problem' exists within PCK research and, as a result, researchers have been having more trouble publishing their studies and getting their papers accepted at meetings of their professional associations. Participants believe PCK's loss of potency in the field stems from the absence of a coherent construct and theoretical foundation for PCK. Consequently, the majority of the participants came to the Summit with a felt need to bring clarity to the work so that those outside the PCK community in science education research can see the value in this line of inquiry.

The rationale and focus of the Summit spoke to two related needs felt by the international community of PCK researchers: One was the need to sustain and further their individual research programs and the other was the need to form a research community unified enough to keep PCK alive as a construct that the field perceives as academically sound, rigorous, generative, and useful. The organizers and participants alike could see that without a better supply of research-based knowledge about PCK, the field's demand will shrink, which would then further diminish the utility of PCK as a contributing concept to improve science teaching, the ultimate goal.

Purposeful and informed selection of participants

As the Summit organizers, we were familiar with both the research and researchers of PCK in science education. This prepared us well to be intentional about inviting participants who not only had a track record of research in PCK, but who had also been developing different (sometimes divergent) conceptual frameworks, instruments, measurements, and uses. In other words, it was the participants' work that was leading the field and also highlighting the need for a discussion about a unified model.

We invited participants from three professional contexts—established academics who have been conducting basic PCK research for many years; new researchers from academia with promising work related to PCK; and professionals working in education research and development organizations including WestEd, BSCS, and Horizon Research. Each of these organizations had been using PCK as a construct for their teacher development and implementation research and had much to offer the conversation.

For the Summit to be effective, we knew that participants had to understand our expectations in terms of both preparation and participation. When we sent the letters of invitation we made these expectations explicit. Thus we invited potential participants to *apply* to attend, not simply to attend, the Summit.

> Because of your extensive work in this area of research, we invite your research team to apply for one or two of the 30 spaces we have available for the Summit. The PCK Summit is scheduled for October 20–25, 2012, in Colorado Springs, Colorado. We anticipate that Summit participants will arrive on October 19th (international) or 20th (domestic) and depart on October 26th. Because of the nature of the Summit, we expect that all participants will be present and participate in the full five days of the meeting. Please let us know if there are extenuating circumstances that prevent your attendance at the entire event.
>
> Are you interested and available to attend the PCK Summit? If so, please respond to Julie Gess-Newsome . . . with an indication of interest or decline and a sense of whether or not you will be inviting a second member from your research team. We would appreciate a response no later than March 15th so that we can offer the spaces to others if you choose not to participate.
>
> To formally submit your initial materials, go to pcksummit.bscs.org to complete and submit the online Letter of Commitment and Overview of PCK Research Program. The web site includes an example of the Overview document for you to use as a model. Please submit your application by April 10, 2012. These materials will help us further organize the conference.
>
> *(8 March 2012)*

The preparation tasks

After the research teams submitted their application to participate in the Summit, which consisted of a Letter of Commitment and an Overview of Research, we reviewed the materials and determined which teams would participate. We first posted these summary papers on the PCK Summit website in a space available only to participants. After the Summit, the site was reorganized to link the participants' Expanded Papers (EPs) to the agenda for the conference and it was made available to anyone who registers for the site (http://pcksummit.bscs.org).

Each research team wrote a structured EP, describing similar aspects of their research projects but in more depth: overview, theoretical background, rationale, methods, results, references, and hyperlinks to related articles. We conceptualized these EPs as the "basis of an analysis and synthesis of the field" that would serve the Summit as well as contribute to a book and journal articles after the Summit. The EPs were all posted to the PCK website. Then both the organizers and the participants devoted considerable time and much disciplined writing, reading, and synthesis work in preparing for the Summit several months prior to the event. Participants were asked to write detailed responses to a set of questions about their research program in PCK, including: their definition of PCK, model used, assessment tools, synopsis of work, and references. Participants were then asked to read all of the responses in preparation for the Summit. We used the following questions to organize the analysis of the papers and as a test of the structure of the agenda:

PCK Summit preparation questions

1. Are there attributes of PCK and teachers' professional knowledge that are similar across multiple EP? Are there other attributes that are unique to a smaller subset of EP? Identify the papers and the attributes.
2. What similarities and differences exist in the measurement tools and analysis methods used to uncover PCK?
3. Are there results across EP that reinforce some of the PCK findings? Are there results that are contradictory? Can you propose explanations for the complementary or contradictory nature of the results?
4. After reading the EP, what questions do you have for specific research teams?
5. After reading the EP, what questions do you have for the group to consider?

After reviewing the range of responses to the preparation questions, we developed the Summit agenda and asked the research teams to present their work during the Summit. What was unique about these presentations was that no one team presented everything about their work. Instead we asked the teams to focus on a particular aspect of their work, such as the challenge in developing an instrument to measure PCK.

This focused and structured preparatory work provided participants with a solid summary of their colleagues' scholarly work and of ways each researcher's work connected (or did not connect) with the work of the other researchers. This created the opportunity to dive into the core of the issues right from the beginning of the Summit. The preparation tasks also primed the intellectual 'juice' that helped animate the discussions at the meeting. The productivity of the Summit was evidence that this approach was better than the alternative of not asking participants to become familiar with one another's work or of asking participants to, on their own, learn about one another's work. Involving each person in an intentional and inclusive sharing of their own work and engagement with one another's work—around core questions that would guide the Summit—was remarkably effective in setting a rigorous tone and 'level playing field' for the Summit, enabling each person to enter with a strong voice for their own work, a regard for and engagement with each other's work, a degree of shared language, and a preview of core problems to discuss. On the follow-up survey, 100 percent of the participants reported that the preparatory work either contributed or greatly contributed to the Summit. Many commented that the papers helped them understand each other's perspectives.

Finally, we asked the participants to be prepared to participate in writing manuscripts following the Summit based on the conversations and discussions that unfolded. We also asked them to consider participating in panel discussions of the Summit synthesis at one or more of the upcoming research conferences, including NARST 2013, ESERA 2013, and/or AERA 2014. We set this expectation prior to the Summit so that it was in people's minds during the Summit and would inform the discussion of next steps at the end of the event.

The external evaluators, in preparing their final report on the Summit, remarked on how impressed they were by how much work people were willing to do before the Summit took place. This is one of many ways it was different from a typical conference. The level of preparation contributed greatly to the success of the Summit and compels us to ask a number of questions such as: What was the motivation for the preparation? Why did people comply? Is it feasible as a model for other events? As the Summit organizers, Carlson, Gardner, and Gess-Newsome suspect that the commitment to preparation was related to the participants' general awareness of the discrepancies in the field of science PCK research and the recognition that these issues needed to be addressed before further progress could be made. In addition, we noticed a strong sense of community among the relatively few number of research groups focused specifically on science PCK. This sense of community coupled with the opportunity to engage in meaningful, in-depth dialogue was a rare opportunity for all of us and therefore worth the effort of preparation.

The selection of the setting

From our initial planning for the PCK Summit we intended to hold the event in a retreat-style setting. We wanted a place that encouraged focus and discouraged distractions. On the other hand, we did not want to be in such a remote location that people felt trapped or had difficulty traveling to the site.

In addition to our criterion that the location supported the focus, thinking, conversation, and collaboration that we envisioned, we also wanted a location with a reputation for quality of service and amenities. We also thought it would help those who had traveled long distances to adjust more easily and participate more fully in the Summit.

In addition to considering the nature of the accommodations and the nature of the work, we kept in mind our total costs and access to support services. In particular, we needed a location that fit our budget, which was based on US federal per diem rates.

With these criteria in mind, we started our search for a suitable location on either coast of the US. We focused on the two coasts because of the increased number of direct flights from international airports. We examined the average costs of flights from the countries of our participants as well as the ease and cost of local transportation to the resort location. Because we did not find any options that met all of our criteria we had to prioritize our criteria.

In the end, we opted for the Cheyenne Mountain Resort located in Colorado Springs. We were able to schedule the conference during a slower time at the resort and they were willing to work with our budget. This location gave us all the amenities we were hoping for as well as proximity to BSCS headquarters and the various support people to help the Summit run smoothly. We did trade-off the immediate proximity of a major airport and most of our participants had to take an additional flight from Denver to Colorado Springs, but the resort has a free shuttle service from the local airport. This location also allowed more participants to drive to the meeting, balancing the budget.

As is evident in the evaluation comments, the participants appreciated our choice of location and felt that it did support the goals of the Summit and the nature of the work. As the organizers, we felt well supported by both the resort staff and the many people from BSCS who helped ensure that all the logistics and technology ran smoothly.

The design and structure of the agenda

We had a very purposeful design to our agenda for the Summit. Because our goal was to create an ongoing conversation that crossed the various lines of research represented by the participants, we needed to develop strategies that did not remind people of presenting their work at a conference in the traditional sense. To do this, we chose to organize the Summit around the themes represented in the preparation tasks. We began with an informal address from Lee Shulman, who first introduced the concept of PCK in 1986. For the first three full days of the Summit, we asked three people to present in sets that focused on some of the dilemmas and tensions that have emerged in PCK research. We alternated these

TABLE 2.1 Abbreviated version of the agenda

Day	Primary work
Saturday evening	Introductions, dinner, keynote address (via Skype) by Lee Shulman and discussion.
Sunday: Content knowledge, orientations, and beliefs in PCK	Two rounds of presentations each day that were organized around focus questions and followed by small group discussions around a related task.
Monday: Models of science PCK	
Tuesday: Assessment of PCK and research results	
Wednesday	Transition from analysis of past work to considering future work, and a break to visit Cheyenne Mountain Zoo.
Thursday	Collaborative work sessions to detail research agendas and map out next steps.

presentation sets with small group work. These small group discussions were designed to promote critical, collaborative inquiry. On the fourth day, following a reflection on the work of the Summit to that point and a discussion of possible next steps, we left the conference center for a behind-the-scenes tour of the local zoo. On the final day, participants worked in affinity groups to flesh out the next steps that included developing a consensus model, articulating a research agenda, considering learning trajectories for teachers, and identifying the implications for policy makers.

Briefly, the agenda played out as indicated in Table 2.1. A more detailed version of the agenda with hyperlinks to the PowerPoint files and EPs can be found at http://pcksummit.bscs.org/node/55.

More detail about the primary work during the Summit

We launched the Summit by re-visiting the origin of PCK through direct interaction with Lee Shulman. In a presidential address at the annual meeting of the American Educational Research Association in 1986, Shulman coined the term pedagogical content knowledge as a way to distinguish the special kind of content knowledge that teachers need to know to teach a subject. The concept resonated strongly with the teacher education and development community and generated quantities of research and activity, especially in mathematics and science education. Launching the Summit with a retrospective by Shulman thus embraced and put the participants in personal touch with the intellectual history of the concept. Shulman delivered his address via Skype, reminiscing about the origin of the concept, noting what he thought he missed in his original work, and strongly encouraging a new generation of educators to continue inquiring into PCK in ways that he did not. Participants referred to Shulman's talk regularly throughout the Summit and it served as a kind of community touchstone.

Each half day was framed around a focus question that lay at the heart of the problem (discrepant concepts, tools, findings, and so on) and that pushed the group inexorably toward a resolution—either to posit a unified model or to identify and agree upon discrepancies that would generate new research of value to the field.

After the initial framing of the day, sessions began in whole-group format with three 10-minute presentations by members of research teams sharing their own work through the lens of the focus question for that day. The conference organizers had asked each team in advance of the meeting to prepare these presentations such that they would address the question of a particular session and its identified discrepancy, challenge, or problem. The organizers had selected and sequenced these short presentations purposefully on the basis of how interesting or provocative a given research team's work was in this particular area of discrepancy. One session, for example, included three teams' sharing of their tools for assessing teachers' PCK. Aligning them this way made the differences and discrepancies visible and available for exploration.

Following the presentations, the organizers divided the participants into three small groups to tackle the questions and challenges driving that session. These small group discussions were of substantial length—one or two hours—so people would not feel rushed and could move beyond superficial conversations. The intention of each small group's focus question was to highlight the diverging views and to compel the participants to see whether they could (or could not) work toward a more unified model of PCK. In each small group session, participants moved from the structured questions toward refinement of their own new ideas and toward identification of where the discussion should go next. Each day, participants worked in different assigned groups on different subtopics related to PCK research; thus they interacted with different people, perspectives, and experiences.

At the end of each day, each small group presented to the whole group in some detail, often with one group member using a diagram on the wall to show their thinking, and with the 25 or so participants clustered in a semi-circle, leaning in, asking questions, commenting, and identifying congruencies and incongruences in the discussions of other groups. The purpose was not only to share thinking, but also to probe for the possibility of a shared model—to see how near the group was getting to the aim of the Summit. Small clusters of participants often continued as the dinner hour neared.

Out of these carefully sequenced and intensive discussions, strands of particular interest emerged organically. The facilitators recognized and named them and, in the last two days, participants chose to work in one of four interest groups for the purpose of taking the work forward beyond the Summit. The four foci included the following:

1. Refining the PCK model
2. Developing PCK in teachers (over a trajectory from pre-service to experts)
3. The research map for PCK
4. Connecting PCK to policy.

On the final day of the Summit, the participants arrived at the point where they could visualize a potential unified model for their work going forward that drew on all of the conversations, disagreements, and iterations from the previous four days. The model that had evolved included situating PCK in the broader framework of teachers' professional knowledge and created clarity around the aspects of PCK that are based on understanding of science concepts (termed topic-specific professional knowledge) and the knowledge and skills used by a teacher in the act of teaching. The proposed operational definition of PCK became: "PCK is the knowledge of, reasoning behind, and enactment of the teaching of particular topics in a particular way with particular students for particular reasons for enhanced student outcomes." From this definition, multiple small groups developed representative graphical models and one model began to capture what most of the participants thought represented the common aspects of the various models. (The details of the model are described in Chapter 3 by Julie Gess-Newsome.)

The last day also brought more progress on the four interest group topics. Participants agreed upon next steps for products resulting from the Summit: a special journal issue, a book, and an interactive website to house instruments and other key documents, videos, and presentations. This book and the PCK Summit website, as well as numerous presentations, are the key products that resulted from the Summit. The website of PCK Summit (pcksummit.bscs.org) contains archival materials from the Summit as well as several options for participating in the Summit asynchronously:

- Keynote address by Lee Shulman with English subtitles (video)
- Hyperlinked agenda with access to papers, videos, and PPT files
- The PCK Summit Story (video)
- FORUMs—six web-based modules that provide a way for small groups to recreate the Summit
- Ongoing list of related presentations.

Keys to success

Two key features contributed to the success of the Summit. First, the participants came to the Summit well prepared and with a commitment to stay focused on the work at hand. In addition, we knew that excellent facilitation skills would be needed to attain the kind of goals we had for the Summit. We saw the recognition of the importance of these elements in the evaluation forms.

One participant commented that, "The leadership team facilitated the development of our thinking without pushing any particular ideas." That and the fact that, as this commenter also said, "The participants were dedicated to the effort!" meant that the discussion neither wandered aimlessly nor was it overly controlled. Rather, the facilitators worked to bring to the fore participants' best and most authentic individual and joint thinking. Most of the attendees did not expect the Summit to have as strong an impact on their thinking as it did. Based on the comments people made in their evaluation surveys, the strength of this impact is credited to the extent to which people were able and willing to question their own assumptions and be open to others' perspectives, even after years and years of work in this area.

The actual design of the facilitation was more complex than met the participants' eyes. As the Summit organizers, we originally planned not to facilitate the meeting, leaving us to participate fully. We opted to invite two neutral facilitators who were knowledgeable about science education but not deeply invested in PCK research and not necessarily invested in the outcome of the Summit. We found as the Summit progressed, however, we did need to play a bigger role in facilitation as we were moving toward consensus because of our understanding of the vision and purpose of the Summit. We had participated fully in the meeting and in doing so had stayed in contact with the flow and energy of discussion. Each day we met with the larger planning team, the external facilitators, and the evaluators to debrief. This helped us to identify the facilitation moves needed the following day to keep the momentum moving toward the meeting goal. We worked to be very responsive to the evolving needs and thinking of the Summit participants. Several times in the last two days, we altered the planned agenda to take advantage of the positive momentum that was building from the small breakout groups. The combination of preparation, a carefully planned agenda, intentional facilitation, and an appropriate degree of flexibility resulted in the Summit making a contribution to the field of science education from the perspective of the original outcomes.

Benefits and contributions

This book, the PCK website, and the presentations the Summit participants have given since the event were made possible because of the many positive outcomes of the Summit including the following:

- Generating a more explicit body of collective wisdom about and critique of the PCK model that has potential to increase the rigor and value of PCK research.
- Identifying and beginning to create better and more coherent definitions, measures, and frameworks for PCK that have the potential to enhance the status and usability of PCK research and direct it for years to come.

- Clarifying the concept of PCK and making its definition more unified so that the construct is more usable and applicable, which can help teacher educators who work in both new and experienced teacher development.
- Strengthening the PCK community and field in ways that contribute back to individual researchers and their formation of a generative and valuable research trajectory.

Outcomes

We think that the Summit has three accomplishments that are not typical of professional meetings. These accomplishments include the formation of professional community, the advancement of a concept, and further development of a particular field of study.

The formation of a community was possible because the participants arrived well prepared and eager for several days of work together. The energy level and intellectual effort that launched the Summit did not lag, but rather was sustained through the last session. Researchers who had put years of work into PCK research were willing to put aside their hard-won 'niche' perspectives and openly explore the prospect of a unified model of PCK for science education research. Participants experienced the Summit as a true manifestation of a professional learning community.

We were able to advance the concept of PCK by proposing a unified model that was discussed and refined through the end of the meeting. Participants worked together and pushed through to the end of the Summit to explicate that model and its many new implications. Every participant engaged with questions about the benefits and challenges a unified model may present to them as individual researchers and to their field.

On the last day of the Summit, all researchers identified multiple next steps for their work, which is a necessary step for furthering this field of study. Many of these plans have already come to fruition: a NARST panel, several sessions at ESERA, a symposium at AERA, this book, and the website. Most of these activities represent new international and collaborative efforts springing from the joint work of the Summit. These activities also are propelling individuals' work forward. The Summit served as a context for both collective and individual advancement.

Acknowledgement

This material is based upon work supported by the National Science Foundation under Grant No. DRL-1108899, a transfer of funds from an NSF grant housed at the University of Missouri, and by the Spencer Foundation. Any opinions, findings, and conclusions or recommendations expressed in this material are those of the author(s) and do not necessarily reflect the views of the National Science Foundation or the Spencer Foundation.

References

Borko, H., & Livingston, C. (1989). Cognition and improvisation: Differences in mathematics instruction by expert and novice teachers. *American Educational Research Journal, 26*(4), 473–498.

Gess-Newsome, J. (1999). Secondary teachers' knowledge and beliefs about subject matter and its impact on instruction. In J. Gess-Newsome & N. G. Lederman (Eds.), *Examining pedagogical content knowledge: The construct and its implications for science education* (pp. 51–94). Dordrecht, the Netherlands: Kluwer Academic Publishers.

Grossman, P. (1990). *The making of a teacher.* New York, NY: Teachers College Press.

Hashweh, M. Z. (1987). Effects of subject-matter knowledge in the teaching of biology and physics. *Teaching and Teacher Education, 3*(2), 109–120.

Magnusson, S., Krajcik, J., & Borko, H. (1999). Nature, sources and development of pedagogical content knowledge for science teaching. In J. Gess-Newsome & N. G. Lederman (Eds.), *Examining pedagogical content knowledge: The construct and its implications for science education* (pp. 95–132). Dordrecht, the Netherlands: Kluwer Academic Publishers.

Shulman, L. (1986). Those who understand: Knowledge growth in teaching. *Educational Researcher, 15*(2), 4–14.

3

A MODEL OF TEACHER PROFESSIONAL KNOWLEDGE AND SKILL INCLUDING PCK

Results of the thinking from the PCK Summit

Julie Gess-Newsome

OREGON STATE UNIVERSITY-CASCADES

Introduction

Educational researchers are interested in how teaching is related to student outcomes. It seems obvious that what a teacher knows should influence how they teach and what students learn. Unfortunately, when examining the relationship between measures of teacher content knowledge (i.e., grade-point average, courses taken, standardized test scores), only weak relationships to student outcomes are found, accounting for less than 1 percent of the variation (Wayne & Youngs, 2003).

When Shulman introduced the idea of PCK as the 'missing paradigm' in the research on teacher knowledge, he described it as one of several knowledge bases needed by teachers. The idea that teachers hold a unique knowledge base, distinct from experts in the discipline that they teach, caught the attention of many researchers, particularly in the fields of science and mathematics. These researchers explored how teachers understand science and combined this knowledge with pedagogical strategies and knowledge of students in order to plan and deliver instruction. This nuanced form of teacher knowledge had the potential to more carefully describe what teachers know and more precisely account for student learning.

Shulman's description of PCK was based on a careful conceptualization of what might constitute a teacher's knowledge base and, as a result, early researchers freely proposed models of PCK to guide their research efforts. The model most often cited is by Magnusson, Krajcik, and Borko (1999), which proposed that PCK was influenced by subject matter knowledge and beliefs, pedagogical knowledge and beliefs, and knowledge and beliefs about context, including students. Within the construct of PCK, they proposed that there were orientations to teaching science that shaped and were shaped by knowledge of science curricula, knowledge of students' understanding of science, knowledge of instructional strategies, and knowledge of assessment of scientific literacy. Other researchers used variations of this model or constructed their own. Instruments were then designed to capture or measure PCK and explore the relationships between PCK and other knowledge bases, classroom practice, and/or student outcomes.

As the research base developed, the divergence in definitions, models, and data collection methods revealed critical differences in the thinking surrounding PCK. For instance: Does PCK exist at the level of science, physics, or force and motion? What is the relationship of teaching orientations to PCK? Does PCK exist as a knowledge base or is it a skill, or both? Is PCK an attribute of a teacher or knowledge held by the community? Can PCK be measured separately from the act of teaching? These questions and others stimulated the need for a focused and extended conversation about PCK and led to the PCK Summit.

The PCK Summit

The PCK Summit (see Chapter 2) brought together 22 science educators from 11 research teams and 7 countries to spend five days together in a retreat setting to examine the construct of PCK. Participants were active PCK researchers recognized as having differing views on PCK. In preparation for the Summit, research teams prepared syntheses of their research using a standardized format that fostered the ability to compare research programs. Through this process, participants were asked to explicitly describe the nature of PCK, their model of PCK and its relationship to other professional knowledge bases, the grain-size of PCK, whether PCK is transformative or integrative (see Gess-Newsome, 1999a), and data collection instruments or tools. These descriptions and their analysis prior to the Summit helped refine questions that would frame the Summit.

Shulman launched the Summit through an informal Skype retrospective about the "notion of inventing pedagogical content knowledge" (see Chapter 1). While Shulman described the roots of PCK as cognitive theory, he also stated that PCK was posed as a "policy claim" for use as a foundation for the development of the National Board Certification of Teachers, and as an "ideological claim" to recognize teachers as professionals with a unique body of knowledge who should be treated with respect, autonomy, and compensation (Shulman, 2012). Shulman identified five weaknesses with PCK—the absence of affect, emotion, and motivation; an overemphasis on teacher thinking versus a teacher's skilled performance in the classroom; the omission of context; the omission of a teacher's vision and goals for education; and, the relationship of PCK to student outcomes.

During the Summit, participants consistently struggled to reconsider their own models of PCK and were challenged to consider the potential of identifying a unified model for PCK or electing to identify several purposefully competing conceptions that could be used to guide future research. Over the week, small groups created and presented models of PCK, explored the relationship of PCK to other professional knowledge bases, and revealed their underlying assumptions. Recursive presentations to the larger group allowed for the evolution of ideas while assumptions were uncovered or challenged. By the last day of the Summit, a small group took the most promising ideas and shaped them into a single model for presentation to the large group, including key definitions, examples, and relationships. I had the honor of refining this thinking into the model presented in this chapter, expanding on the thinking initiated at the Summit—so it was through the contributions of all of the Summit participants that this model exists.

A model of teacher professional knowledge and skill that includes PCK

Early in our conversations, it became apparent that too many ideas were packed into PCK. Particularly troubling were the five weaknesses identified by Shulman. The model of teacher professional knowledge and skill (TPK&S) presented here is quite different from that originally presented by Magnusson et al. (1999). Many previously competing or confusing ideas have been unpacked. The model identifies the overarching role of teacher professional knowledge and situates PCK within that model, including all of the complexity of teaching and learning.

We believe that this model offers explanatory power for existing research, provides a more robust and predictive way to think about teacher knowledge and action, and allows for extant research to be situated within the model or reconceptualized based on relationships and definitions presented.

As an overview, the model of TPK&S (Figure 3.1) originates in the generic teacher professional knowledge bases (TPKB). This is the generalized professional knowledge that results from research and best practice. Knowledge from the TPKB informs and is informed by topic-specific professional knowledge (TSPK). This new category of knowledge contributes several things: (1) It makes explicit that content for teaching occurs at the topic level (i.e., force and motion) and not at the disciplinary level (i.e., physics or science); (2) this knowledge blends subject matter, pedagogy, and context; and, (3) it is recognized as public knowledge, or knowledge held by the profession, allowing it to assume a normative role. Different than the rest of the model that follows, the two knowledge bases described thus far are context free.

In the model of TPK&S, teacher affect is recognized as making a contribution to teacher knowledge, skill, and practice. These beliefs and orientations act as amplifiers or filters to teacher learning and mediate teacher actions. It is in the classroom context that we can examine PCK. Unique to this model, PCK is defined as both a knowledge base used in planning for and the delivery of topic-specific instruction in a

Model of teacher professional knowledge **31**

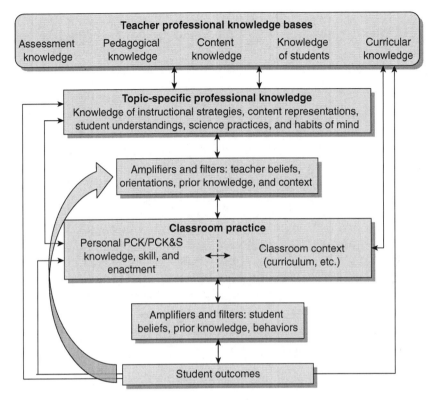

FIGURE 3.1 Model of teacher professional knowledge and skill including PCK and influences on classroom practice and student outcomes

very specific classroom context, *and* as a skill when involved in the act of teaching. To make thiscontribution clear, the model introduces the idea of pedagogical content knowledge and skill (PCK&S). Finally, student outcomes are explicit in this model. Student learning is not an automatic product of instruction: Student amplifiers and filters also impact the results of outcome measures. The model of TPK&S is recursive and dynamic. Both student outcomes and classroom practices have the ability to further inform classroom practice, TSPK, and the TPKB. These feedback loops underscore the complexities of teaching and learning and provide leverage points for growth in teacher knowledge and skill.

Teacher professional knowledge bases

As with Shulman's work, the model of TPK&S includes general knowledge bases for teaching. The TPKB identified in the model include knowledge of assessment, pedagogy, content, students, and curriculum, but other categories of knowledge could be included as well. The importance here is not that an exhaustive set of knowledge bases be named, but that we recognize and define the kind of knowledge that falls into this category. This knowledge is created by experts in the field and often falls beyond the typical knowledge of teachers. Cochran-Smith and Lytle (1992) called this the knowledge *for* practice. This is a formal body of knowledge determined and codified by researchers or experts. Teachers are seen as the consumers of this knowledge as translated for use in teacher education programs or professional development. As a professional knowledge base, it is generic (not content specific) and normative and can be used to construct assessments to determine what teachers know. For example, assessment knowledge might include knowledge of the design and use of formative and summative assessments and how to use results from those assessments to design or modify instruction. Pedagogical knowledge might include strategies for classroom management and student engagement, for example, questioning techniques, instructional strategies to support differentiation based on student need, or how to design a lesson plan. Content knowledge is the academic content of the discipline. Using the dimensions included in the *Next Generation Science Standards* (Achieve Inc., 2013), content knowledge includes the science and engineering practices used to generate knowledge, the disciplinary core ideas, and the recognition of cross-cutting concepts. Knowledge of students encompasses student cognitive and physical development, understanding student differences that might require instructional differentiation, and how to capitalize on personal and community assets to enrich instruction. Curricular knowledge might include the goals of a curriculum, curriculum structures, the role of a scope and sequence, and the ability to assess a curriculum for coherence and articulation. All of these knowledge elements can be identified by the education community, taught generically across the disciplines that a teacher might teach, be used to define desired teacher knowledge, and then support the construction of measurements of what teachers know.

Topic-specific professional knowledge

While the TPKB are generic, their power lies in their application to teaching a topic. TSPK is both topic specific and, in most instances, specific to a student developmental level. Knowledge within this category would include determining effective instructional strategies; selecting multiple representations; organizing content to use specific examples to highlight and build overarching ideas; understanding incoming student knowledge or misconceptions; and knowing how to integrate science and engineering practices, cross-cutting concepts, and the nature of science within a topic. To engage in these activities, visioning a specific topic and grade level is necessary. For instance, when considering the topic of forces and motion for a third-grade classroom, knowledge in this category would include selecting from and sequencing the manipulation and measurement of the impact of different forces on the motions of an object, and/or using simulations to explore the same concepts; selecting modes to represent evidence in tables, graphs, oral presentations, or in written form; understanding student background experiences (i.e., pushing someone on a swing) or their misconceptions (an object that is not moving has no forces acting on it); and how the topic lends itself to the integration of cause and effect, making observations, taking and recording measurements, making predictions based on patterns, creating explanations from evidence, and how the generation of knowledge relates to the nature of science.

In describing this knowledge, it sounds much like the knowledge that has been previously associated with PCK, but there is an important and critical difference. TSPK is clearly recognized as codified by experts and is available for study and use by teachers. It is a public understanding held by the community, is relatively static and visible, and can be easily recorded in text, diagrams, or tables (West, Fensham, & Garrard, 1985). In contrast, it is not private knowledge, which is held by an individual, is relatively more dynamic, and is more difficult to precisely describe. TSPK is canonical, generated by research or best practice, and can have a normative function in terms of what we want teachers to know about topic- and context-specific instruction. It can be identified and described to construct measures, tests, or rubrics to determine what teachers know, might act as the basis for creating a learning progression for teachers, and should be used as a framework for the design of professional development.

One example of a manifestation of TSPK can be found in the content representations (CoRe) developed by Loughran and his team (Loughran, Berry, & Mulhall, 2012). CoRes are representations of how a community of teachers thinks about the knowledge needed to teach a particular topic at a given grade level. The process of creating a CoRe starts with agreement about the big ideas related to a specific topic that are important for developing a robust student understanding. Once the big ideas are identified, teachers work as a group to answer the questions: What do you intend students to learn about this idea? Why is it important for students to know this? What else might you know about this idea that you don't intend students to know yet? What difficulties or limitations are connected with teaching this idea? What do you know about student thinking about this idea? What other factors influence your teaching of this idea? What instructional strategies will you use and why? How will you monitor student understanding or confusion around this idea? In answering these questions, groups of teachers co-construct a visible representation of their collective TSPK. These questions are similar to those found in the scaffolding provided by Page Keeley's *Science Curriculum Topic Study* (2005). In answering such questions, teachers access canonical knowledge about their topic and organize it in a way that will be useful for planning instruction.

Professional development using the *Framework for K-12 Science Education* (National Research Council, 2012) and the *NGSS* offer similar opportunities for exploration and content deepening so that teachers can increase their TSPK. To be clear, making a distinction between TSPK and PCK is an important contribution of this model. Decoupling professional knowledge from personal knowledge *and skill* clarifies concepts which were previously conflated in many attempts to describe, measure, or capture PCK.

As previously noted, TSPK is derived from the TPKB once attention is turned to the teaching of a specific topic. As such, growth in one knowledge base has the potential to increase knowledge in the other. One way to envision the recursive nature and growth of these two knowledge bases may be similar to the interplay between deductive and inductive teaching models. In a deductive model, one starts from a broad generalization (the TPKB) and then moves to examples (TSPK). The latter is used to test the understanding of the former. In an inductive model, the examples are reflected upon and used to develop robust understandings of the general principles. With active and potentially externally facilitated reflection, it is possible to see how growth in one knowledge base may increase growth in the other.

Teacher amplifiers and filters

Up to this point, the focus of the model of TPK&S has been on knowledge that is held by the profession and accessed by teachers. But in order to personalize knowledge, it must pass through the lens of the teacher. As a free agent, a teacher has the opportunity to embrace, reject, or modify new knowledge, skills, and practices. Based on a teacher's beliefs (i.e., teaching is about the actions of the teacher versus the learning of the student), their views about the societal goals for schooling (knowledge for knowledge's sake, for problem-solving, or to promote social justice), their orientation toward preferred instructional strategies (didactic or experiential), or the preferred organization of the content of their discipline (for biology, four potential approaches include cellular, ecological, systems, or phylogenic), teachers may approach the learning of new knowledge and its application to the classroom differently. For instance, a teacher who believes that teaching is telling might reject conceptual change learning strategies that begin with an understanding of what a student knows in order to design instruction to challenge those understandings. In this case, a teacher's belief would act as a filter. While the teacher may learn the steps involved in conceptual change practices (and be able to repeat them accurately on a knowledge test), she would reject using them in instructional practice. In another case, a teacher might enthusiastically infuse their curriculum with instruction about the nature of science. With the introduction of the *NGSS*, such a teacher might actively seek ways to simultaneously design instruction that integrates disciplinary core ideas, science and engineering practices, and cross-cutting concepts. Here, a commitment to teaching the nature of science would act as an amplifier for a change in practice. In addition, teacher affect, such as motivation, dissatisfaction, efficacy, or risk-taking, can also influence what a teacher learns and chooses to implement in practice. In short, incoming teacher affect and knowledge influence learning and act as an amplifier or filter between knowledge and practice.

Teachers also have a personal knowledge base that might act as an amplifier or filter. Teachers with highly structured and deep content knowledge have the potential to profit differently from content deepening experiences than teachers with limited knowledge or misconceptions (Gess-Newsome, 1999b). Novice teachers apply new knowledge and skills to instructional planning differently than veterans (Borko & Livingston, 1989). While veteran teachers may attend professional development opportunities and leave with new ideas and skills, novice teachers may be so distracted by issues related to classroom management that their intentions to put new practices into the classroom can be thwarted.

Contextual variables can influence what a teacher knows and how knowledge may or may not be used. Access to high-quality professional development at the pre-service or in-service levels can influence practice, as well as the nature of the professional development and whether it is focused on generic or topic-specific knowledge and skills. Research shows that professional development based on generic teaching strategies can actually decrease teacher effectiveness (Milken Family Foundation, 2000), and asking teachers to transfer generic teaching strategies to their specific topics is much less effective than topic-specific and classroom-embedded professional development (Smylie, 1989).

The idea of amplifiers and filters as well as contextual supports for learning helps explain why professional development may not have a straightforward impact on teacher classroom practice. The variability imposed by teacher amplifiers and filters, the impact of context on teaching, and the decisions that teachers make about instruction all increase the uniqueness of each teacher and classroom and provide a viable explanation for this lack of correspondence.

Amplifiers and filters certainly mediate the translation of TSPK to classroom practice, but is it possible for classroom practice to influence teacher affect and knowledge as well? There has been a long-standing debate about whether teacher beliefs need to change before a change in practice can be observed, which raises the question does changing teacher practice have the potential to change teacher knowledge and beliefs (McLaughlin, 1990)? The answer may be both. As student outcomes are recognized as a primary driver of teacher change (Smylie, 1989), and as interactions between knowledge, affect, and practice are dynamic, the combination may create unpredictable and idiosyncratic implications for different teachers.

The removal of teacher orientations and beliefs from the construct of PCK and placing it as an amplifier or filter for classroom practice is a contribution of the model of TPK&S. Removing orientations and affect outside the realm of PCK is more consistent with the literature that has carefully considered this topic (Friedrichsen, Van Driel, & Abell, 2011) and provides greater explanatory power than when embedded within the PCK construct.

Classroom practice: The interaction of personal PCK and the classroom context

Where the TPKB and TSPK can be thought of as context free, relatively static, visible, and clearly identified as a knowledge base, what happens in a classroom is different. The action is fast. Instructional moves may be planned or occur in response to something unexpected. In the act of teaching, the influence of knowledge and belief is blurred and the private and personal understandings that are used to make decisions are dynamic and, in many cases, tacit. Classroom practice is the location of PCK. As a result of the Summit and based on the contributions of John Loughran, we came to a consensus around the following definitions of personal PCK and a related construct—PCK and skill (PCK&S):

- Personal PCK is the *knowledge* of, *reasoning* behind, and *planning* for teaching a particular *topic* in a particular *way* for a particular *purpose* to particular *students* for enhanced *student outcomes* (Reflection *on* Action, Explicit).
- Personal PCK&S is the *act of teaching* a particular *topic* in a particular *way* for a particular *purpose* to particular *students* for enhanced *student outcomes* (Reflection *in* Action, Tacit or Explicit).

There are several features of these definitions that are important to note. First, PCK is clearly defined as personal knowledge, in contrast to the public knowledge bases used earlier in the model. Second, PCK is context specific including the teaching of a particular topic in a particular way for a particular purpose to particular students. PCK is not generalized but lives in a specific experience. Research supports this claim: PCK and associated classroom instruction vary by topic, particularly across high and low knowledge topics (Carlsen, 1991, 1993) and for topics within and outside an area of content expertise (Hashweh, 1987).

Second, there are two time periods identified where PCK is employed with important consequences. In the first definition, PCK is the application of knowledge to teaching. PCK can be found in the instructional plans that teachers create and in the reasons behind their instructional decisions. PCK is therefore Reflection *on* Action (Schön, 1983) and it is purposeful, explicit, and somewhat easily captured. This is the knowledge that teachers bring forward to design and reflect on instruction. For instance, careful questioning and think-aloud protocols can be used to not only understand what a teacher planned (the what), but also the rationale for their instructional decisions (the why).

In PCK&S, we recognize that what a teacher does in the classroom is also based on their PCK, but with some powerful differences. Here, teachers are in the moment, attempting to carry out instructional plans but also needing to monitor student involvement and adjust instruction based on rapid clues. Understanding teacher decision-making here requires Reflection *in* Action and is much more elusive. The knowledge used is much more dynamic, sometimes explicit but often fleeting and tacit, and can only be captured in think-aloud interviews as teachers review teaching videos and attempt to remember what they were thinking that influenced what they did and why. PCK&S in action can also be inferred by researchers based on analysis of what they see in classroom practice. While extrapolating what teachers do in an attempt to understand the 'why' is more brittle than direct knowledge obtained from the teacher, such an analysis can provide insight into what students experience in a classroom. Each type of information provides a different window into how the teaching/learning experience is lived by the teachers and students.

A third important element of this definition has to do with skill. In the original conceptions of PCK, the emphasis was on the knowledge that teachers drew on to inform their teaching. This focus made sense when much of the conceptualization around PCK was designed to help establish tools (e.g., the National Board Certification of Teachers) to assess teachers' knowledge. But as PCK grew to include interactive classroom contexts, a tension developed between what teachers knew and what they were able to do. Two issues were evident: First, just because a teacher knows something doesn't mean that it would be directly translated into practice (remember the teacher amplifiers and filters). Second, just because a teacher recognized an appropriate next instructional move, they may or may not have the skill set to implement it effectively. Not all teachers have equally mastered the skills of teaching. Distinguishing PCK from PCK&S allows researchers to more clearly explain what they are measuring and why, while examining teacher knowledge and practice.

Within the specificity of classroom practice, there is an acknowledgement that the context of the classroom plays an important role. Beyond what teachers know and believe, instruction is shaped by a specific classroom context. For instance, the types of curriculum materials, supplies, and supports available will impact the type of instruction a teacher can deliver. The number of classroom preparations that are assigned to an individual teacher, the amount of planning time available, and the assignment of responsibilities outside the classroom (i.e., coaching, clubs) can limit the amount of time and attention that a teacher can dedicate to instructional planning for any given class. Other school features, such as political and cultural influences of parents and/or community values, disruptions to the school day, and the number of competing types of school reform initiatives, can also influence teaching decisions. Not all of these contextual features are within the control of the teacher. Mary Kennedy (2010) identified these features of the teaching context as contributing to teacher attribution error and warned that diminished attention to these very real pressures overestimates the role and influence of a given teacher on the instruction they can deliver and the student outcomes they can produce.

Learning from the act of teaching is an obvious and important aspect of the profession of teaching. For Cochran-Smith and Lytle (1992), this is knowledge in practice and is generated by teachers as the result of reflection on their teaching practice. Such knowledge grows as teachers individually, collectively, or with a facilitative expert, consider instructional actions and consequences and seek larger perspectives. In this way, personal knowledge can contribute to and grow the public and professional knowledge bases. In creating such knowledge, teachers may restructure their existing professional or topic-specific knowledge bases and/ or rethink their beliefs. By trying new practices and examining what occurs in the classroom, teachers may challenge and change their incoming beliefs. By considering new beliefs and trying out associated practices in an incremental fashion, a teacher may adopt new instructional practices and beliefs.

Student amplifiers and filters

Just like teachers, students have agency in the educational process. Despite our best attempts, students can elect (or not) to engage with the learning process. External influences on student achievement include socio-economic status, parental involvement, and parent and community expectations. Student success is influenced by such things as: demographics (age, gender, race, ethnicity, native language); intelligence and working memory; background knowledge and misconceptions; motivation, self-regulation, ability to pay attention, and persistence; self-concept and goal orientation; health, nutrition, and level of physical activity; and school attendance. This wide variety of influences can act as amplifiers or filters for student learning, thus increasing explanations for the variation in student outcomes and decreasing the ability to directly trace the impact of classroom instruction to results of student measures.

Beyond the impacts of student amplifiers and filters on student outcomes, they also influence what occurs in the classroom. Student behavior and reactions can support or suppress teacher motivation, practice, or ability to learn from teaching experiences. For instance, a teacher who meets student resistance and experiences classroom management issues while trying to implement activity-based instruction may resort to lecture-based teaching strategies, resulting in a decreased willingness to implement new instructional strategies in the future.

Student outcomes

The student amplifiers and filters help us understand why the relationship between instruction and student outcomes is not direct. For example, value-added models attempt to measure a teacher's contribution to student achievement based on comparison to student growth in other years and against student growth seen in other classrooms. Despite the political appeal of using student outcomes as a measure of teacher quality, these metrics show weak or nonexistent relationships to the content and quality of classroom practice (Polikoff

& Porter, 2014). An additional confounding variable in student outcomes is the sometimes questionable quality of instruments we use. Few instruments meet psychometric quality indicators (i.e., reliability and validity). Others lack the sophistication to collect the student learning data that we value. With limited high quality instrumentation, data collection may not be as nuanced or sensitive to change as needed.

While student outcomes are the 'downstream' products of educational research, their influence is felt across the model. Student achievement and examination of student work are powerful learning opportunities for teachers and strong sources of teacher motivation. Such attention to student knowledge and growth can contribute to gains in TSPK, and can help challenge or reinforce teacher amplifiers and filters. Likewise, student outcomes have the potential to modify student amplifiers and filters by increasing or decreasing student motivation and other learning behaviors.

Implications for research and professional development

PCK research has been in progress for the last 30 years. In many ways, we have been measuring a construct that we had not fully defined or developed. However, this work has helped us as a research community to identify both strengths and weaknesses in early conceptualizations of PCK, to explore the nature of the relationships within teacher professional knowledge, and to seek explanations for anticipated relationships that were not borne out by empirical evidence. Through our individual and collective work, and the conversations during and resulting from the PCK Summit, we have developed a more robust model of TPK&S, including PCK; and have a new tool to guide the conceptualization of future research as well as reinterpret sometimes surprising results from the past, while also highlighting the complex and sophisticated nature of content-specific practice.

In the model of TPK&S, we attended to many concerns expressed by the research community and Lee Shulman. This model is much more explicit about defining public and private knowledge, disentangling constructs that have previously all been labeled as PCK. In particular, TSPK distinguishes the knowledge held by the community versus the knowledge in action that exists in PCK. The model also recognizes that PCK is both a knowledge base and a skill, recognizes the use of knowledge during and surrounding instruction, and establishes PCK and much of the related knowledge base as being grounded in the context of a specific topic and related to instruction to specific students and within a specific school context. The model of TPK&S also includes affect and its influence, for both teachers and students.

With clarification of the construct, some ideas presented in the past can be removed from the conversation or considered differently. I will use three personal examples. In my introduction to the 1999 PCK book (Gess-Newsome,

1999a), I discussed the idea of PCK being integrative or transformative. Based on our conversations at the PCK Summit and with the formulation of this model, that conversation is no longer helpful. By distinguishing TSPK from PCK, the relationship between the knowledge bases clarifies the tension that I felt between these two terms. In the same volume, I wrote a chapter about subject matter, considering it at the time as the content knowledge aspect of the teacher professional knowledge base. In the chapter, I identified five ways that the research on teachers' subject matter could be categorized. With the model of TPK&S, I would reassign sections. Conceptual knowledge may stay with the TPKB, but many of the other sections would more appropriately be embedded in the teacher amplifiers and filters of PCK. Finally, in a two-year exploration of changes in biology teachers' PCK and related knowledge bases as a result of professional development and curriculum implementation (Gess-Newsome, Carlson, Gardner, & Taylor, 2010), we sought to measure changes in academic content knowledge, pedagogical knowledge, PCK, classroom practice, and student outcomes. While the ambitious nature of our research contained elements of the model, we were disappointed that significant changes in teacher knowledge and practice did not result in clear pathways of influence to student outcomes. Now, with the model of TPK&S, it is more obvious why variation within teachers may have been greater than the differences across teachers and students.

Beyond refining future research and re-examining past research, the model of TPK&S helps target opportunities for professional development. The definition of PCK&S continues to support long-held assumptions in our work (Gess-Newsome et al., 2010) and are supported by the research of others: PCK&S exists on a continuum from weak to strong; PCK&S can be strengthened through teaching experience, professional development, or other interventions; and teaching experience does not necessarily result in an increase in PCK&S. Being explicit about developing TSPK in professional development would target the types of knowledge that have the greatest potential for translation of knowledge and skill to shape teachers' practice. The more closely those professional development activities can attend to the specific topics and the specific students, the greater the potential for knowledge and skill use. In addition to developing teacher knowledge, we must be cognizant of teacher affect and the potentially filtering or amplifying effects that might impact teacher engagement with learning and implementation. While teachers may benefit greatly from professional development opportunities, we need to be sensitive to the teaching contexts within which they must operate and recognize and measure the contextual variable that might mediate what they are able (or willing) to do in practice. Finally, if student outcomes are the metric that we value, we need to create tools that are more sensitive to the inputs that we are trying to measure across the model.

References

Achieve Inc. (2013). *Next generation science standards*. Retrieved from www.nextgenerationscience.org/next-generation-science-standards (accessed November 24, 2014).

Borko, H., & Livingston, C. (1989). Cognition and improvisation: Differences in mathematics instruction by expert and novice teachers. *American Educational Research Journal, 26*(4), 473–498.

Carlsen, W. S. (1991). Effects of new biology teachers' subject-matter knowledge on curricular planning. *Science Education, 75*(6), 631–647.

Carlsen, W. S. (1993). Teacher knowledge and discourse control: Quantitative evidence from novice biology teachers' classrooms. *Journal of Research in Science Teaching, 30*(5), 417–481.

Cochran-Smith, M., & Lytle, S. (1992). Relationships of knowledge and practice: Teacher learning in community. *Review of Research in Education, 24*, 249–305. Washington, DC: American Educational Research Association.

Friedrichsen, P., Van Driel, J., & Abell, S. A. (2011). Taking a closer look at science teaching orientations. *Science Education, 95*, 358–376.

Gess-Newsome, J. (1999a). Pedagogical content knowledge: An introduction and orientation. In J. Gess-Newsome & N. G. Lederman (Eds.), *Examining pedagogical content knowledge: The construct and its implications for science education* (pp. 3–20). Dordrecht, the Netherlands: Kluwer Academic Publishers.

Gess-Newsome, J. (1999b). Secondary teachers' knowledge and beliefs about subject matter and its impact on instruction. In J. Gess-Newsome & N. G. Lederman (Eds.), *Examining pedagogical content knowledge: The construct and its implications for science education* (pp. 51–94). Dordrecht, the Netherlands: Kluwer Academic Publishers.

Gess-Newsome, J., Carlson, J., Gardner, A., & Taylor, J. (2010). Project PRIME: Building science teachers' pedagogical content knowledge through educative curriculum materials and professional development. Retrieved from BSCS.org\ProjectPRIMEPapers (accessed February 4, 2015).

Hashweh, M. Z. (1987). Effects of subject matter knowledge in the teaching of biology and physics. *Teaching and Teacher Education, 3*(2), 109–120.

Keeley, Page. (2005). *Science curriculum topic study: Bridging the gap between standards and practice*. Thousand Oaks, CA: Corwin Press.

Kennedy, M. M (2010). Attribution error and the quest for teacher quality. *Educational Researcher, 39*, 591–598.

Loughran, J., Berry, A., & Mulhall, P. (2012). *Understanding and developing science teachers' pedagogical content knowledge* (2nd ed.). Rotterdam, the Netherlands: Sense Publishers.

Magnusson, S., Krajcik, J., & Borko, H. (1999). Nature, sources, and development of pedagogical content knowledge for teaching. In J. Gess-Newsome & N. G. Lederman (Eds.), *Examining pedagogical content knowledge: The construct and its implications for science education* (pp. 95–132). Dordrecht, the Netherlands: Kluwer Academic Publishers.

McLaughlin, M. W. (1990). The Rand change agent study revisited: Macro perspectives and micro realities. *Educational Researcher, 19*(9), 11–16.

Milken Family Foundation. (2000). *How teaching matters: Bringing the classroom back into discussions of teacher quality*. Princeton, NJ: ETS. Retrieved from www.ets.org/research/pic (accessed November 24, 2014).

National Research Council. (2012). *A framework for K-12 science education: Practices, crosscutting concepts, and core ideas*. Washington, DC: National Academies Press.

Polikoff, M. S., & Porter, A. C. (2014) Instructional alignment as a measure of teaching quality. *Educational Evaluation and Policy Analysis, 36,* 399–416.

Schön, D. A. (1983). *The reflective practitioner: How professionals think in action.* New York, NY: Basic Books.

Shulman, L. S. (1987). Knowledge and teaching: Foundations of the new reform. *Harvard Educational Review, 57*(1), 1–22.

Shulman, L. (2012*). Dr. Lee Shulman Keynote Presentation – 2012 PCK Summit.* Retrieved from http://pcksummit.bscs.org/node/68 (accessed November 24, 2014).

Smylie, M. A. (1989). Teachers' views of the effectiveness of sources of learning to teach. *The Elementary School Journal, 89*(5), 543–558.

Wayne, A. J., & Youngs, P. (2003). Teacher characteristics and student achievement gains: A review. *Review of Educational Research, 73,* 89–122.

West, L. H. T., Fensham, P. J., & Garrard, J. E. (1985). Describing cognitive structures of learners following instruction in chemistry. In L. H. T. West & A. L. Pines (Eds.), *Cognitive structure and conceptual change* (pp. 29–49). New York, NY: Academic Press.

PART II
Research developments and trajectories

4

SUPPORTING GROWTH OF PEDAGOGICAL CONTENT KNOWLEDGE IN SCIENCE

Kirsten R. Daehler
WESTED

Joan I. Heller & Nicole Wong
HELLER RESEARCH ASSOCIATES

Our program of research has investigated the development of teachers' pedagogical content knowledge (PCK) in science as a result of their participation in professional development intentionally designed to strengthen PCK. This chapter traces the co-evolution of our research, our professional development model, our notions of PCK, and our understanding of how best to support growth of teachers' PCK.

Broadly, we view PCK as the intersection of knowledge about content and teaching—that is, knowledge for teaching topic-specific content. Our early conceptions of PCK were rooted in the core elements introduced in Shulman's original formulation—*teachers' knowledge of learners*, such as understanding students' thinking and reasoning and what makes a specific topic easy or difficult for learners; and *teachers' knowledge of teaching*, such as ways of formulating, sequencing, and representing the subject matter to make it comprehensible to learners (Shulman, 1986, 1987). While the PCK Summit, as presented in this volume, highlighted the many components comprising PCK, we have focused our studies on teachers' abilities to: (1) organize instruction around an accurate, precise, and coherent set of interrelated conceptual learning goals; (2) anticipate, elicit, interpret, and address particular challenges the content poses for their students; and (3) sequence and represent that content during instruction in a way that advances their students' understanding. Teachers use or enact this professional knowledge while actively engaged in content-specific teaching and while planning, analyzing student work, and reflecting on their instruction.

The historical backdrop of the last two decades in the US has played a significant role in shaping our work. With consistently low student achievement scores, an underprepared teaching force, implementation of rigorous standards, and a dearth of high-quality professional development opportunities for teachers, our nation has been in dire need of a solution. The landmark report, *Taking science to school: Learning and teaching science in grades K–8*, produced by the National Research Council in 2007 called for a comprehensive professional development program that is "conceived of, designed, and implemented as a coordinated system" to support students' attainment of high standards (Duschl, Schweingruber, & Shouse, 2007, p. 347).

With support from the National Science Foundation (NSF), the US Department of Education's Institute of Education Sciences (IES), the Stuart Foundation, and the W. Clement and Jessie V. Stone Foundation, a team of science educators from WestEd and researchers from Heller Research Associates and the University of California, Berkeley responded to this challenge to improve student achievement by developing and studying the Making Sense of SCIENCE (MSS) model for teacher learning. The MSS model builds on the work of Carne Barnett-Clarke and her mathematics colleagues at WestEd (Barnett-Clarke & Ramirez, 2004), and uses a case-based approach to teacher education, informed by the work of Lee and Judy Shulman.

At present, MSS resources have grown to nearly a dozen courses for teacher learning that cover core topics in earth, life, and physical science (e.g., matter, organisms, earth systems) for K–12 teachers. Some courses have been co-published and widely disseminated by the National Science Teachers Association. Since 1998, more than 20 states across the US have invested in training science educators to lead MSS courses with thousands of teachers, providing tens of thousands of hours of professional development, and reaching hundreds of thousands of students.

The MSS theory of action posits that teacher professional development improves student achievement through intermediate effects on teachers' content knowledge (CK) in science and their PCK, as shown in Figure 4.1. We have tested different links in this causal chain by examining the impact of our professional development courses on all of these outcomes. In increasingly rigorous quasi-experimental and experimental studies, we have found that MSS teachers and their students consistently show significant gains compared to control groups on measures of science CK, with non-native English speakers and low-performing students making the greatest gains (Heller, Daehler, & Shinohara, 2003; Heller, Daehler, Wong, Shinohara, & Miratrix, 2012).

PCK journey

In this chapter, we detail the interrelated co-evolution of our professional development model, our research, and our understanding of how to support the

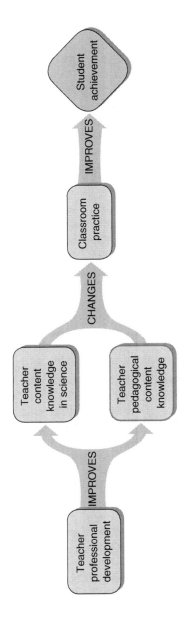

FIGURE 4.1 Making sense of SCIENCE theory of action

Source: Adapted from Horizon Research's ATLAST Theory of Action model http://www.horizon-research.com/atlast

development of PCK. Over the past two decades, our professional development model has gone through three major research-based iterations that reflect shifts in our understanding of how to support PCK development: (1) PCK Cases; (2) the Learning Science for Teaching series; and (3) Making Sense of SCIENCE courses.

Phase I: PCK cases

The roots of our current MSS model extend back to the late 1990s, when the approach began as a collection of teacher-written cases about teaching physical science topics (e.g., electric circuits, sinking and floating, light). Each PCK case described a slice of teaching and a content-based instructional dilemma—for example, the challenge of finding an accurate and accessible model to help students understand the flow of electrical current in a circuit. The cases highlighted common areas of student difficulty, featured classroom artifacts, and served as a basis for engaging teachers in in-depth discussions. Wall charts like the sample shown in Figure 4.2 were used to document the group's conversation during facilitated whole-group discussions about the cases.

One of our early studies (Heller, Daehler, & Kaskowitz, 2004) demonstrated that these case discussions supported growth in PCK. This study followed twelve teachers and tracked how their CK and PCK changed over time as they participated in six case discussions over several months. During in-depth interviews,

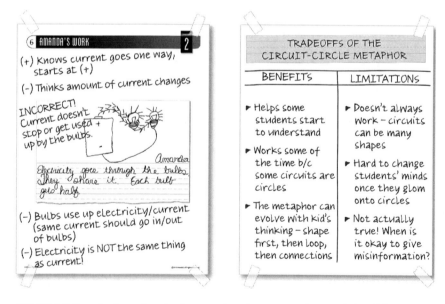

FIGURE 4.2 Sample charts showing how teachers interpret student work in a PCK case and identify the tradeoffs of a common metaphor used in instruction

Supporting growth of PCK **49**

conducted before and after the teachers' participation, teachers were shown a student assessment task, for example a picture of two bulbs connected in a parallel circuit, and were asked: How would you go about helping your students understand what happens when one bulb is unscrewed? What do you think would be hard about this task for students? Later, teachers were shown a sample incorrect student response (see Figure 4.3) and were asked to analyze the student work and describe the instructional approach they would take with this student. The interviews elicited rich information about: (1) teachers' own science understandings; (2) what they anticipated as student difficulties; (3) how they would help students understand specific science content, for example, how electrical current flows in a parallel circuit; (4) their interpretation of a sample student response; and (5) how the teacher would go about helping that particular student develop a stronger understanding of a specific concept.

After participating in six case discussions, teachers showed gains in both their CK and PCK, as measured by content tests and interviews. During the pre-interview, teachers typically named one general challenge without elaboration, such as, "parallel circuits are hard." During the post-interviews, however, teachers had a more nuanced and accurate understanding of the science, which allowed them to anticipate multiple, detailed student difficulties related to learning about circuits, for example:

> Resistance is very hard . . . the fact that . . . the resistance of light bulbs in a series circuit causes the entire circuit to use less electricity, so it reduces flow. And how on earth could that be true if, in a parallel circuit, it's brighter, there's more flow in it . . . That's just very, very hard to get across. Also that the number of bulbs and how they are arranged in the

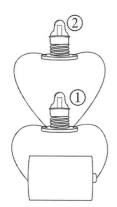

What would happen if you unscrewed the #2 light bulb?

brighter

Please explain what you would see in terms of how the flow of electricity affects the brightness of the light.

When I took out a light the other one was brighter. All the electricity goes to the #1 light. That is why it is bright.

FIGURE 4.3 Excerpt from PCK interview prompt with sample incorrect student response

circuit affects the way the battery kicks out juice, and the fact that you've got two batteries, it's different than having one . . . Light bulbs are tricky too. Because . . . the kids don't really think of them as part of the circuit unless you explicitly teach that or have them dissect a bulb so that they can actually look at the wire and the two places the wire touches and forms part of the circuit.

Many teachers demonstrated increased complexity and accuracy in their analysis of student work. During the post-interviews it was more common for teachers to speculate about what might have led to the student's incorrect answer than during the pre-interviews, as shown in the following response.

I'm wondering if this student [work shown in Figure 4.3], if he is incorrect, he's transferring knowledge from a series circuit to a parallel circuit. But he's transferring the knowledge from a series circuit, not if you take a bulb out, but instead of having two bulbs being lit up, versus just one bulb. That's what it looks like to me.

Through participating in PCK case discussions, many teachers also became better able to make explicit links between specific student difficulties and proposed instructional interventions, and demonstrated increased complexity in their descriptions of teaching strategies. For example, teachers emphasized having students explicitly consider and trace different pathways for the current in a circuit.

I would again ask them to conceptualize where the electricity is flowing. They know that electricity originates in the D cell, with the chemical reaction, and that it's trying to get from the negative back to the positive side. So if we unscrew Bulb 2, it no longer has a route through Bulb 2, but it still does have an alternative route through Bulb 1. So I'd want them to think about that. Think about when Bulb 2 was screwed in, it had two routes, and therefore it was taking both routes. But when Bulb 2 was unscrewed, it only has one route.

Our rubric for analyzing these teacher interviews was informed by prior work done in the context of Barnett's Math Case Methods (MCM) project (Ball, 1988, 1990, 1991; Barnett, 1991; Gordon & Heller, 1995). Gordon and Heller examined whether teachers who participated in math case discussions came to reason differently about the mathematics content and teaching they had encountered in those discussions. This pedagogical reasoning was conceptualized metaphorically as the act of traversing a complex, interconnected web of mathematical information and meanings related to a particular component of content being taught, in combination with a set of considerations about the teaching and learning of that content.

Gordon and Heller's analysis of PCK focused on teachers' responses to the interview question: Could you explain how you might go about helping students understand problems like "2.4 × 0.5" (on post, "4.8 × 0.5")? This revealed that some features of pedagogical knowledge for teaching content can be assessed along two major dimensions—the *semantic complexity* of the content described by the teacher and the *pedagogical complexity* of the teacher's thinking. Semantic complexity can be thought of as the richness of the mathematical or scientific meanings incorporated in the teacher's thinking about teaching and learning (Leinhardt, 1985). Pedagogical complexity can be thought of as the extent to which the teacher evidences careful and explicit analytical thinking to form judgments about instructional approaches, materials, and procedures. From analyses of interviews with MCM participants, three levels of pedagogical complexity emerged, each of which includes the following three dimensions:

- *Focus on Students*—description of what students do, know, think, understand, or find difficult, with respect to particular aspects of content.
- *Emphasis on Meaning-making*—descriptions and explanations, representations, or strategies for illustrating meanings of both quantities and the multiplication process.
- *Critical Analysis of Practice*—analysis of multiple instructional practices, materials, and processes, along with attention to the relationship between features of instruction and particular purposes with respect to student learning and thinking.

This model of pedagogical reasoning was used to characterize how twelve new and continuing participants in the MCM project reasoned about the instructional problem posed during the interview. Analysis revealed that none of the six new participants began in or moved to the strongest levels of pedagogical or semantic complexity, even when their mathematical CK scores were high. In contrast, all six of the continuing participants were at the strongest levels of pedagogical and semantic complexity by the end of the school year, and all had high mathematical CK scores. Although based on a limited sample of teachers, these patterns suggest that PCK develops over time and more sophisticated knowledge about teaching seems to be associated with strong CK. At the same time, strong CK by itself is not sufficient for developing strong PCK, which means other factors must support the growth of this kind of specialized knowledge for teaching.

Building on this math work, our analysis of teachers' involvement in PCK case discussions in science reinforced several hunches about what supports growth in teacher knowledge. When audio records of case discussions were closely examined, we found that teachers who had weaker CK struggled to identify common misconceptions in the student work, often because they shared the same incorrect ideas. Weaknesses in teachers' CK also limited their abilities to analyze the tradeoffs between various instructional decisions, leading to statements about general approaches to teaching (e.g., direct instruction versus inquiry) rather than rich, content-specific conversations that sharpened and refined their pedagogical reasoning. Over time, it became apparent that significant deficits in teachers' own science CK impeded their ability to strengthen their PCK (Daehler & Shinohara, 2001). In summary, we came to understand that teacher CK is necessary for developing PCK, but is not sufficient on its own; teachers' own CK is inextricably interrelated with their knowledge about how to teach that content; and weak content knowledge inhibits teachers' engagement in PCK-rich discussions. These findings signaled an opportunity to modify our professional development model by strengthening teachers' CK to support further growth in PCK.

Phase II: Learning science for teaching (LSFT) series

In this second phase, we made several major revisions to our professional development model. First, we moved from a collection of cases to a series of eight 3-hour sessions that were carefully sequenced to cover core science concepts related to a given topic (e.g., electric circuits), along with a focus on common misconceptions associated with that same topic. Second, to better prepare teachers for more fruitful case discussions we front-loaded the content by starting each session with a 70-minute science investigation. In contrast to most hands-on activities in professional development, which are designed to help teachers implement a curriculum by guiding teachers through the student activities, LSFT focused on adult-level investigations in which teachers solidified their own understandings of core science concepts.

During the science investigation, teachers worked in small groups to conduct hands-on investigations, and engaged in whole-group discussions to make sense of the science. For example, in the first session of electric circuits, groups were provided with a battery, a bulb, and a wire, and challenged to find as many ways as possible to make the bulb light. Based on this experience, groups developed their own working definition of a 'complete circuit' and then used it to make predictions about other circuits. A facilitated whole-group discussion followed, in which teachers shared the circuits they built that lit, did not light, and surprised them. They looked for patterns in their data and summarized what this helped them understand about circuits. Next, teachers regrouped the data according to complete and incomplete circuits, which predictably led them to discover a tricky aspect of the science: Some complete circuits do not result in a lit bulb. To solidify this important understanding, teachers were prompted to describe the relationship between complete, incomplete, lit, and unlit circuits, through drawings, writing, and verbal discussion (Shinohara & Daehler, 2008).

In 2007, we undertook a large-scale research project funded by the NSF that included an efficacy study of the newly redesigned LSFT professional development. The study was conducted over a two-year period, in eight sites across six states in the US. It involved 49 districts, more than 260 elementary teachers, and nearly 7,000 students, largely from underserved populations. This randomized, controlled trial compared the differential effects of three related but systematically varied interventions, including: a *Teaching Cases* course with discussions of pre-structured written cases of classroom practice (Barnett-Clarke & Ramirez, 2004; Daehler & Shinohara, 2001); a *Looking at Student Work* course involving analysis of teachers' own student work in conjunction with concurrent teaching (Little, 2004; Little, Gearhart, Curry, & Kafka, 2003); and a *Metacognitive Analysis* course with teachers engaging in metacognitive reflection on their own learning experiences (Mundry & Stiles, 2009; White, Frederiksen, & Collins, 2009). Each intervention consisted of 24 hours of contact time, divided into eight 3-hour sessions, and all three included an identical science component that incorporated hands-on investigations, sense-making discussions, and readings. However, the PCK components of each course were varied to test different approaches to focusing on teaching and learner thinking.

Conducting research at this scale presented new challenges, one being the need for a cost-effective means of assessing PCK with hundreds of teachers. Our solution was to develop written, constructed-response items, using questions similar to our PCK interviews. The written PCK items asked teachers to analyze samples of student work, interpret strengths and weaknesses in the students' understanding of electric circuits, and describe instructional strategies for addressing those difficulties. The coding scheme for analyzing teachers' responses focused on recording specific science learning goals teachers said they would target, and recording the instructional representations and activities they mentioned to help students make sense of phenomena.

This study provided strong evidence of efficacy for all three interventions, in that each intervention produced significant increases in teacher and student outcomes. Results of hierarchical linear modeling (HLM) analyses showed all three interventions caused sizable gains in teacher CK related to electric circuits, and these increases were significantly greater than control group teachers ($ES = 1.8$–1.9, $p < 0.001$). In addition, students of these teachers outperformed students of control teachers by more than 40 percent ($ES = 0.36$), with English learners making the greatest gains ($ES = 0.72$–0.76). HLM analyses also showed the Teaching Cases and Looking at Student Work courses raised teachers' PCK post-test scores significantly when compared with scores of control teachers ($ES = 0.9$ and 0.8, respectively), whereas the Metacognitive Analysis course did not increase PCK (Heller et al., 2012). This study confirms that teacher PCK can be strengthened through professional development focused on science content, student thinking, and analysis of practice, in ways that benefit student achievement.

Furthermore, this LSFT study provided an opportunity to determine whether the impact on teacher CK solely accounted for the impact on student achievement or whether other teacher outcomes might be partially responsible. This question has important policy implications, because if teacher CK solely accounts for student outcomes, this would support decisions to strengthen *only* teachers'

CK in science as a means of producing student learning gains. To test this, we compared the results using an HLM model that included teacher CK (and a set of relevant student and teacher covariates) to a model that had both teacher CK and the intervention type (i.e., Teaching Cases). These models were found to be significantly different, and all three interventions had significant positive effects, which indicated expected student gains *beyond those gains due to the teachers' CK*. We concluded that each of the three teacher interventions did something to improve student test scores beyond that of merely improving teachers' CK— something that could well be strengthening teacher PCK. This evidence of professional development impact on teacher pedagogical knowledge reinforced our efforts to understand and measure this knowledge.

These findings led us to ask: What changes in teacher PCK may have contributed to increases in student science achievement? To address this question, we analyzed teachers' responses to PCK questions according to several dimensions, including *conceptual learning goals* and *engaging students in meaning-making* (see Table 4.1). The interventions that most strongly led to teachers mentioning at least one specific conceptual learning goal for their students were Looking at Student Work (78 percent of teachers) and Teaching Cases (70 percent of teachers), followed by 62 percent of Metacognitive Analysis teachers. These proportions were approximately double those of the control teachers.

Furthermore, nearly 40 percent of control teachers described having a student only do hands-on work with bulbs, batteries, and wires (for example, "I would have them build it"), with no reference to strategies for helping students make sense of what they observed, whereas fewer than 14 percent of any intervention-group teachers did so. In contrast, the largest proportion—30 percent—of Teaching Cases teachers referred explicitly to strategies for helping students make sense of what they observed (such as by tracing electrical current through the circuit or creating a T-chart to compare drawings of circuits that did and did not

TABLE 4.1 Percent of teachers giving each category of response to written pedagogical content knowledge question, by experimental condition

Response to item, "What might the teacher do next to move this student toward further understanding of electric circuits?"	Teaching Cases	Looking at Student Work	Meta-cognitive Analysis	Control
n	67	60	53	69
Mention any conceptual learning goal	70.1	78.3	62.3	36.2
Mention more than one conceptual learning goal	19.4	25.0	18.9	7.2
Teacher has students do hands-on activity only	10.4	8.3	13.2	39.1
Teacher has students do hands-on activity and a meaning-making activity	29.9	13.3	17.0	10.1
At least one strategy involving meaning-making	47.8	26.7	22.6	15.9
More than one strategy involving meaning-making	14.9	6.7	5.7	4.3

light the bulb) as compared with 10 percent of control teachers. Teaching Cases produced the highest proportion of teachers who mentioned at least one way of engaging students in meaning-making, close to 50 percent, versus only 16 percent of control teachers.

In summary, data from the experimental study established that: (1) two of the three interventions (Teaching Cases and Looking at Student Work) improved teacher PCK; (2) all three interventions improved student test scores by doing more than merely improving teachers' CK—something that could well be strengthening PCK; and, (3) the Teaching Cases course was especially effective at increasing teachers' explicit focus on conceptual learning goals for students, references to engaging students in active roles as learners, and describing strategies for helping students make sense of key science ideas. The courses that most improved both teacher PCK and teacher and student test scores emphasized science content situated in activities and scenarios involving student curricula and instruction, in combination with analysis of student work and classroom pedagogical practice. Based on these findings, policymakers should invest in professional development that emphasizes analysis of student learning, pedagogy, and content, rather than focusing on general pedagogy or purely on content.

Phase III: Making Sense of SCIENCE

Findings from the LSFT study have shaped our current professional development model—Making Sense of SCIENCE. Currently, we think about improving student achievement through a cascade of influences beginning with teacher professional development that is rich in talk about scientific meanings, and focused on student thinking and critical analysis of practice. The current MSS model uses the same two core components as our LSFT teaching cases model (science investigations and teaching cases) while adding greater opportunity for teachers to reflect on what they learn during the professional development and to make connections to their own students and classrooms. Furthermore, in response to a nationwide push for science teachers to explicitly support disciplinary reading, writing, and discourse for all students, and to help teachers meet the growing need to support English learners in their classrooms, each MSS course was designed with a specific literacy focus. In addition, to fit the implementation needs for a summer institute, the MSS model was redesigned into five days (30 hours of learning) with four main components:

- *Science Investigations*—hands-on collaborative activities engage teachers in foundational science content and practices that are related to the accompanying teaching cases.
- *Teaching Investigations*—case discussions engage teachers in examining student thinking and analysis of detailed instructional scenarios. The materials, written by classroom teachers, contain student work, student/teacher dialogue, context information, and discussions of teacher thinking and behavior.

- *Literacy Investigations*—reading/writing/discourse activities intended to help teachers learn how to more effectively support students' development of science literacy skills, help students make sense of the science, communicate in science-specific ways, and develop their academic language proficiency.
- *Classroom Connections*—opportunities for teachers to read about, reflect on, and discuss key science and literacy concepts and consider how these concepts pertain to their own work with students.

Given that the LSFT study showed different benefits in PCK for the Teaching Cases and Looking at Student Work interventions, we decided to combine both approaches in the current MSS model. During the five-day core course, teachers discuss teaching cases, then they meet in professional learning communities for five additional two-hour sessions during the school year, to: (1) examine student work from their own classrooms; (2) evaluate assessment tasks that elicit student understanding; (3) examine classroom artifacts for evidence of student understanding; and, (4) plan instructional 'next steps' to address particular learning gaps. This school-year component is supported by detailed protocols for teacher-led meetings, as well as a task bank of topic-specific student assessments, lists of learning objectives and common yet incorrect ideas, and sample sets of student work.

Each MSS course comes with a *teacher book* that presents all the materials teachers need to participate, including teaching cases, handouts, and session reviews that summarize the key concepts and outcomes and feature illustrations of common but incorrect ways students think about related concepts. To support scale-up and broad use, each MSS course is also accompanied by a *facilitator guide* that provides detailed yet flexible procedures, in-depth background information, guiding questions and charts for each whole-group discussion, and other tips for leading successful professional development.

While we continue to have a myriad of questions about how best to support the growth of teacher PCK, when we reflect on what we know from our research and development work over the years, and compare our work with that of colleagues at the 2012 PCK Summit, we can identify key ingredients that we believe are part of the 'secret sauce' that contribute to growth in teacher PCK. These include:

- *Intertwine science learning with science teaching*. For example, in MSS courses, although the science activities are designed for adults, the content is tightly coupled to the science featured in each accompanying teaching case, such that teachers deepen their own understanding of the science in the context of thinking about children's ideas and classroom experiences. In addition, by using teaching cases that feature pedagogical-content dilemmas, teachers have the opportunity to examine instructional decisions related to teaching core science concepts, including analyzing a variety of metaphors, models, and other representations to help make the concepts comprehensible to students (and themselves), thus reinforcing their science understandings. In addition, after engaging in science investigations, teachers in MSS courses are asked to be metacognitive about what supported and hindered their own learning, as well as what implications their own experiences might have for teaching their own students. In this way, the science and science teaching are always tightly coupled.

- *Provide a high-quality curriculum for teacher learning that models exemplary instruction for science learning.* When engaged in MSS science investigations, teachers experience top-notch curricular materials that showcase effective, research-based practices for science learning. This includes the use of a variety of representations to keep ideas 'on the table' as objects of and for thought (e.g., graphs, images, diagrams; Wong, 2009), as well as multi-modal learning opportunities (e.g., reading, writing, discourse, individual, small group, whole group) and a focus on practicing scientific practices (e.g., asking questions, developing explanations, engaging in scientific argumentation).
- *Push for deep conceptual understanding of both the science and science teaching.* MSS courses have been accused of 'going for the jugular.' This is perhaps because the course development process begins by identifying vexing aspects of the science related to a given topic and then designing learning opportunities that push teachers to examine these tricky issues first-hand. This means teachers often experience cognitive dissonance when they face their own conceptual limitations. Nevertheless, because teachers are immersed in a deep level of thinking about genuinely tough concepts, they often end up with a more relaxed stance about not understanding and come to trust that learning is a process. Through their own experiences, they learn the value of raising the rigor in their own classrooms in ways that result in students' developing deeper understandings of science.
- *Leverage collaborative sense-making.* MSS courses are based on a belief that teachers can learn challenging science by working together to make sense of their own experiences and deeply explore their own understandings/misunderstandings. Toward this end, approximately 50 percent of the learning involves teachers working in small groups, so their thinking happens in the context of other teachers. When working in groups of three, teachers examine data and classroom artifacts in ways that value a variety of viewpoints. As teachers share their own knowledge and experiences, they gain new insights and challenge each other's interpretations, which lead teachers to appropriate each other's ideas.
- *Foster a community of professionals.* Participants in MSS courses frequently comment on the ways in which teachers are treated with utmost respect and supported as they engage in peer-to-peer conversations and rigorous discourse. It is key that teachers hold the locus of authority in their own learning and develop an identity as life-long learners who are part of a professional community.

Current and future directions

We are currently engaged in examining aspects of teachers' instructional strategies and classroom discourse, to help us understand the processes by which the teachers' professional development experience might influence student achievement. Building on our prior work, and as an outgrowth of conversations with colleagues during the PCK Summit, we will characterize teachers' *enacted PCK* by analyzing the accuracy of the science content communicated by the teachers, the ways teachers elicit students' science ideas during instruction, and the opportunities teachers give students to make sense of science ideas and to read, write, and talk in science-specific ways.

While existing research now confirms teacher PCK (and student achievement in science) can be strengthened through targeted professional development, many unanswered questions remain about how best to do this, for example: What features of the professional learning experience are essential? Are there more efficient or effective ways of developing teacher PCK? What happens if video cases are used instead of written narrative cases? What are cost-effective ways of assessing PCK? Will teachers need to engage in professional development for every topic they teach to develop the specialized PCK they need, or do some elements of PCK transfer across content areas? What supports are needed and what barriers exist to scaling? We look forward to the interesting research and development work required to begin addressing these questions. We also look forward to the ongoing collaborations and the collegial conversations that enhance this work, such as that made possible by the PCK Summit of 2012.

References

Ball, D. L. (1988). *Knowledge and reasoning in mathematical pedagogy: Examining what prospective teachers bring to teacher education* (Unpublished doctoral dissertation). Michigan State University.

Ball, D. L. (1990). Prospective elementary and secondary teachers' understanding of division. *Journal of Research in Mathematics Education, 21,* 132–144.

Ball, D. L. (1991). Research on teaching mathematics: Making subject matter knowledge part of the equation. In J. Brophy (Ed.), *Advances in research on teaching* (Vol. 2, pp. 1–48). Greenwich, CT: JAI Press.

Barnett, C. S. (1991). Building a case-based curriculum to enhance the pedagogical content knowledge of mathematics teachers. *Journal of Teacher Education, 42*(4), 263–272.

Barnett-Clarke, C., & Ramirez, A. (2004). Case discussions. In L. B. Easton (Ed.), *Powerful designs for professional learning* (pp. 75–84). Oxford, OH: National Staff Development Council.

Daehler, K. R., & Shinohara, M. (2001). A complete circuit is a complete circle: Exploring the potential of case materials and methods to develop teachers' content knowledge and pedagogical content knowledge of science. *Research in Science Education, 31*(2), 1–24.

Duschl, R. A., Schweingruber, H. A., & Shouse, A. W. (Eds.). (2007). *Taking science to school: Learning and teaching science in grades K-8.* Washington, DC: National Academic Press.

Gordon, A., & Heller, J. I. (1995). *Traversing the web: Pedagogical reasoning among new and continuing Math Case Methods participants*. Paper presented at the annual meeting of the American Educational Research Association, San Francisco, CA.

Heller, J. I., Daehler, K. R., & Kaskowitz, S. R. (2004, April). *Fostering pedagogical content knowledge about electric circuits through case-based professional development*. Paper presented at the annual meeting of the National Association for Research in Science Teaching, Vancouver.

Heller, J. I., Daehler, K., & Shinohara, M. (2003). Connecting all the pieces: Using an evaluation mosaic to answer an impossible question. *Journal of Staff Development, 24*, 36–41.

Heller, J. I., Daehler, K. R., Wong, N., Shinohara, M., & Miratrix, L. (2012). Differential effects of three professional development models on teacher knowledge and student achievement in elementary science. *Journal of Research in Science Teaching, 49*(3), 333–362.

Leinhardt, G. (1985). Instructional time: A winged chariot? In C. W. Fisher & D. C. Berliner, (Eds.), *Perspectives on instructional time* (pp. 263–282). New York, NY: Longman Press.

Little, J. W. (2004). "Looking at student work" in the United States: Countervailing impulses in professional development. In C. Day & J. Sachs (Eds.), *International handbook on the continuing professional development of teachers* (pp. 94–118). Buckingham, UK: Open University Press.

Little, J. W., Gearhart, M., Curry, M., & Kafka, J. (2003). Looking at student work for teacher learning, teacher community and school reform. *Phi Delta Kappan, 85*(3), 184–192.

Mundry, K., & Stiles, K. E. (Eds.). (2009). *Professional learning communities for science teaching: Lessons from research and practice*. Arlington, VA: National Science Teachers Association Press.

Shinohara, M., & Daehler. K. R. (2008). Understanding science: The role of community in content learning. In A. Lieberman & L. Miller (Eds.), *Teachers in professional communities: Improving teaching and learning*. New York, NY: Teachers College Press.

Shulman, L. S. (1986). Those who understand: Knowledge growth in teaching. *Educational Researcher, 15*(2), 4–14.

Shulman, L. S. (1987). Knowledge and teaching: Foundations of the new reform. *Harvard Education Review, 57*(1), 1–22.

White, B., Frederiksen, J., & Collins, A. (2009). The interplay of scientific inquiry and metacognition: More than a marriage of convenience. In D. Hacker, J. Dunlosky, & A. Graesser (Eds.), *Handbook of metacognition in education* (pp. 175–205). Mahwah, NJ: Lawrence Erlbaum Associates.

Wong, N. (2009, April). *Empowering conceptual understanding and scientific reasoning through external representations*. Paper presented at the annual meeting of the American Educational Research Association, San Diego, CA.

5

SCIENCE TEACHERS' PCK

Understanding sophisticated practice

Rebecca Cooper & John Loughran
MONASH UNIVERSITY

Amanda Berry
LEIDEN UNIVERSITY

> Pedagogical content knowledge (PCK) is an academic construct that represents an intriguing idea. It is an idea rooted in the belief that teaching requires considerably more than delivering subject content knowledge to students, and that student learning is considerably more than absorbing information for later accurate regurgitation. PCK is the knowledge that teachers develop over time, and through experience, about how to teach particular content in particular ways in order to lead to enhanced student understanding . . . [it is] a corner stone of teachers' professional knowledge and expertise . . . in order to recognize and value the development of their own PCK, teachers need to have a rich conceptual understanding of the particular subject content that they teach. This rich conceptual understanding, combined with expertise in developing, using and adapting teaching procedures, strategies and approaches for use in particular classes, is purposefully linked to create the amalgam of knowledge of content and pedagogy that Shulman (1986, 1987) described as PCK.
>
> *(Loughran, Berry, & Mulhall, 2012, p. 9)*

Introduction

Intrigued by the construct of pedagogical content knowledge (PCK), the authors of this chapter have been involved in a long-standing research program investigating the nature and development of PCK of pre-service and in-service science teachers and, more recently, science teacher educators. As we were all high school science teachers prior to beginning work as university academics, we value a practitioner perspective in researching PCK and as such, have sought through our work, to elicit and represent science teachers' expertise in ways that speak meaningfully to teachers as well as researchers, and that support the continuing articulation and development of science teachers' PCK.

Our approach to researching PCK was based on the assumption that expert teachers have well-developed PCK that has grown over time and through particular kinds of experiences—all of which we were trying to capture and portray. We viewed PCK as a tacit form of teachers' professional knowledge that is often topic, person, and context specific. Yet, our research also indicated that teachers hold a shared knowledge (or collective PCK) around key notions of teaching and learning particular science topics.

In this chapter, we present first an overview of our research program including the development of our particular research approach using CoRes (Content Representations) and PaP-eRs (Pedagogical and Professional-experience Repertoires), see the appendices for an example of each. Then, we discuss the current trajectory of our work investigating the PCK of science teacher educators, based on a study by the first author. Finally, we propose possible lines of future research based on issues that have emerged through our work and from our conversations with colleagues at the PCK Summit, held in Colorado, USA.

Starting points

Our research into science teachers' PCK was supported by three consecutive Australian Research Council (ARC) grants (over nine years). The overall aim of the project, driven by the ideas noted in the introductory quotation, was to develop ways of capturing, documenting, and portraying experienced science teachers' PCK so that it might be useful from a teacher's point of view.

We hold the view that teaching is a sophisticated business even though it is not necessarily seen that way from outside the profession—and sometimes from within. We thought that if we could capture and portray experienced science teachers' PCK, if we could develop ways of making it concrete for others, then it might help to highlight the complex nature of teaching and illustrate the importance of teachers' professional knowledge of practice. In so doing, we envisaged PCK as offering real possibilities for conceptualizing science teaching as considerably more than assembling an array of "activities that work" (Appleton, 2006).

Uncovering and explicating science teachers' PCK proved to be a difficult task, because teachers' knowledge of practice is largely tacit (Polanyi, 1962). As a consequence, when we began to work with science teachers, although we thought we knew what PCK was, the teachers with whom we worked found it difficult to give us examples of PCK in their practice. Although they were recognized as expert science teachers and had an understanding of what we were trying to do, the tacit nature of their knowledge meant that they did not have a language to share that knowledge with us.

Across a range of approaches to collecting data with our participants, there was a noticeable mismatch between our hopes and expectations and what we were able to capture and portray. When we thought we could see examples of PCK in teachers' practice, we were disappointed with the follow-up discussions and inquiries. Teachers were unable to explicate their thinking about their teaching in the ways we sought, which made us feel as though *we* were offering the pedagogical reasoning underpinning their practice rather than it genuinely coming from them.

Over time, we developed a set of prompts that we found very useful for tapping into teachers' thinking about their practice. The prompts took time to develop and emerged as a consequence of listening carefully to that which teachers considered important in shaping their thinking about their teaching. As we developed and refined the prompts, we found that they functioned well in uncovering the thinking that underpinned the expert practice we were observing. When we used the prompts as specific cues for discussing teaching within a given science unit, topic, or theme, we began to access aspects of teachers' content-specific pedagogical reasoning that helped to provide insights into their tacit knowledge of practice.

The prompts took on new significance when we introduced the notion of 'Big Ideas' as a way of understanding how teachers conceptualized the particular science content. Through the Big Ideas (i.e., ideas that teachers see as crucial to students' understanding of a specific topic), teachers began to discuss science in ways that went well beyond sharing propositional knowledge. This combination of Big Ideas and specific prompts led to the development of what we later termed a CoRe that became a powerful tool for unpacking science teachers' PCK.

The value of the CoRe as a data collection tool helped us to better access and explore teachers' thinking about their practice, but creating ways of making that thinking visible through practice was still lacking. When we began to ask teachers for examples of elements of the CoRe in their own practice, the CoRe became a vehicle for 'concretizing' issues, ideas, and reasoning in action. We discovered the importance of what we later termed PaP-eRs, as an essential complement to the CoRe. PaP-eRs were developed as short narratives based on teachers' accounts of teaching a specific science topic over time to particular groups of students. PaP-eRs were constructed in different ways to display the range of approaches to and thinking about teaching that was so evident in what we heard and saw in their practice. A CoRe and its associated PaP-eRs became a two-part methodological tool for uncovering and explicating science teachers' PCK. However, when we shared our CoRes and PaP-eRs with teachers to offer them examples of PCK, it quickly emerged that these representations were both understood and appreciated. Hence, as we built up a series of CoRes and associated PaP-eRs, we recognized their value to teachers as resource folios on particular science topics.

Resource Folios (see Loughran, Berry, & Mulhall, 2006, 2012) have proved useful for working with in-service and pre-service teachers in exploring and examining their understandings of PCK, and in the development of their science teaching practice.

CoRes and PaP-eRs

CoRes and PaP-eRs have been taken up in different ways by different groups of people. For example, CoRes have been adopted by teachers as an approach to curriculum planning and as a science faculty professional development activity when planning a unit of work. Similarly, many science education researchers internationally have adopted CoRes as a data collection tool (see, Bertram & Loughran, 2012; Hume, 2010; Nilsson & Loughran, 2011; Williams & Lockley, 2012). CoRes have also been used as a way of introducing pre-service teachers to PCK to begin to develop their PCK (Woolnough, 2009) as well as promoting the PCK development of university chemistry educators (Garritz & Ortega-Villar, 2012).

Different studies have illustrated how the CoRe has been used as both a research tool and a representational product and have affirmed our experiences that the task of developing a CoRe challenges teachers' thinking. Studies consistently reveal that individually, teachers often struggle to construct Big Ideas and to answer the prompts of the CoRe. However, when working in small groups, they are better able to articulate their ideas as a consequence of discussing and testing each other's thinking. In some situations we found it was helpful to have a facilitator to stimulate and focus the discussion. For example, identifying Big Ideas often presents a challenge to a group of teachers as their ideas and thinking vary greatly across the group; a facilitator can help teachers focus and frame their thinking. As a consequence, the notion of Big Ideas (top row of a CoRe) has emerged as important in framing thinking about teaching the particular topic under consideration, because the conceptual nature of the topic comes to the surface in new and challenging ways.

Because CoRes highlight the importance of thinking about a science topic through Big Ideas, they focus attention on the role of content in a new and different way for many teachers. The CoRe highlights that the development of PCK is not about content knowledge as information but about conceptual understanding of the content *for* teaching. The majority of prompts (the left-hand side of a CoRe) probe deeper understandings of the content and, for that reason, require a consideration of not only how it might be taught, but also, importantly, how it might (or might not) be learned. Thus, teaching as the simple delivery of content knowledge is immediately challenged when thinking about PCK using the construct of a CoRe. As a consequence, it causes teachers to think differently about what they are doing, how, and why in teaching a specific science topic.

PaP-eRs provide 'windows' into how aspects of a CoRe might be recognized and realized in practice. However, our work with experienced teachers suggests that although they enjoy reading them, they find writing PaP-eRs is hard work and not something that they want to invest too much of their time in doing. Our experience also highlights how, for pre-service teachers, writing PaP-eRs appears to offer a form of scaffolding that encourages and supports the development of their reflection on practice. Analyzing a PaP-eR can also be an effective means for teachers to begin to recognize aspects of PCK and consider that which influences their pedagogical reasoning. PaP-eRs can therefore be seen as another way of looking into practice to better understand what PCK looks like when it is well developed.

We believe that PCK can be developed through experience, although the nature of that experience matters; some types of experiences seem to be more helpful than others in enhancing teachers' PCK. Working with a CoRe appears to be a catalyst for teachers to see the value of pursuing their understanding of science teaching through the notion of PCK. Through our research we came to the view that the development of PCK is a non-linear process related to teachers' professional contexts, situations, and personal beliefs. The CoRes and PaP-eRs developed through our research are helpful in supporting teachers to articulate and discuss their understandings of teaching and learning specific science topics and enhancing their professional knowledge of practice; and that is important in illustrating teaching as a sophisticated business.

Moving beyond the initial project: PCK for science teacher educators

The first author of this chapter, Rebecca, began as a teacher participant in the original project that led to the development of CoRes and PaP-eRs. Initially, the idea of PCK intrigued her as a way of thinking differently about her science teaching. Then, when she took up an academic position in science teacher education, PCK became a topic of interest for her in new ways; both in teaching and research. The following vignette illustrates how Rebecca's thinking about and experience in pursuing PCK influenced her understanding of the construct.

Grasping the notion of PCK

> The idea of PCK resonated strongly with me as a high school science teacher since it provided a way of describing not only what I wanted to do when I was teaching a particular science concept, but also helped me to explore the reasoning behind my thinking and actions. Journal writing and peer observation were strongly encouraged in the science faculty of my school, both for personal reflection and facilitating faculty collaboration and discussion. So PCK (although we didn't necessarily call it that to start with)

became both a personal challenge and a publicly discussed/observed notion for me. The personal challenge was to reflect on my teaching beyond recall of classroom events and to really delve into what my priorities were for student learning and thus, how my practice could support these priorities. The faculty discussions and peer observations were, in effect, ways of generating collective PCK, although I didn't really recognize it that way, at the time. It was an attempt to tap into that tacit professional knowledge that we held as individuals, and then to bring it out and question it through observation and discussion. While this was a valuable form of professional learning at the time, I also see that reflecting on this experience over time is equally valuable in terms of my understanding and development of PCK. In other words, grasping the notion of PCK has been, and continues to be, an ongoing process shaped by my context and experiences.

As I began the transition from high school science teacher to science teacher educator I started to recognize differences between my science teacher PCK and my developing science teacher educator PCK. I felt that while some aspects of my knowledge of teaching science were transferable into this new context, there were also other aspects that were significantly different for a science teacher educator. Through grappling with the notion of PCK, as well as my shift in roles, I came to see that I had developed three distinct ways of thinking about PCK: (1) as a way of framing my teaching of science concepts; (2) as a construct that pre-service science teachers needed to be aware of and begin to develop for themselves; and (3) as a source for informing my developing understanding of teaching as a science teacher educator.

In terms of the first way of thinking about my PCK for teaching science concepts, I began to see that my PCK about a given piece of science content was indeed just that, *my PCK*, and in a sense, not so helpful to pre-service science teachers. They did not have my experiences of thinking about this construct, they did not understand science concepts in the same way that I did, nor did they have my teaching experience or understandings of student learning. Further, we did not share a common language for talking about teaching. So how then could I help these pre-service teachers understand, develop and value something so complex? These types of issues generated a need in me to better understand the intricacies of PCK and how I could best use it as a science teacher educator.

I began team-teaching with a colleague, where it became common practice for us to challenge each other's teaching approach in front of our pre-service teachers while we were teaching. We wanted the students to see into our decision-making processes, and also to highlight the idea that teachers can perceive and react to situations differently. Further to this, it was also a way of forcing us to articulate our thinking for ourselves as well as for our pre-service teachers. Post-class debriefings with my colleague led us to question, as science teacher educators, what our PCK actually comprised, and what knowledge we were beginning to develop about PCK that was particular to our work as science teacher educators.

This ongoing grappling with the notion of PCK became formalized as my PhD research: which started out as an exploration of the development of science teacher educators' PCK at different career stages, and possible links between their PCK development and their approach to teaching about science teaching. Interestingly, as my research progressed, I was confronted with issues of how to access the PCK of participating science teacher educators, just as my co-authors had experienced the same situation in developing their research approach with experienced science teachers. Mostly, the science teacher educators who participated in my research talked about the development of their *pedagogical knowledge* (PK) for teaching pre-service science teachers, rather than their *PCK*. They did not connect specific science content for teaching with talking about their pedagogical approach. Perhaps also, these science teacher educators' emphasis on PK was indicative of a shifting emphasis between different knowledge types as their various experiences, contexts or expectations influenced how they thought about and enacted their teaching knowledge at different career stages, as a teacher or as a teacher educator, which in turn, influenced their PK/PCK development? Thus, my research became focused on science teacher educators' PK at different career stages even though I had set out to examine their PCK.

Researching PCK has been important in my development as a teacher and teacher educator and has now begun to influence the approach I take to supporting pre-service teachers in their learning about science teaching. My involvement in the research that led to CoRes and PaP-eRs provided a base on which to extend my own knowledge of practice as a teacher educator and, as a consequence, has become a catalyst for my ongoing research into science teacher educators' PCK. My research brought me through a cycle of questioning, clarifying and re-questioning PCK as a construct and its usefulness for teacher educators. I have asked myself questions such as: Is there a point where unpacking PCK development just gets too complex, a point where it is no longer really useful in teacher education? Is that knowledge so personal and complex and idiosyncratic that we can't even begin to use it in teacher education programs? Is the knowledge that science teacher educators develop in their teaching of science teaching PCK or is it something else?

Returning to my ways of thinking about PCK outlined above: (1) as a way of framing my teaching of science concepts; (2) as a construct that pre-service science teachers needed to be aware of and begin to develop for themselves; and (3) as a source for informing my developing understanding of teaching as a science teacher educator, it is the last point that has really captured my interest.

I am not convinced that the knowledge that the science teacher educators that I worked with could (or should) be labeled as PCK. My research suggests that there are many shifts in focus that science teacher educators are confronted by in their work with pre-service teachers. These shifts include two in particular, that of moving from being focused on their development as a science teacher educator to being more focused on their students' learning, and a shift from holding science content as central to their efforts to being more concerned with quality teaching and assessment strategies. Perhaps it is better to describe the situation as not so much a shift in focus, but rather a rethinking about learning and teaching science more generally. It is difficult for teacher educators to manage these shifts in focus, but in observing them through my research, I am left questioning the nature of PCK and the knowledge that science teacher educators develop as they progress through their teaching about science teaching careers.

An emerging research agenda: Science teacher educators' PCK

Studies into the shift from teacher to teacher educator have illustrated that there are a number of challenges faced in making that transition (Boyd & Harris, 2011; Bullock, 2009; Davey, 2013; Dinkelman, Margolis, & Sikkenga, 2006; Kitchen, 2005; Murray & Male, 2005). However, one aspect of that transition that has not yet been examined is associated with how a teacher educator's PCK develops and is influenced by the change in their teaching context. Despite the recognition of the demanding issues associated with professionally developing as a teacher educator (Loughran, 2014), thus far the subject-specific nature of that professional development has received very limited attention in the research literature. It would seem reasonable to suggest that if science teachers' PCK is to be developed in meaningful ways, and that such development was to be initiated in teacher preparation programs, then one outcome might be that a vision for ongoing professional growth as a science teacher might be more clear and explicit. That would then mean that science teacher educators' PCK, the ways it develops, and how it shapes their teaching of science teaching should come into sharp focus on the research agenda of science education.

Some notable starting points that have yet to gain serious traction in the literature include the work of Smith (2000), an elementary science teacher educator who described aspects of her professional development in relation to what she defined as three kinds of PCK—knowledge of pre-service teachers' backgrounds as science learners; pre-service teachers' ideas about science and scientists; and pre-service teachers' view of learning to teach science. Another example is Abell, Rogers, Hanuscin, Lee, & Gagnon's (2009) study on the development of PCK of teacher educators related to the different roles they perform at various phases of their careers (i.e., observer, apprentice, partner, independent instructor, and mentor); and

Berry and Van Driel's (2012) study on the development of expertise of a small group of science teacher educators from Australia and the Netherlands.

Interestingly, Abell et al. (2009) argued that a parallel form of PCK exists for science teacher educators whereby the subject matter knowledge needed includes both science content knowledge *and* knowledge for teaching science. These researchers were of the view that a science teacher educator's PCK included "knowledge about curriculum, instruction and assessment for teaching science methods courses and supervising field experiences, as well as . . . knowledge about pre-service teachers and orientations to teaching science teachers" (p. 79). Their study led them to propose a model of learning to teach prospective science teachers centered on explicitly attending to individual components of PCK for science teaching as well as opportunities to integrate those components into practice. In many ways, Rebecca's vignette (above) illustrates a number of connections with Abell et al.'s work and highlights again the fact that PCK offers new ways of conceptualizing aspects of the work of science teacher educators that extend well beyond sharing tips and tricks of practice. A focus on PCK in science teacher education though must not just be about 'delivering' it to student teachers; the development of science teacher educators' PCK adds another layer of sophistication to the nature of their work and the ways in which they can better teach about science teaching.

In considering the experiences articulated through the vignette and considering the links to the work of others who have been drawn to similar ideas, an interesting research agenda emerges based on an exploration of questions such as: How does a change in the teaching context (from school to teacher education) influence understandings of PCK? What does PCK look like from a science teacher educator's point of view and why? Such an agenda could be productive and informing for science teacher education and open up new avenues for better understanding how learning about science teaching might be enhanced.

Tamir (1991) was of the view that science teacher educators should have "elements of professional knowledge integrated with elements of personal knowledge" (p. 267), which suggests that the ability of science teacher educators to make their PCK explicit could be a shaping force in helping them recognize how to best address the shift from first-order to second-order teaching (Murray & Male, 2005). There is a need for science teacher educators to have a strong working knowledge and practice of PCK. Yet there is another layer for science teacher educators to be well versed in and that includes knowing about pre-service teachers' development and how that might be shaped and impacted in the long term if PCK is a serious focus for their ongoing professional learning. Perhaps this 'double layer' of knowledge for science teacher educators offers insights into how to better help pre-service teachers make the shifts in their development, using PCK as a form of scaffolding, for what it means to develop and grow as science teachers and to have a vision for that development into the future.

Conclusion

We have found that researching PCK has been an ongoing challenge, and while CoRes and PaP-eRs have helped to reveal a lot about expert science teachers' knowledge, really, what we have is a more comprehensive understanding of the notion of PCK. Our engagement with PCK has demonstrated to us in very personal ways why it is a somewhat elusive construct and how it is that different researchers interpret it in a diversity of ways (Smith and Banilower—Chapter 7— arrived at a similar conclusion). Perhaps the idea that PCK remains somewhat elusive is part of its allure? Broadening our research agenda to include a consideration of PCK for science teacher educators opens up many exciting possibilities. We see it as a way of creating new opportunities to think more deeply about what it means to be a science teacher educator and how (through a serious focus on PCK) pre-service teachers of science might develop a more meaningful approach to their learning about science teaching.

It is interesting to ponder the conditions in education when Shulman (1986) was originally pushing the idea of PCK as a special form of knowledge that teachers may have and actively develop and Berliner (1986) was questioning what it meant to be an expert pedagogue. Politically, these academics were responding to simplistic views of teaching that too easily dominated the landscape and undermined teaching as a profession. Now, years later, similar conditions seem to be buffeting the world of teacher education across continents and nations. Perhaps a serious focus on researching the nature and influence of science teacher educators' PCK might help to bolster the teaching profession in new ways and highlight the importance of teacher education as something that develops and supports a profession involved in a sophisticated and complex business.

Note

1 These are described in the PaP-eR: Seeing things differently.

References

Abell, S. K., Rogers, M. A. P., Hanuscin, D. L., Lee, M. H., & Gagnon, M. J. (2009). Preparing the next generation of science teacher educators: A model for developing PCK for teaching science teachers. *Journal of Science Teacher Education*, 20(1), 77–93.

Appleton, K. (Ed.). (2006). *Elementary science teacher education: International perspectives on contemporary issues and practice*. Mahwah, NJ: Lawrence Erlbaum Associates.

Berliner, D. C. (1986). In pursuit of the expert pedagogue. *Educational Researcher*, 15(7), 5–13.

Berry, A., & Van Driel, J. H. (2012). Teaching about teaching science: Aims, strategies, and backgrounds of science teacher educators. *Journal of Teacher Education*, 64(2), 117–128.

Bertram, A., & Loughran, J. J. (2012). Science teachers' views on CoRes and PaP-eRs as a framework for articulating and developing pedagogical content knowledge. *Research in Science Education,* doi: 10.1007/s11165-011-9227-4

Boyd, P., & Harris, K. (2011). Becoming a university lecturer in teacher education: Expert school teachers reconstructing their pedagogy and identity. In T. Bates, A. Swennen, & K. Jones (Eds.), *The professional development of teacher educators* (pp. 20–34). London: Routledge.

Bullock, S. M. (2009). Learning to think like a teacher educator: Making the substantive and syntactic structures of teaching explicit through self-study. *Teachers and Teaching: Theory and practice, 15*(2), 291–304.

Davey, R. L. (2013). *The professional identity of teacher educators: Career on the cusp?* London: Routledge.

Dinkelman, T., Margolis, J., & Sikkenga, K. (2006). From teacher to teacher educator: Experiences, expectations, and expatriation. *Studying Teacher Education: A journal of self-study of teacher education practices, 2*(1), 5–23.

Garritz, A., & Ortega-Villar, N. A. (2012, March). *Interviews and content representation for teaching condensed matter bonding: An affective component of PCK?* Paper presented at the National Association for Research in Science Teaching, Indianapolis, IN.

Hume, A. (2010). A pedagogical tool for science teacher education: Content Representation (CoRe) design. *Science Teacher Education, 59,* 29–38.

Kitchen, J. (2005). Looking backward, moving forward: Understanding my narrative as a teacher educator. *Studying Teacher Education, 1*(1), 17–30.

Loughran, J. J. (2014). Professionally developing as a teacher educator. *Journal of Teacher Education,* doi: 10.1177/0022487114533386

Loughran, J. J., Berry, A., & Mulhall, P. (2006). *Understanding and developing science teachers' pedagogical content knowledge.* Rotterdam, the Netherlands: Sense Publishers.

Loughran, J. J., Berry, A., & Mulhall, P. (2012). *Understanding and developing science teachers' pedagogical content knowledge* (2nd ed.). Rotterdam, the Netherlands: Sense Publishers.

Murray, J., & Male, T. (2005). Becoming a teacher educator: Evidence from the field. *Teaching and Teacher Education, 21*(2), 125–142.

Nilsson, P., & Loughran, J. J. (2011). Understanding and assessing primary science student teachers' pedagogical content knowledge. *Journal of Science Teacher Education, 23*(7), 699–721.

Polanyi, M. (1962). *Personal knowledge: Towards a post-critical philosophy.* London: Routledge and Kegan Paul.

Shulman, L. S. (1986). Those who understand: Knowledge growth in teaching. *Educational Researcher, 15*(2), 4–14.

Shulman, L. S. (1987). Knowledge and teaching: Foundations of the new reform. *Harvard Educational Review, 57*(1), 1–22.

Smith, D. C. (2000). Content and pedagogical content knowledge for elementary science teacher educators: Knowing our students. *Journal of Science Teacher Education, 11,* 27–46.

Tamir, P. (1991). Professional and personal knowledge of teachers and teacher educators. *Teaching and Teacher Education, 7*(3), 263–268.

Williams, J., & Lockley, J. (2012). Using CoRes to develop the pedagogical content knowledge (PCK) of early career science and technology teachers. *Journal of Technology Education, 24*(1), 34–53.

Woolnough, J. (2009, September). *Developing preservice teachers' science PCK using Content Representations.* Paper presented at the European Science Education Research Association, Istanbul.

Appendix 1: Abbreviated version of a CoRe

This CoRe is designed for students in Lower Secondary School, i.e., Years 7–9.	IMPORTANT SCIENCE		
	A: Matter is made up of small bits that are called particles.	**B:** There is empty space between particles.	**C:** Particles are in constant motion.
What you intend the *students* to learn about this idea.	If we break up substances, the smallest bit of substance we can get is a particle.	The relative distances between particles differ in solids, liquids, and gases.	Particles of matter are always moving. The speed of particles can be changed (by heating/cooling, pressure change) . . .
Why it is important for students to know this.	Because it helps to explain the behavior of everyday things, e.g., diffusion.	Because it explains the ability to compress things and helps to explain events such as expansion and dissolving.	Because it explains what happens in phase changes, e.g., the need to contain gases is evidence the particles are moving.
What else *you* know about this idea (that you do not intend students to know yet).	At this stage 'particles' is used in a general sense without discriminating between atoms and molecules. Subatomic structure. Chemical reactions. Ions. More complex properties of materials. . . .		
Difficulties/limitations connected with teaching this idea.	The use of particular science models is not necessary to comprehend science in everyday life . . .	There is a big difference between macro (seen) and micro (unseen) levels . . .	That macro properties are a result of micro arrangements is hard to understand. . . .
Knowledge about students' thinking which influences your teaching of this idea.	Many students will use a continuous model (despite former teaching).	The notion of 'space' is very difficult to think about—most students propose there is other 'stuff' between the particles . . .	Students have commonly encountered 'states of matter' but do not understand the ideas in terms of particle movement . . .

Other factors that influence your teaching of this idea.	Maturity—stage of psychological development, readiness to grapple with abstract ideas. Dealing with many different student conceptions at once. Knowledge of context (students' and teacher's). Using the term 'phase' suggests the idea of a continuum ...		
Teaching procedures (and particular reasons for using these to engage with this idea).	**Probes of student understanding:** e.g., students draw a flask containing air, then re-draw the same flask with some of the air removed. Probes promote student thinking ...	**POE (Predict-Observe-Explain:** e.g., squashing syringe of air (ask students to predict the outcome based on different models of matter ...)	**Translation activities:** e.g., role-play, modeling, drawing. For example, my life as a Carbon Atom; or, write about what you would see if you were inside a particle of water ...
Specific ways of ascertaining students' understanding or confusion around this idea (include likely range of responses).	.... Explaining thinking and defending views. Making predictions about new situations. Tracking one's own learning, e.g., "I used to think ... " Asking questions such as, What is something that has been bothering you from yesterday's lesson? ...			

Appendix 2: Abbreviated version of a PaP-eR

(This is part 1 of a 3-part PaP-eR, for the complete PaP-eR refer to Loughran, Berry, & Mulhall, 2006, 2012.)

Teaching about the concept of nothing

Part 1: The idea of 'nothing' is problematic

> This PaP-eR portrays how a teacher links her experience of teaching about the idea of empty space with the history of the idea of empty space/aether/vacuum. This helps her understand why the idea of nothing in the gaps between gas molecules is difficult for her Year 7 students to grasp.

The students were busily making models to show how they thought the particles were arranged in solids, liquids and gases. Prior to this class they had learned that the particles in a solid are packed closely together in a regular pattern, that in a liquid they are still close together but the arrangement is not regular and has spaces which enable the particles to slide over each other, and that in a gas the particles are far apart with no pattern at all.

Hannah, one of the more able students, raised her hand:

> 'Ms. Smith, you know how particles are further apart in a gas – what's in the gaps?'

Ms. Smith had been waiting for a question like this. If it had not come from one of the students she would have raised it herself. It was only after she had been teaching for some years that she had begun to realise that the answer to this question was a difficult one for many students to imagine. Each time she taught the Particle Theory she found that even when students "knew" from their lessons that nothing was between the spaces in a gas, they said or asked things which indicated that they actually thought there was something in the gaps.

Ms. Smith told the class:

> 'Let's think about Hannah's question. Put on your magic glasses[1] and tell me what you see when you look at a gas?'
> 'Gas particles with big spaces between them!'
> 'What do you see when you look at the big spaces?' Ms. Smith asked.
> 'Lots of tiny air particles!' was the reply.

As Ms. Smith had often reflected, in many ways this kind of response was not surprising. If we poured all the water out of a jug, we would say it had nothing in it. Yet we would understand that it contained air. Thus, in everyday life, "nothing" was often a synonym for "air".

But the problem went deeper than that. Looking back over the history of scientific ideas about the world, humankind had often struggled with the idea of "nothing", of a void. There had been a number of different kinds of "something", or aethers, which had been proposed as filling the spaces in which there was no matter. These had been postulated in order to explain various scientific phenomena such as how particles could affect each other's behaviour without touching and the wave-like nature of light, questions that were still being grappled with by modern physics. However, Ms. Smith did not discuss these ideas with her students – the ideas were complex and required a level of scientific knowledge that was well beyond that of her students at this stage. But they helped Ms. Smith to understand that Hannah's question was not a trivial one, that it was worth spending some time developing an understanding of the scientific idea of "nothing".

6
TRACING A RESEARCH TRAJECTORY ON PCK AND CHEMISTRY UNIVERSITY PROFESSORS' BELIEFS

Kira Padilla & Andoni Garritz

FACULTAD DE QUÍMICA, UNIVERSIDAD NACIONAL AUTÓNOMA DE MÉXICO,
CIUDAD UNIVERSITARIA, AVENIDA UNIVERSIDAD 3000, 04510 MÉXICO, D.F.

Events in a PCK research trajectory

Andoni Garritz started working on PCK in 2003, advising the master degree thesis of Rufino Trinidad with whom he wrote his first PCK paper in Spanish (Garritz & Trinidad, 2004). Vicente Talanquer, a good friend at the University of Arizona, USA, sent Lee Shulman's papers (1986, 1987) to Garritz. Garritz was fascinated with Shulman's transformation of George Bernard Shaw's sentence, "He who can, does. He who cannot, teaches" to "Those who can, do. Those who understand, teach." From his first reading, Garritz appreciated both remarkable papers.

Shortly afterwards, upon reading about CoRes and PaP-eRs (Loughran, Mulhall, & Berry, 2004), Garritz decided to implement these tools with 16 Latin-American teachers for the topic, Particulate Structure of Matter. He presented this work at the 2005 European Science Education Research Association (ESERA) conference in Barcelona (Garritz, Porro, Rembado, & Trinidad, 2005). The symposium inspired a great deal of interest and discussion about the work, among audience members, yet it was difficult to publish the research until some years later (Garritz, Porro, Rembado, & Trinidad, 2007).

In 2000, Kira Padilla completed her PhD in Valencia, Spain, on teachers' thinking about the chemical concept, 'amount of substance.' On her return to Mexico in 2004, she began working with Garritz on chemistry professors' PCK. They used Loughran et al.'s (2004) CoRe and PaP-eRs to document and portray PCK, using interviews as a data collection strategy. In 2007, at the ESERA conference at Malmö, Padilla presented a study of "Undergraduate professors' PCK of amount of substance," later published in the special issue on PCK of the *International Journal of Science Education* (Padilla, Ponce-de-León, Rembado, &

Garritz, 2008). While in Malmö, Padilla met Jan Van Driel and arranged to do postdoctoral research with him. Padilla had in mind a specific topic—quantum chemistry teachers' PCK. In 2008, she moved to the Netherlands to carry out this project. Padilla and Van Driel published their first co-authored paper on this topic in *Chemistry Education Research and Practice* (Padilla & Van Driel, 2011).

Curiously, in 2008 and for different reasons, Garritz and Padilla became interested in how emotions influence teaching. Garritz was on sabbatical in Badajoz, Spain, with Vicente Mellado and Lorenzo Blanco, who were exploring the affective dimension of teaching/learning activities with two psycho-pedagogy doctoral students, María Brígido, (science education) and Ana Caballero (mathematics education). During Padilla's postdoctoral research, she noted many emotional aspects in the transcription of her interviews with six quantum chemistry professors. Garritz (2010) and Padilla (Padilla & Van Driel, 2012) began publishing their first papers in English on the affective domain in PCK and so were pleased when Shulman, in his keynote address at the PCK Summit, recognized the affective dimension as a missing aspect in his initial thinking about PCK. Additional research threads emerged as Garritz and Padilla began exploring PCK related to inquiry (Espinosa, Labastida, Padilla, & Garritz, 2011), stoichiometry (Padilla & Garritz, 2014), and the nature of science. These events have been important in shaping our ways of thinking about and investigating the construct of PCK and have shaped our research trajectory. In particular, teacher beliefs and the affective domain in PCK research have become an important focus of our research attention, an area thus far neglected in the literature.

Our conceptions of epistemological beliefs

To relate this chapter with our transformed thinking about PCK we will focus on our conception of beliefs before, during, and after the Summit. We describe our present conception of beliefs by describing our recent research study of a topic rarely found in the literature: Beliefs of Higher Education Professors.

Both authors participated in the PCK Summit Forum 2, Beliefs, Teaching Orientation and PCK, with a presentation titled, "What is the role and relationship of personal orientations or beliefs to PCK?" (see https://www.youtube.com/watch?v=GgNd4XbE0iA). In the presentation, Kira stated, "From our personal point of view, beliefs are those personal constructions that influence attitudes, behaviors and knowledge" and "PCK is composed of knowledge and beliefs." While we still hold this to be true, we have adapted our view as a result of our discussions at the Summit and the resulting consensus model of PCK that was developed there (see Chapter 3). Initially, we considered knowledge and beliefs to occupy a kind of 'superposition' influencing all other aspects of PCK. However, our experiences from the Summit suggested to us that, instead, knowledge and beliefs act as filters that join with personal orientations and context (see Figure 3.1) in shaping a teacher's PCK. After the Summit, we decided to work further on the beliefs construct by interviewing professors at our university to capture their epistemological beliefs about science teaching and learning, and how they solve the paradox of bringing together research and teaching. Our research question was: How do professors, with extensive teaching experience and a primary focus on research, draw upon their epistemological beliefs in their teaching practice?

Many different definitions of beliefs appear in the literature, as has been discussed by Jones and Carter, (2007, pp. 1068–1069), but they define *epistemological beliefs* as:

> Sets of beliefs about knowing and learning that play a mediating role in the processing of new information. Teachers' personal epistemologies emerge from formal and informal learning experiences and serve as mental exemplars for constructing and evaluating their own teaching practices.
>
> *(p. 1077)*

Science teachers' epistemologies affect their instructional behavior in science classrooms and have a "pervasive influence on them" (Van Driel, Verloop, & de Vos, 1998, p. 678). They "frame their teaching paradigms" (Jones & Carter, 2007, p. 1075) and encompass teachers' attitudes with respect to various aspects such as pedagogy, students, subject matter, and curriculum. Bandura (1989, p. 66) identified the concept of self-efficacy and defined it (in the context of teaching) as belief in one's capacity to successfully implement a given instructional strategy and accomplish desired outcomes. Park and Oliver (2008) include self-efficacy as a sixth component of PCK, as "related to teacher beliefs about their ability to enact effective teaching methods for specific teaching goals and was specific to classroom situations/activities" (p. 270). Our interest in the role of beliefs thus led us to prefer the PCK model with six components as presented by Park and Oliver (2008), instead of the five components of Magnusson, Krajcik, & Borko (1999).

Epistemological beliefs questionnaire

One of the first studies on the topic of teachers' beliefs was that of Nespor (1987) who noted that although teachers may share similar subject matter knowledge, they are likely to teach in different ways related to factors such as subject matter conceptions, career influences, and experience on teaching practices. Prawat (1992) discussed "four questionable sets of beliefs about teaching and learning" (p. 357) that influence many aspects of teacher behavior: (1) the tendency to think of both learner and content as relatively fixed entities; (2) 'naive constructivism'—the tendency to equate activity with learning; (3) the perpetuation of a distinction between comprehension and application, learning, and problem-solving; and (4) the popular view of curriculum as a fixed agenda, a daily course to be run that consists of pre-set means.

Based on the studies of Nespor (1987), Prawat (1992), and Pajares (1992), we developed a 12-question interview protocol to investigate university teachers' beliefs, with some of the questions taken from empirical studies reported in the literature (Luft & Roehrig, 2007; Markic, Eilks, & Valanides, 2008; Simmons et al., 1999; Thomas, Pedersen, & Finson, 2001; Veal, 2004). We conducted semi-structured interviews with ten university professors, based on the following questions:

1. How do you describe yourself as a teacher in the classroom? What is the role you play?
2. Which are the main strengths you have as a teacher? What weaknesses would you like to improve upon?
3. Describe your view of your students.
4. How do you believe your students learn best? How do you know that your students understand a concept when learning is occurring in the classroom?
5. How do you manage the educational environment (classroom, school, etc.) to maximize student learning?
6. What are the characteristics of a good learner?
7. What types of higher-order skills do you try to develop in your students and what strategies do you normally use?
8. What deserves higher priority: students or curriculum?
9. What are the principles on which your teaching is based?
10. How do you decide what to teach, how to represent it, how to ask students about the topic, how to manage misunderstandings, and what not to teach?
11. Describe the best situation of teaching/learning that you have experienced.
12. Would taking a teacher-training course benefit your teaching practice? Why/why not?

Interview categorizations

Each interview lasted from 30 to 90 minutes. All of the interviews were digitally recorded, transcribed, and coded. For the data analysis, a set of categories was developed (see Table 6.1) derived from the ideas generated through the interviews. Both authors read all the interviews and classified each sentence, then discussed both classifications until a consensus was reached.

Teachers' personal views

This category was divided into subcategories representing the role professors played in the classroom, (i.e., their personal views as teachers). This category included how they think they are viewed by students and authorities in the classroom; their perceived teaching strengths and weaknesses; and insightful information about the importance of teachers in the teaching–learning process.

TABLE 6.1 Teachers' beliefs categories

Teacher's personal views	Role in the classroom
	Strengths
	Weaknesses
	How I think they see me in the classroom
	About the lecturer
Teaching orientations	Planning
	Decision-making
	Focus
	Main principles of teaching
About students	Students play a relatively passive role
	Good learner
	Real view of students
About learning	Scientific thinking skills
	Learning contexts
About the content	As a fixed entity
	Contextualization
	Priority: student or content

Teaching orientations

In this category we included planning, decision-making, focus, and teaching principles. This category includes data about how the university professors teach, how they plan for teaching, how they make decisions about what to include/ or not when teaching a concept, and how they assess learning. One important subcategory was the principles on which they thought their teaching was based.

About students

For this category, we drew upon Prawat's (1992) research on elementary, middle, and high school teachers' beliefs about students as spectators of the teaching/ learning process, or keepers of information, indicating whether students play a passive or active role in the classroom. In addition, we asked the professors about their images of a good learner and their general views of students.

About learning

For this category, we included the professors' beliefs about the scientific thinking skills that could be developed by their students, as well as information about their particular learning context.

About the content

In this category, we drew upon Prawat (1992) who reported that teachers think the content is a fixed entity and that they contextualize the content to make it more comprehensible for their students. We also included the priority teachers give to students' comprehension or learning difficulties versus finishing the curriculum on time.

The sample

Given our interest in university professors' beliefs and how they influence practice, we conducted interviews with university researchers who also lectured at least six hours a week (in accordance with university rules for teaching hours). The researchers worked in the fields of chemistry, physical chemistry, chemical engineering, or biology. All had merits in research, recognized by their membership in the two highest levels of the National Research System in Mexico. The ten professors ranged from 45 to 66 years of age. Two of the professors were female and all had 20 years (or more) of teaching experience. To maintain confidentiality, we use numbers (1–10) to denote their identity, and we use 'she' when referring to any of them.

Results

Teachers' personal views

All of the professors viewed themselves as committed teachers who like to teach and work with students. P1, P9, P10, and P8 stated their goal was for students to understand scientific ideas and phenomena. Some of the professors (e.g., P9) considered themselves as courageous and active people in the classroom, even enthusiastic actors (P4, P2, and P5). Almost all expressed emotions and feelings about themselves and their students as they described trying to build good relationships with students—acknowledged as important because students can be shy and fearful of asking questions or interrupting the lecture. P10 was the only one who did not take into account students' feelings, as her main focus was on content. P7, P2, and P5 were strict in the classroom and with students, with classroom rules that must be followed by all.

Participants' views of themselves as teachers were related to how they saw their role in the classroom. P5 and P6 saw the classroom as a stage where the teacher must act. P6 claimed, "teaching is more acting than knowledge." While P5 viewed the teacher as an actor, she recognized herself as discursive, meaning that she was a didactic teacher, but with the flexibility of an actor performing. At the other extreme, P10 expressed a very traditional view, emphasizing content. In addition, some of the professors saw themselves as guides or facilitators of knowledge as illustrated in the following quotes:

The teacher's function is to show students the path, but they have to decide whether to follow the way or not.

(P8)

I'm just a facilitator, someone who lets them acquire knowledge; maybe some kind of guide that can help them.

(P6)

I do my best to capture the attention of students. I treat, at the climax of the play I do in each class session, hitting them with the beauty of science, the most important concepts and conclusions about nature.

(P2)

We asked the professors to identify their strengths as teachers. Order and clarity in the lecture was a strength identified by three professors. Strong content knowledge was identified by seven of the professors. Doing research in their field as a means of helping them keep up-to-date in the subject they taught was mentioned by four professors (P2, P10, and P4). P8 and P6 had more than 30 years of teaching experience, and they described this as a strength. P8 was a student in a pedagogical soviet school when she was young, and she considered this to be one of her main strengths. It is important to note that P8 was the only one who had taken a teaching course early in her career, and this experience continued to influence her teaching. The level of formality and relationship with students was another strength mentioned by two of the professors. They found it important to mark homework and exams as soon as possible, were punctual, and followed the university protocols. P7 remarked on the importance of professional dress; she never taught wearing jeans or sneakers. P10 was one of the most traditional teachers. She claimed that her main strength was being a good speaker who tried not to be boring, and that she recognized when she did not know something.

When asked about their perceived weaknesses in teaching, there were a variety of responses. P1 and P10 identified difficulties in assessing students. P10 admitted that she did not know the best way to assess students' comprehension of material. P1 recognized that she did not like assessing, because she admitted that she usually gets angry at the low level of student answers. P8 also mentioned the lack of students' commitment and dedication that upset her and acknowledged that students noticed her feelings. P7 conceded that a lack of tolerance was her main weakness and, as P8 said, "students notice it." P4 pointed out that her main weakness was not being able to closely monitor students' learning; which she felt was due to her heavy workload.

P3 and P9 experienced difficulty making concepts and ideas understandable for students. P9 admitted that she was not a good speaker and many times could not find the right words to convey her ideas effectively. P3 felt students became bored in her lectures because she had difficulty in making the lecture interesting; however, students did not say, "I do not understand."

Finally, one interesting case was that of P5, who claimed that her main weakness was her, "belief that students are more interested than they really are." Once she realized that students were not very interested in the content, it was often too late to change her teaching. P5 thought that students lacked some fundamental skills such as efficient reading or writing skills. P5 was a didactic teacher, and another weakness she recognized was that the subject she taught was so complicated that it made it quite difficult to have a different teaching orientation.

Only two professors responded to the question about how they were perceived by their students. Both thought students perceived them as are strict, but felt they could not change their strictness. P5 tried to have students reflect on why they were studying the subject and what goal they wanted to achieve. She felt that, above all, "students have to believe that I am able to take them there." We see that as related to Bandura's concept of self-efficacy. Interestingly, P5 and P10 expressed that the teacher is not as important as one may think. P5 explained that the professor is just a guide; the success of the learning process does not depend on this guide, rather it depends primarily on the students. P10 was of the view that, "the best teachers are books."

Teaching orientations

All professors claimed that they planned their courses before the term began; some had been giving the same lecture for a long time and rarely made any significant changes. They were mostly didactic in approach, although some of them (e.g., P7 and P4) held problem-solving workshops as a different approach to helping their students learn.

Two main ideas were reported by the professors related to making decisions; the first related to the program and the second related to assessment. Teachers decided whether to add or remove some concepts in the program for different reasons. For example, P8 was reflective and made these decisions based on whether students had been successful or not in learning a specific concept. In contrast, P5 was of the view that the professor did not have the right to change the program; "they just have to decide how much emphasis should be given to specific concepts." Some of the professors reflected on the cognitive demand for students and based on that they chose strategies to use for the next concepts. Interestingly, P9 asserted that she felt she was a better teacher for upper-level students than for those in the lower level, and she saw this feeling reflected in the students' faces—she could see that the upper-level students understood. As a consequence, she put less effort into teaching lower-level students.

When asked about the main principles of teaching, all affirmed that in the emotional domain, respect was fundamental. There needs to be a relationship of mutual confidence between teacher and students that comes from communication, motivation, and an ethical approach. On the conceptual level, all thought that professors needed to master their content; on the pedagogical level, some commented that teachers should have specialized pedagogical skills and abilities.

> [Teaching] is a two-sided act, on one side is the teacher who has to put the best of her and on the other side is a group of students that have to give the best of themselves.
>
> *(P8)*

> Teaching or the relationship between learner and teacher is a confidence contract, and it is a very simplistic formula: the teacher believes that students would learn, and students believe that the teacher could teach. If this hierarchy is clear and this idea is present then there is a deal, so it is possible to work.
>
> *(P5)*

About students

All participants claimed that many students show no interest in what they are doing; they thought students preferred to memorize answers rather than design and rationalize a strategy. All of the professors employed different strategies to avoid this problem; for example, P10 encouraged students to clarify their own doubts. She only listened, supervised, and gave advice to complement students' ideas. All expressed a similar view about student passivity, venturing that students did not have a commitment to, nor interest in, what they were studying—a phenomenon that appeared in undergraduate and graduate students alike. However, they ascribed that to a kind of cultural phenomenon caused by students' upbringing because parents did not teach their children to appreciate such things.

Respect was another idea that was mentioned. Participants were of the view that students did not respect their teachers and abused professors' respect for them. It seemed there were two extremes related to this point: Some of the students (the minority) are really good, and at the other end, the majority of students seek an easy way to pass the course.

With this in mind, when we asked the professors about the characteristics of a good student, they all answered with reference to the following: A good student should have creativity; curiosity; ask good questions; be dedicated; have the capacity for inquiry, writing and reading skills, critical thinking skills; and, lastly, be autonomous. P8 asserted that a good student is "a person who wants to learn and has the will to do it."

About learning

The concept of scientific thinking skills was closely linked to their images of a good student, because all wanted to promote such skills. For example, P1 tried to make students interpret and understand different kinds of representations, such as chemical structures, graphs, and mathematical formulas. P7 taught analytical chemistry and wanted her students to develop analytical criteria to solve different kinds of problems in different contexts. To accomplish this goal, she asked students to read scientific papers to generate their own questions and answers. P3 also used this strategy to develop analytical reading skills. The other professors wanted students to think critically, find relationships between concepts, and ask good questions. Some professors discussed ideas related to the nature of science. For example, P10 stated, "They have to understand that the whole of scientific knowledge is supported by scientific research."

About content

All professors asserted that a good teacher must have an excellent understanding of the content to be taught. In terms of their views about the content, some saw their subject material as fixed and could not be changed; others, particularly those who taught in upper levels, saw that the content could vary, according to what might be interesting and relevant to a particular group of students.

All of the professors tried to contextualize the content, although some were more successful than others. Mostly, they reported that as the subject became more theoretical, the examples were less contextualized. P10 thought that if she contextualized the content, then students could "understand that all knowledge is based on scientific methods, research and experimentation, and if they understand that, then they could have a critical view and develop an awareness of the social context."

When the professors were asked if they prioritized the curriculum or the students, six indicated the curriculum. The reason given was at the undergraduate level there "is some knowledge that students must have." The university requires a general exam for each subject that all students must take. Two professors (P3 and P4) stated that they prioritized their students, P3 answered, "students, because it is a formative subject. My goal is that students have learned to think . . . introduce them to the subject. I focus on students, but I do not leave the subject out."

Concluding remarks

It is clear that from the professors' answers that their beliefs influence their teaching as illustrated through such things as how they viewed their students as mostly passive; their perceptions of the lack of students' fundamental skills; and the way they prioritized the needs of the University program to cover necessary content, over students' understanding.

Another aspect that was common among this group was that they used teaching approaches, with only slight differences among them, for example, in the use of workshops. All believed that being a content expert was fundamental for teaching; however, not all recognized the need for pedagogical knowledge. All enjoyed teaching, although P10 preferred doing research over teaching. Teaching was a very important activity for them, which, in essence, did not conflict with their research (P4 mentioned the difficulties of balancing workload with doing a good job of teaching), and considered both were enhanced simultaneously.

Assessment was an important idea that we did not specifically ask about in the interviews; however, several professors identified assessment as one of their primary weaknesses. Based on the assessment goal and the strategy used, it appeared to generate conflict for at least some of them. Some commented that the course goal was not to assess, but to learn. Others, like P5, affirmed that assessment was one of the most important activities and should reflect the students' scientific thinking skills, so P5 invested a lot of time in assessment. Four of the professors asked students to write and to explain ideas in addition to the procedural knowledge they had to acquire.

Finally, the data illustrated that the participants had developed self-efficacy for teaching, that is, through their beliefs about their ability to successfully implement a given instructional strategy—because they felt comfortable with their role in the classroom and believed they were doing it with propriety.

The PCK Summit both challenged and strengthened our conceptions of PCK. After participating in the beliefs forum, we developed this study of university professors' beliefs about teaching. In future studies, we plan to explore how professors' beliefs are reflected in their classroom practices.

References

Bandura, A. (1989). Social cognitive theory. In R. Vasta (Ed.), *Annals of child development. Vol. 6. Six theories of child development* (pp. 1–60). Greenwich, CT: JAI Press.

Espinosa, J. S., Labastida, D. V., Padilla, K., & Garritz, A. (2011). Pedagogical content knowledge of inquiry: An instrument to assess it and its application to high school in-service science teachers. *US-China Education Review*, 8(5), 599–614.

Garritz, A. (2010). Pedagogical content knowledge and the affective domain of scholarship of teaching and learning, *International Journal for the Scholarship of Teaching and Learning*, 4(2), 1–6. Retrieved from http://digitalcommons.georgiasouthern.edu/cgi/viewcontent.cgi?article=1246&context=ij-sotl (accessed November 25, 2014).

Garritz, A., & Ortega-Villar, N. A. (2013). El aspecto afectivo en la enseñanza universitaria. Cómo cinco profesores enseñan el enlace químico en la materia condensada [The affective aspect in university teaching. How five Professors teach chemical bonding in condensed matter]. In Vicente Mellado Jiménez, Lorenzo J. Blanco Nieto, Ana Belén Borrachero Cortés, & Janeth A. Cárdenas Lizarazo (Eds.), *Las emociones en la enseñanza y el aprendizaje de las ciencias y las matemáticas [Emotions in the teaching and learning of sciences and mathematics*], (volumen II, Capítulo 12., pp. 277–304). Badajoz, España: Editorial Deprofe, Universidad de Extremadura. Retrieved from http://www.eweb.unex.es/eweb/dcem/Capitulo12.pdf (accessed November 25, 2014).

Garritz, A., Porro, S., Rembado, F. M., & Trinidad, R. (2005). *Latin-American teachers' pedagogical content knowledge of the particulate nature of matter*. Paper presented at the meeting of the European Science Education Research Association Conference, Barcelona, Spain.

Garritz, A., Porro, S., Rembado, F. M., & Trinidad, R. (2007). Latin-American teachers' pedagogical content knowledge of the particulate nature of matter. *Journal of Science Education, 8*(2), 79–84.

Garritz, A., & Trinidad-Velasco, R. (2004). El conocimiento pedagógico del contenido [Pedagogical Content Knowledge], *Educación Química, 15*(2), 98–102.

Jones, M. G., & Carter, G. (2007). Science teacher attitudes and beliefs. In Sandra K. Abell & Norman G. Lederman (Eds.), *Handbook of research on science education* (Chapter 35, pp. 1067–1104). Mahwah, NJ: Lawrence Erlbaum Associates.

Loughran, J., Mulhall, P., & Berry, A. (2004). In search of pedagogical content knowledge in science: Developing ways of articulating and documenting professional practice. *Journal of Research in Science Teaching, 41*(4), 370–391.

Luft, J. A., & Roehrig, G. A. (2007). Capturing science teachers' epistemological beliefs: The development of the teacher belief interview. *Electronic Journal of Science Education, 11*(2). Retrieved from http://ejse.southwestern.edu/article/view/7794 (accessed November 25, 2014).

Magnusson, S., Krajcik, J., & Borko, H. (1999). Nature, sources, and development of the PCK for science teaching. In J. Gess-Newsome & N.G. Lederman (Eds.), *Examining pedagogical content knowledge: The construct and its implications for science education*, (pp. 95–132). Dordrecht, the Netherlands: Kluwer Academic Publishers.

Markic, S., Eilks, I., & Valanides, N. (2008). Developing a tool to evaluate differences in beliefs about science teaching and learning among freshman science student teachers from different science teaching domains: A case study. *Eurasia Journal of Mathematics, Science and Technology Education, 4*(2), 109–120.

Nespor, J. (1987). The role of beliefs in the practice of teaching. *Journal of Curriculum Studies, 19*, 317–328.

Padilla, K., & Garritz, A. (2014). Stoichiometry's PCK of university chemistry professors. In Dennis W. Sunal, Cynthia Szymanski-Sunal, E. Wright, Cheryl L. Mason, & Dean A. Zollman (Eds.), *Research based undergraduate science teaching, Volume 6* of the series *Research in Science Education*, (pp. 499–523). Charlotte, NC: Information Age Publishers.

Padilla, K., Ponce-de-León, A. M., Rembado, F. M., & Garritz, A. (2008). Undergraduate professors' pedagogical content knowledge: The case of "amount of substance." *International Journal of Science Education, 30*(10), 1389–1404.

Padilla, K., & Van Driel, J. H. (2011). The relationships between PCK components: The case of quantum chemistry professors. *Chemistry Education Research and Practice, 12*, 367–378.

Padilla, K., & Van Driel, J. H. (2012). Relationships among cognitive and emotional knowledge of teaching quantum chemistry at university level. *Educacion Química, 23*(Extraord2), 311–326.

Pajares, M. F. (1992). Teachers' beliefs and educational research: Cleaning up a messy construct. *Review of Educational Research, 62*(3), 307–332.

Park, S., & Oliver, J. S. (2008). Revisiting the conceptualization of pedagogical content knowledge (PCK): PCK as conceptual tool to understand teachers as professionals. *Research in Science Education, 38*, 261–284.

Prawat, R. S. (1992). Teachers' beliefs about teaching and learning: A constructivist perspective. *American Journal of Education, 100*(3), 354–395.

Shulman, L. S. (1986). Those who understand: Knowledge growth in teaching. *Educational Researcher, 15*(2), 4–14.

Shulman, L. S. (1987). Knowledge and teaching: Foundations of the new reform. *Harvard Educational Review, 57*(1), 1–22.

Simmons, P. E., Emory, A., Carter, T., Coker, T., Finnegan, B., Crockett, D., . . . Labuda, K. (1999). Beginning teachers: Beliefs and classroom actions. *Journal of Research in Science Teaching, 36*(8), 930–954.

Thomas, J. A., Pedersen, J. E., & Finson, K. (2001). Validating the draw-a-science-teacher-test checklist (dastt-c): Exploring mental models and teacher beliefs. *Journal of Science Teacher Education, 12*(3), 295–310.

Van Driel, J. H., Verloop, N., & de Vos, W. (1998). Developing science teachers' pedagogical content knowledge, *Journal of Research in Science Teaching, 35*(6), 673–695.

Veal, W. R. (2004). Beliefs and knowledge in chemistry teacher development. *International Journal of Science Education, 26*(3), 329–351.

7

ASSESSING PCK

A new application of the uncertainty principle

P. Sean Smith & Eric R. Banilower

HORIZON RESEARCH, INC.

Introduction

The title of this chapter intentionally invokes Heisenberg's Uncertainty Principle, which states that the position and momentum of a particle cannot be measured precisely at the same time. Our experience with pedagogical content knowledge (PCK) has been almost entirely from a measurement perspective and, although we do not treat PCK as a particle, our experience of attempting to measure it has been characterized by uncertainty. Each time we thought we were getting close to locating PCK, it seemed to change directions on us. The major source of uncertainty is the lack of a clear, widely agreed-upon definition of PCK that can be operationalized for assessment. Our experience has led us to the conclusion that although PCK is a powerful construct, it is not yet adequately specified for assessment purposes.

Researchers are pursuing a number of valuable strands of work in PCK. Many are focused on identifying the kinds of experiences that develop PCK in teachers (e.g., Park & Oliver, 2008; Van Driel, Verloop, & de Vos, 1998). Others are primarily concerned with how a teacher's PCK changes over time (e.g., Schneider & Plasman, 2011). Still others focus on how PCK grows in a community (e.g., Loughran, Milroy, Berry, Gunstone, & Mulhall, 2001). Our assessment perspective was driven by the broader context in which we were working. Specifically, we were studying the relationships among teacher professional development, changes in teacher beliefs and knowledge (including PCK), changes in classroom practice, and student learning. Further, we were interested in establishing these relationships quantitatively, and this interest necessitated assessments. When we began our work more than ten years ago, PCK assessments for the areas we were interested in did not exist. As a result, we initiated a substantial assessment development effort, which we describe in this chapter. First, however, it is important to describe our theoretical stance on PCK.

Theoretical stance on PCK

From an assessment perspective, the importance of being very clear about what 'counts' as PCK is paramount. Our PCK journey, like that of most PCK researchers, began with Shulman's definition that PCK is an amalgam of content knowledge and pedagogical knowledge (Shulman, 1986). Adopting this definition has certain implications. First, PCK is more than the sum of the parts; having knowledge of content and pedagogy is not the same as having PCK. Second, because PCK is inextricably tied to content knowledge, PCK is specific to a discipline (e.g., biology) and, as many hold (e.g., Hashweh, 2005; Magnusson, Krajcik & Borko, 1999), to a topic within a discipline (e.g., ecosystems). Perhaps it is even specific to an idea within a topic (e.g., the idea of a parasitic relationship between two organisms).

Facets of PCK

We adopted a model of PCK put forth by Magnusson et al. (1999) that suggests PCK exists as facets, such as knowledge of students' understanding of science, knowledge of instructional strategies, and knowledge of assessment of scientific literacy. The model also posits a central role played by orientations (Grossman, 1990). In our work, we did not attempt to trace the influence of teachers' orientations on their PCK. We focused our assessment efforts at the facet level, adapting those in the Magnusson et al. model as follows:

1. Knowledge of students' understanding of science:

    a. *Knowledge of how to sequence ideas for students.* This facet refers to knowledge of which ideas are pre-requisites for later ideas and how to progress from less complex to more complex ideas. This form of knowledge encompasses learning progressions (e.g., Corcoran, Mosher, & Rogat, 2009; Smith, Wiser, Anderson, & Krajcik, 2006).
    b. *Areas of student difficulty.* Teachers need to know what ideas students are likely to bring with them and where they are likely to struggle, which may be due to: (1) the concepts being abstract (or lacking connection to students' experiences); (2) students not yet having developed the needed problem-solving strategies; or (3) students' prior knowledge being contrary to the targeted scientific concepts (often referred to as misconceptions).

2. Knowledge of content-specific strategies that can build students' conceptual understanding. Such strategies may take a number of forms, including:

- a. *Activities* (e.g., investigations, discrepant events) that confront students with phenomena that provide evidence for the targeted idea.
- b. *Representations* of content (models, examples, analogies) that are particularly effective in revealing the subtle aspects of a content area; these are especially important in understanding phenomena that are not easily or directly observable.
- c. *Questions* that, if asked at the right point in a sequence of instruction, can move students' thinking forward.

3. Knowledge of methods of assessing science learning. This domain includes knowledge of activities/representations/hypothetical scenarios that can be used to elicit and diagnose the thinking of students. Teachers need to know how to discern what ideas students have about a content area, prior to, during, and after instruction on a topic.

It is important to note that the empirical knowledge base in each of these facets is quite thin relative to the number of science topics. Some topics—e.g., force and motion—have a rich research base on student preconceptions and misconceptions, which includes research on how resistant these ideas may be to change (Langford & Zollman, 1982; Watts & Zylberszstajn, 1981). Most topics do not have such an extensive research base on student thinking or the other facets.

Personal vs. canonical PCK

Clearly, PCK exists within an individual teacher and, in that sense, PCK is personal. Further, some argue that all PCK is context dependent; it is formed through preparing to teach, teaching, and reflecting on the teaching of a particular topic to a particular group of students for a particular purpose (Loughran, Mulhall & Berry, 2004). Although we agree that PCK is personal in this sense, we also argue that just as there is canonical (or normative) science content knowledge, there is canonical PCK; that is, PCK that is widely agreed upon and formed through research and/or collective expert wisdom of practice. Further, we see personal and canonical PCK as related. As shown in Figure 7.1, canonical PCK becomes personal through application—preparing to teach, teaching, or reflecting on teaching. Personal PCK may also grow entirely separately from canonical PCK through teaching-related experiences. As personal PCK accumulates across many teachers, it may become canonical.

Implications for assessment

All assessment requires an agreed-upon standard. Assessments of teachers' science content knowledge use canonical science as the standard. One ramification of our assessment perspective is that we believe a teacher's PCK, just like a teacher's science content knowledge, can be correct or incorrect as judged against

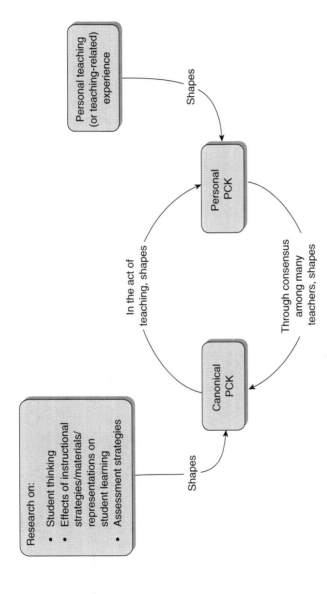

FIGURE 7.1 Canonical PCK becomes personal through application

canonical PCK. (Some would argue incorrect PCK is not PCK at all, but that is a philosophical question beyond the scope of this chapter.) For example, we know that elementary students tend to think that air does not have mass (e.g., Séré, 1985); PCK for teaching about matter—gases in particular—should include strategies for confronting this aspect of student thinking. PCK can also be judged against the components of PCK. For example, if a teacher's PCK incorporates incorrect science content knowledge, then the resulting PCK would, by definition, be incorrect. PCK might also be incorrect if it is contrary to firmly established principles of cognitive science—few would argue that deep conceptual understanding will result solely from memorizing a page of definitions.

Finally, from a measurement perspective, we argue that PCK, like all forms of knowledge, is a latent characteristic. It cannot be observed directly; we can only make inferences about it from observable behaviors, including written responses to questions, interview responses, or teaching practice (including lesson plans and other artifacts of instruction).

Attempts to assess PCK

Rationale for the work

As described above, we were interested in exploring relationships among teacher knowledge, professional development, instructional practice, and student learning based, in part, on the findings of two literature reviews. Abell (2007) conducted an extensive review of research on science teacher knowledge and found that:

- the literature base on teacher knowledge on the whole is quite thin;
- there is no sense that the research is cumulating; researchers are not building on each other's work but instead are introducing new constructs related to teacher knowledge and discarding them relatively quickly;
- the field needs research on the relationship between teacher knowledge and student learning, but is missing the foundational work needed to enable such studies.

Horizon Research, Inc. (HRI) reached similar conclusions in a comprehensive literature review as part of the NSF-funded *MSP Knowledge Management and Dissemination Project* (Heck, Smith, Taylor, & Dyer, 2007). To be included, each study had to meet all of the following criteria:

- teachers' knowledge was studied empirically, through a specific measure (e.g., multiple-choice test, open-response written items, interviews) or through systematic analysis of samples of teachers' work;
- the subjects or participants in the study were practicing in-service teachers within grades pre-Kindergarten through 12;
- the study was published after 1990.[1]

The initial search (using both the ERIC and EBSCO databases) yielded just over 1,000 articles. Screening out non-empirical articles and studies that did not include objective measures of teacher knowledge winnowed the pool down to 104 studies, the vast majority of which focused on teachers' subject matter knowledge (e.g., Kruger, 1990; Parker & Heywood, 2000). No studies were found relating teachers' PCK to student learning in science.

Assessment approach

We did not set out to completely fill this gap in the literature. We did, however, design a study to yield knowledge that would generalize across multiple science topics by selecting three topics in middle-grades science: (1) flow of matter and energy in living systems; (2) force and motion; and (3) plate tectonics. The original content statements were taken directly from *Benchmarks for Science Literacy* (AAAS, 1993).

These topics were then unpacked into discrete, assessable statements, or 'sub-ideas,' which provided guidance to item writers and ensured that the items assessed subtleties of the content hidden in the general statement. In addition to unpacking the topic, we reviewed the literature on student/adult thinking related to the content. We associated the misconceptions (or prior/alternative conceptions) with the sub-ideas, providing further guidance to item writers.

In developing the teacher assessments, we attempted to measure teacher knowledge in three domains. Two were described earlier as 'facets' of PCK: (1) knowledge of student understanding about the content; and (2) knowledge of content-specific strategies that can build students' conceptual understanding. We thought that the best chance of measuring canonical PCK was in these facets. The third domain was knowledge of disciplinary content.

To enable large-scale research, we set out to create tools that would be minimally burdensome for both the test taker and the researcher. Accordingly, we opted for a multiple-choice format, even though such items, like all item formats, have limitations.[2] We attempted to address some of their limitations by using the literature on misconceptions to generate distractors (Sadler, 1998).

We began developing multiple-choice items for each of the three science topics by asking approximately 100 middle-grades science teachers to respond to open-ended questions about students' ideas and teaching of the concepts. Examples of these questions are shown in Figures 7.2 and 7.3, with sample responses shown in quotes. Our primary purpose was to generate distractors for the multiple-choice items, and they accomplished that purpose. The responses also provided a window into teachers' thinking about the content, both in what they wrote and what they did not write (e.g., in the instructional strategies question, none of the teachers noted the incorrect idea of light energy being transformed into matter suggested in the student's response). In addition, responses to instructional strategies questions revealed teachers' thinking about teaching the content and perhaps about their teaching orientations.

> What are the most common *incorrect and/or naïve* ideas middle school students have prior to instruction on plate tectonics that teachers should be prepared to address in their instruction? Please list 3–5 different ideas.
>
> - "Earth's surface is one solid piece."
> - "Plates and continents are the same thing."
> - "When plates spread apart, they leave a large open gash in Earth's surface."
> - "Plates do not move; it is impossible to move something as massive as a plate."
> - "Plates move only when we have earthquakes."
> - "All mountains are the result of volcanic activity."
> - "Earth is getting bigger because of seafloor spreading; Earth grows as new material is formed."
> - "All land will disappear because of subduction, resulting in a water world."

FIGURE 7.2 Open-ended teacher task about student thinking

> Students plant beans under several different conditions and watch them grow over a few weeks. During a discussion about the plants' growth, a teacher asks her students "Why did the plants in the sunlight grow better than those in the dark?" One student says,
>
> "The plants in the light absorbed the light from the Sun, and turned it into sugars that helped them grow."
>
> What could the teacher do to help move this student forward in his thinking about the role of sunlight in plant growth?
>
> Sample teacher responses:
>
> - "Discussion of photosynthesis and the chemical reaction that takes place. Show the student the chemical equation and show them what takes place."
> - "Have students design and conduct experiments testing various variables on plants/seeds to decide which variables affect plant growth and the ability to make sugars and the amount of sugars (benedict's indicator can be used for the presence/quantity of sugar present in leaf extracts)."
> - "Grow several plants in the light, some with water and some without. Water is just as important as sunlight."
> - "Diagram a plant with leaves—showing chlorophyll in leaves, CO_2 moving in, water moving up, etc."

FIGURE 7.3 Open-ended teacher task about instructional strategies

Using the teachers' responses and our literature review, we began writing multiple-choice questions. To assess knowledge of student thinking about a topic, we wrote items such as, "Which of the following misconceptions are students likely to exhibit in a study of plate tectonics?" However, scoring responses to such items as correct or incorrect requires a robust empirical literature. And although the research base in some content areas, particularly in the physical sciences, has identified prevalent misconceptions (e.g., Driver, Guesne, & Tiberghien, 1985), it is not yet strong enough to argue the *relative prominence* of misconceptions. For that reason, asking teachers to choose one answer in such questions was not a valid assessment of their knowledge of student thinking.

Multiple-choice items assessing teachers' knowledge of instructional strategies proved to be invalid on different grounds. Such items seemed to be more about teachers' beliefs or attitudes than about their knowledge. The question in Figure 7.4 illustrates this issue. The case could be made that both choices A and C are correct, depending on one's beliefs about effective instruction. (Note: Choices B, D, and E are incorrect because they do not address the incorrect idea that a force can be transferred from one object to another.) Furthermore, teachers sometimes chose a hands-on activity over a lecture or reading simply because they believed hands-on to always be more effective than other strategies, regardless of what ideas the activity addressed. Although attitudes, beliefs, and orientations are important determinants of instruction and of PCK, our focus was assessing teachers' knowledge of particular facets of PCK. After many attempts to write such items, we recognized that even in force and motion, where the literature is relatively robust, the empirical basis is not strong enough to judge the relative effectiveness of two or more activities that reasonably address the same idea.

Ultimately, we constrained our assessment items to teacher knowledge of disciplinary content for two reasons. First, disciplinary content knowledge is the foundation on which all facets of PCK are built. Second, it has proven to be the most assessable domain of teacher knowledge to date. We developed three types of items for assessing teacher content knowledge, each set in instructional contexts: (1) knowledge of science content; (2) assessing teacher content knowledge through the analysis of student thinking; and (3) assessing teacher content knowledge through instructional decision-making. The instructional contexts have proven useful by making it obvious that our tests are written for teachers, not students.

Your local miniature golf course invites your middle school science class to their annual event—"The Physics of Golf." Before beginning play, you are planning to ask each student to describe the forces acting on the ball as it rolls toward the cup on the 1st hole—a hole that is straight and level. Most of the students answer, "The force that the putter gave to the ball." What would you do next to move these students' in their understanding thinking forward.

A. Review with the students the scientific definition of force.
B. Have them hit several golf balls with varying force to see how fast the ball goes.
C. Facilitate a class discussion to draw out all the students' ideas about forces.
D. Have them hit golf balls on different surfaces with varying amounts of friction.
E. Move on to the next topic; these students seem to have a good understanding of what a force is.

FIGURE 7.4 Multiple-choice item assessing teachers' knowledge of instructional strategies

At the same time, the instructional contexts have led some who have reviewed the questions to suggest that they measure PCK, simply because of the contexts. We argue that they do not, and explain why by illustrating each item type. (The correct answer in each item appears in bold text in the figures that follow.) To do so, it is important to understand the two principles that carried the most weight for ensuring item validity—necessity and sufficiency (Stern & Ahlgren, 2002). (Taylor and Smith (2009) describe the full set of criteria.) An item meets the necessity criterion if it requires that the respondent know the target content in order to answer correctly. Put another way, respondents should not be able to answer correctly without knowing the content (e.g., by using test-taking strategies). An item meets the sufficiency criterion when knowledge of the targeted content is all the respondent needs to know to answer correctly; answering the item correctly requires no knowledge outside the target content. To answer the question in Figure 7.5, knowledge of science content is both necessary and sufficient; PCK is not necessary.

The second type of item requires teachers to *apply* their content knowledge in analyzing or diagnosing a sample of student thinking (see Figure 7.6). A teacher must understand the science content in order to answer correctly. However, additional analysis of the question is required because more than one of the choices includes a correct science statement, unlike the question in Figure 7.5. In Figure 7.6, the statements in choices A, B, and C are correct in terms of the physics, but only C *also* applies to what the students said. This feature is present in all items of this type; teachers must evaluate the students' thinking in relation to the physical scenario in order to choose the correct answer. However, knowledge of student thinking (the most closely related PCK facet) is not necessary. Therefore, we argue that the question does not assess PCK.

The third type of item (Figure 7.7) asks teachers to apply their content knowledge in choosing among instructional strategies. To answer these questions, teachers must not only evaluate the science content, but also consider the student's thinking in relation to the content and then evaluate each instructional strategy. As with the second type of item, more than one answer choice has a

---

In a unit on the flow of matter and energy in living systems, students were asked to describe what happens to the light energy from the Sun that plants absorb. Which one of the following student answers is correct?

A. **Some of the energy is changed into chemical energy.**
B. Some of the energy is changed into sugars.
C. All of the energy is changed into heat when sugars are made.
D. All of the energy is used up while making sugars.

FIGURE 7.5 Item that requires science content knowledge but not application

> A teacher gives her physical science class the following thought experiment: "Standing at the edge of an ice rink, you give a hockey puck a gentle push toward the middle of the rink. This is a special ice rink that has absolutely *no friction*. About how far do you think the puck would go before it stops?"
> Virtually all the students agree that the answer depends on how hard you push the puck with your foot. Which of the following best represents the students' understanding of forces and motion?
> A. They do not understand the idea that forces combine to create a single net force on an object.
> B. They do not understand the idea that force is directly proportional to an object's acceleration.
> **C. They do not understand the idea that an object's motion will not change unless an unbalanced force acts on it.**
> D. They correctly understand the motion of the puck.

FIGURE 7.6 Item that requires teachers to apply their content knowledge in analyzing or diagnosing a sample of student thinking

> In a class discussion, a teacher asks his students to describe Earth's plates. One student says, "There are thousands of plates that are moving and causing changes to Earth's surface."
> Based on this statement, which one of the following should the teacher do next to further this student's understanding of Earth's plates?
> A. Discuss the types of geological features plate movement can cause.
> **B. Have students outline the boundaries of the plates on a map.**
> C. Introduce students to the specific ways in which plates move.
> D. Demonstrate how the plates move as a result of convection.

FIGURE 7.7 Item requiring teachers to apply their content knowledge in choosing among instructional strategies

correct science statement, but only one has a correct science statement *and* is relevant to the instructional context. However, science content knowledge is sufficient to answer the question; knowledge of instructional strategies (the most closely related PCK facet) is not needed.

As we illustrated, a content analysis of the questions strongly suggests that they do not measure PCK. In addition, we administered our force and motion questions to a group of physics doctoral students at a local university. Only individuals without teaching experience were included. All of the students answered the multiple-choice questions correctly, further suggesting that content knowledge is sufficient.

Insights developed

We stated at the outset that we approached PCK from an assessment perspective. Many, but not all, of the insights we have gleaned through our work also relate to assessing this elusive construct.

As a field, we are better at eliciting teachers' PCK than assessing it

Open-ended tasks have promise for eliciting teachers' PCK, even when the knowledge is tacit. Two of the most widely known tools are the CoRes (Content Representations) and PaP-eRs (Pedagogical and Professional experience Repertoires), with which teachers represent their PCK in writing (Loughran et al., 2004). Another promising approach is interviewing teachers about instructional scenarios. For example, teachers can be presented with a hypothetical scenario and asked how they would respond. Alternatively, interviewers can present teachers with video of their own teaching and ask them to describe the thinking that shaped their instructional moves (Calderhead, 1981). In either case, interviews have the advantage of probing for rich detail. One implication, however, is that the interviewer needs to have deep PCK to probe effectively.

Regardless of the approach, the challenge is not so much eliciting teachers' PCK as assessing it. Assessment implies judging correctness, which leads to the next insight.

Efforts to assess PCK are hindered by a lack of consensus on what the construct is and a very thin empirical research base

Regardless of the question format (multiple choice or constructed response, written or interview), assessment involves judgments about the correctness of a response. We have developed many teacher assessments of science content knowledge, and making such judgments in that context is usually straightforward. It involves comparing the response to currently accepted scientific thought. As a field, science education researchers lack the needed consensus for assessing much of what is considered PCK. It is important to point out that researchers in mathematics education have had a similar experience. The Learning Mathematics for Teaching project is well known for the teacher assessments it has developed. They, too, initially set out to assess teacher PCK. Describing their efforts to write such assessment items, the researchers wrote:

> The uneven research base across domains [of PCK] was noticeable, leading us to mark off the territory in slightly different ways. For instance, although we found substantial research on student errors and strategies in mathematics, we uncovered less about what representations work best for particular mathematical topics. Such insight would be needed to write items that

would tap knowledge of "representations most useful for teaching specific content" (Shulman, 1986). Without these items and this category, faithfully representing pedagogical content knowledge as conceived in the theoretical literature was not possible.

(Hill, Schilling, & Ball, 2004, pp. 14–15)

Our experience assessing PCK has been characterized, as the chapter title implies, by uncertainty, which we attribute to the fact that PCK is a complex, multidimensional construct specific to a topic/idea. It combines science content knowledge and pedagogical knowledge, two constructs that are themselves complex. This complexity has contributed to the lack of consensus on what PCK is. An assessment approach that has promise is focusing on facets of PCK rather than the broad construct. This approach is still accompanied by many challenges discussed in this chapter, but the field is more likely to reach consensus on a definition of knowledge of student understanding, for example, than PCK writ large. In this chapter, we suggested two additional facets: knowledge of instructional strategies that promote conceptual learning and knowledge of assessment strategies. These also have multiple components, as we described.

Instruments that purport to assess PCK may in fact be assessing content knowledge or beliefs about instruction

Through our work, we have had the opportunity to review many teacher assessments, some of which are described as PCK measures. When we applied the criteria of necessity and sufficiency to multiple-choice questions, we found that in many cases, content knowledge was sufficient to select the correct response, even though the questions were set in instructional contexts. We have made the same argument about our own items when others have suggested they assess PCK. Our stance is that because content knowledge is sufficient to answer the questions, they do not assess PCK.

Other questions seem to tap teachers' beliefs rather than their PCK. For example, a multiple-choice question may ask teachers about potential instructional moves and present options that are some variation of hands-on, lecture, reading, or demonstration. However, it is difficult to think of a science topic for which there is enough research to say that a hands-on approach, for example, is better than a lecture.

We are skeptical about the prospects for measuring PCK in a multiple-choice format for most science topics

Our efforts to assess PCK were motivated by an interest in exploring quantitative relationships between PCK and other variables, including instructional practice and student learning. This approach necessitated large sample sizes and, for this reason, we constrained ourselves to multiple-choice measures of teacher knowledge. We have become skeptical that multiple-choice approaches to assessing PCK are viable, at least in the near term. Sadler and colleagues have developed a successful approach to measuring one facet of PCK (knowledge of student misconceptions) in a small number of topics using multiple-choice questions (Sadler, Sonnert, Coyle, Cook-Smith, & Miller, 2013). Their work is important and groundbreaking, but it represents a relatively small region of the PCK landscape. Our experience suggests that developing valid and reliable multiple-choice assessments for other facets of PCK (e.g., knowledge of instructional strategies) will be much more difficult, which in turn implies that establishing quantitative relationships between these facets of PCK and other variables is still a long way off.

The PCK Summit: A critical incident in the evolution of our thinking

This chapter began with one science metaphor; it ends with another. In evolution, the idea of punctuated equilibrium suggests that a species remains relatively stable over geologic time and that change occurs in comparatively short time periods, sometimes precipitated by an external event (Gould & Eldredge, 1977). The Summit was such an event in the evolution of our thinking about PCK. Although we went to the PCK Summit with an assessment orientation, we were aware of other perspectives from the literature. However, interacting with other participants who brought different perspectives reshaped our thinking, helped us develop new insights, and deepened our appreciation for these perspectives.

One perspective shared by several Summit participants is that PCK is, by definition, personal. That is, PCK is specific to a particular teacher, teaching a particular topic to a particular group of students for a particular purpose. Being able to hear this perspective firsthand and ask questions of those who hold it was enlightening. The experience also suggested that some perspectives are incompatible with each other. For example, an assessment perspective seems incompatible with the perspective that all PCK is personal; assessment requires a canon against which to judge assessment responses, but if all PCK is personal, there is no canon. Despite such fundamental disagreements, there was substantial common ground. For example, participants who held each perspective were very interested in how PCK develops in an individual teacher.

Our notion of canonical PCK was challenged at the Summit. The term itself was troublesome for some, particularly those who held that all PCK is personal. We have begun to think in terms of 'collective' rather than canonical PCK. Collective PCK includes knowledge established through empirical research (e.g., effective strategies for teaching the concept of natural selection to middle-grades students) as well as the knowledge that cumulates from expert practitioners' experience. Further, we began to see this latter source of collective PCK as the primary source for many science topics. As described earlier in this chapter, most science topics have scant empirically based PCK. At the same time, there are perhaps hundreds of expert practitioners for each science topic, and this source of knowledge has gone largely untapped. It may be that gathering and organizing the knowledge of these individuals is easier and less costly than establishing PCK through research in classroom settings.

We are still interested in assessing PCK. Assessment efforts have challenged the field to define the construct more clearly, and assessment is critical for understanding the relationship between teacher knowledge and education outcomes. The emphasis of our work, however, has shifted from assessing PCK through multiple-choice items to creating novel open-ended tasks and interview prompts that elicit teachers' PCK. Teacher interviews conducted by someone with deep knowledge of the topic seem to be the most promising approach for eliciting a teacher's PCK. But, as noted earlier in the chapter, the larger challenge for assessment is scoring teacher responses. To address this challenge, we have begun testing a method for collecting and synthesizing PCK from empirical research literature and expert practitioners. The method will be applied in a number of science topics, carefully documenting topic-specific differences so that others can learn from and use the approach in their own work.

Acknowledgement

The work described in this chapter was supported by the National Science Foundation under grant numbers 0335328 and 0928177. Any opinions, findings, and conclusions or recommendations expressed in this material are those of the authors and do not necessarily reflect the views of the National Science Foundation.

Notes

1 1990 was chosen as a cutoff because of the significant shift in thinking about K-12 science content that occurred at about this time with the beginning of the standards movement, marked by the publication of *Science for All Americans* (AAAS, 1989), *Benchmarks for Science Literacy* (AAAS, 1993), and the *National Science Education Standards* (NRC, 1996).
2 For example, well-constructed open-ended items may elicit more depth of understanding, but they are more time intensive for both the researcher (in terms of scoring costs) and the test taker (in terms of time required to complete the assessment). In addition, scoring requires the training of raters to establish inter-rater reliability.

References

Abell, S. K. (2007). Research on science teacher knowledge. In S. K. Abell & N. G. Lederman (Eds.), *Handbook of research on science education* (pp. 1105–1149). Mahwah, NJ: Lawrence Erlbaum Associates.

AAAS (American Association for the Advancement of Science). (1993). *Benchmarks for science literacy: Project 2061*. New York, NY; Oxford: Oxford University Press.

Calderhead, J. (1981). Stimulated recall: A method for research on teaching. *British Journal of Educational Psychology, 51*(2), 211–217.

Corcoran, T., Mosher, F. A., & Rogat, A. (2009). *Learning progressions in science: An evidence-based approach to reform* (CPRE Research Report # RR-63). Consortium for Policy Research in Education, University of Pennsylvania.

Driver, R., Guesne, E., & Tiberghien, A. (1985). *Children's ideas in science.* Milton Keynes, UK; Philadelphia, PA: Open University Press.

Gould, S. J., & Eldredge, N. (1977). Punctuated equilibria: The tempo and mode of evolution reconsidered. *Paleobiology, 3,* 115–151.

Grossman, P. L. (1990). *The making of a teacher: Teacher knowledge and teacher education.* New York, NY: Teachers College Press.

Hashweh, M. Z. (2005). Teacher pedagogical constructions: A reconfiguration of pedagogical content knowledge. *Teachers and Teaching, 11*(3), 273–292.

Heck, D., Smith, S., Taylor, M., & Dyer, E. (2007). *Review of empirical research on teachers' mathematics and science content knowledge and its effects on teaching practice and student outcomes.* Chapel Hill, NC: Horizon Research, Inc.

Hill, H. C., Schilling, S. G., & Ball, D. L. (2004). Developing measures of teachers' mathematics knowledge for teaching. *Elementary School Journal, 105*(1), 11.

Kruger, C. (1990). Some primary teachers' ideas about energy. *Physics Education, 25*(2), 86–91.

Langford, J. M., & Zollman, D. (1982). *Conceptions of dynamics held by elementary and high school students.* Paper presented at the Annual meeting of the American Association of Physics Teachers, San Francisco, CA.

Loughran, J., Milroy, P., Berry, A., Gunstone, R., & Mulhall, P. (2001). Documenting science teachers' pedagogical content knowledge through PaP-eRs. *Research in Science Education, 31*(2), 289–307.

Loughran, J., Mulhall, P., & Berry, A. (2004). In search of pedagogical content knowledge in science: Developing ways of articulating and documenting professional practice. *Journal of Research in Science Teaching, 41*(4), 370–391.

Magnusson, S., Krajcik, J., & Borko, H. (1999). Nature, sources and development of pedagogical content knowledge for science teaching. In J. Gess-Newsome & N. G. Lederman (Eds.), *Examining pedagogical content knowledge: The construct and its implications for science education* (pp. 95–132). Norwell, MA: Kluwer Academic Publishers.

Park, S., & Oliver, J. S. (2008). Revisiting the conceptualisation of pedagogical content knowledge (PCK): PCK as a conceptual tool to understand teachers as professionals. *Research in Science Education, 38*(3), 261–284.

Parker, J., & Heywood, D. (2000). Exploring the relationship between subject knowledge and pedagogic content knowledge in primary teachers' learning about forces. *International Journal of Science Education, 22*(1), 89–111.

Sadler, P. M. (1998). Psychometric models of student conceptions in science: Reconciling qualitative studies and distractor-driven assessment instruments. *Journal of Research in Science Teaching, 35*(3), 265–296.

Sadler, P. M., Sonnert, G., Coyle, H. P., Cook-Smith, N., & Miller, J. L. (2013). The influence of teachers' knowledge on student learning in middle school physical science classrooms. *American Educational Research Journal, 50*(5), 1020–1049.

Schneider, R. M., & Plasman, K. (2011). Science teacher learning progressions: A review of science teachers' pedagogical content knowledge development. *Review of Educational Research, 81*(4), 530–565.

Séré, M. G. (1985). The gaseous state. In R. Driver, E. Guesne, & A. Tiberghien (Eds.), *Children's ideas in science* (pp. 105–123). Milton Keynes, UK; Philadelphia, PA: Open University Press.

Shulman, L. S. (1986). Those who understand: Knowledge growth in teaching. *Educational Researcher, 15*(2), 4–14.

Smith, C. L., Wiser, M., Anderson, C. W., & Krajcik, J. (2006). Implications of research on children's learning for standards and assessment: A proposed learning progression for matter and the atomic-molecular theory. *Measurement: Interdisciplinary research and perspectives, 4*(1), 1–98.

Stern, L., & Ahlgren, A. (2002). Analysis of students' assessments in middle school curriculum materials: Aiming precisely at benchmarks and standards. *Journal of Research in Science Teaching, 39*(9), 889–910.

Taylor, M., & Smith, S. (2009). How do you know if they're getting it? Writing assessment items that reveal student understanding. *Science Scope, 32*(5), 60–64.

Van Driel, J. H., Verloop, N., & de Vos, W. (1998). Developing science teachers' pedagogical content knowledge. *Journal of Research in Science Teaching, 35*(6), 673–695.

Watts, D. M., & Zylbersztajn, A. (1981). A survey of some children's ideas about force. *Physics Education, 16*(6), 360–365.

8
FROM PORTRAYING TOWARD ASSESSING PCK

Drivers, dilemmas, and directions for future research

Soonhye Park & Jee Kyung Suh
UNIVERSITY OF IOWA

A shift from portraying PCK toward assessing PCK

Our research on PCK started with capturing and portraying key features and the nature of PCK to better understand how it looked and developed over time. This line of research was drawn from an assumption grounded in cognitive science that teacher knowledge bases guide instructional practices that in turn impact student learning. Among multiple knowledge bases required for teaching, PCK has been suggested as a critical contributing factor to quality teaching both theoretically and empirically (Baumert et al., 2010; Shulman, 1986, 1987). What then, are the differences in PCK between teachers who enact quality teaching and those who do not? Why do some teachers develop sophisticated PCK necessary for quality teaching whereas others do not? What is the mechanism through which teacher PCK is translated into instructional practice? What are the mediating factors in such a translation process? These questions led us to devote our effort to describing and identifying characteristics and representative examples of PCK, its developmental mechanism, and its relation to practice.

It was our belief that such research would provide insight into strategies and interventions for supporting teachers' PCK development (which is imperative to support students' science learning). In pursuing this line of research, our focus was on teacher PCK more in relation to instructional practices than to student learning, assuming that effective practice shaped by PCK will yield effective student learning. However, Fenstermacher and Richardson's (2005) conceptualization of quality teaching caused us to reframe our research program to pay more attention to student learning. They argued that the presumption that what teachers do determines whether students learn is a naïve conception of the relationship between teaching and learning. Rather, teaching and learning are related to each other in highly complex ways that go beyond a direct causal connection. Thus, teaching and learning need to be understood as independent phenomena to advance our understanding of their relationship. Based on this notion, any determination of quality teaching must account for both the worthiness of what teachers try to do (called 'good teaching') and the realization of intended student learning outcomes (called 'successful teaching'). They warned that quality teaching is more than the combination of good teaching and successful teaching, because good instructional practices enacted by the teacher is only one of the four critical conditions that yield student learning. The other three conditions are: student willingness and effort to learn; supportive social surroundings; and, opportunity to teach and learn. Learning is therefore more likely to occur when all four conditions work together.

Fenstermacher and Richardson's (2005) work informed our research in two significant ways. First, that teachers are not the sole factor influencing student learning led to considering contextual factors not only for portraying and capturing PCK, but also in assessing and measuring PCK. Second, their argument for multifaceted relationships between teaching and learning reinforced our recognition that for PCK to be useful in informing practice and policy, the relationship between PCK and student learning must be empirically examined. This calls for research that directly examines whether PCK matters in student learning, and if so, how and why it matters especially with large sample sizes to increase the probability that significant effects will be detected. A critical element to this kind of research is measurement instruments of both teacher PCK and various student learning outcomes. While measures of student learning outcomes are relatively substantial, PCK measures applicable to a large number of teachers, especially in science, are scant and that is why we have been working on the development of PCK measures. PCK measures that are reliable, valid, and feasible for large-scale use are an important stepping stone to investigating links between PCK, teaching practices, and student learning outcomes.

Table 8.1 compares two lines of PCK research that we have developed, including the three types of education research questions categorized by the National Research Council (NRC, 2002). It is important to point out that our change in research focus was a gradual evolution through an expansion of the research scope to achieve our ultimate goal: *To develop a theoretical model of PCK rooted in firm empirical evidence that explains how to improve science learning for all students and why/how it works.*

Achieving this goal requires a sophisticated understanding of causal effect relationships among different variables associated with teacher PCK, instructional practices, and student learning as a systematic whole. To this end, a thorough understanding of the construct of PCK is necessary, especially to establish plausible hypotheses about PCK's connections to other variables and their mechanisms.

To date, our understanding of PCK is limited and we have not even reached agreement on what it is (Park & Oliver, 2008a). This calls for a continued effort

TABLE 8.1 Comparison between two lines of research on PCK

Area of PCK research		Portraying and capturing PCK	Assessing and measuring PCK
Research goal		Understand how to support PCK development to improve instructional practices.	Understand the impact of PCK on student learning and how it works.
Research focus		Nature and characteristics of PCK, its development, and its relation to instructional practice.	Relationships between PCK and variables associated with student learning.
Underlying assumption		Teacher PCK guides instructional practices that to foster student learning.	Teacher PCK is one of the factors that impacts student learning.
Research question	Description	• What are the characteristics of experienced high school chemistry teachers' PCK? (Park & Oliver, 2008a) • What is the process through which the constituting components of PCK are integrated? (Park & Chen, 2012) • How does the National Board Certification process influence candidate teachers' PCK development? (Park & Oliver, 2008b)	• How has a survey-type measure of teacher PCK been developed and validated? (Park et al., 2013) • How is a teacher's PCK score related to the degree to which his/her instruction is reform oriented? (Park, Jang, Chen, & Jung, 2011)
	Causal effect	• What are the effects of a particular intervention on teacher PCK? • What are the effects of teacher PCK on a particular variable that affects student learning? • What are the effects of teacher PCK on student learning outcomes?	
	Mechanism or process	• How and why do the effects identified in the causal effect questions above occur?	
Methodological approach		• Qualitative research methods. • Quantitative methods used to embellish a primary qualitative study.	• Quantitative research methods. • Qualitative methods used to help develop quantitative measurement instruments. • Qualitative methods used to explain quantitative findings.

to elucidate the complexities of PCK through in-depth descriptive studies to identify uncovered aspects of PCK, illuminate unforeseen relationships, and generate new insights. Such research will help build clear conceptual frameworks and strong theoretical foundations for developing PCK measures and further addressing questions related to causal effect relationships and mechanisms. In this regard, our descriptive research on PCK continues to be coupled with the endeavor of assessing and measuring PCK. Parallel advancement in both areas through reciprocal influences will enable us to garner strong empirical evidence and theoretical descriptions that can influence teaching practices, student learning, and educational policies.

Conceptual framework and procedures

Conceptualization of PCK

Defining what is to be assessed is a necessary first step in any measurement process. Since Shulman (1986) fashioned the concept of PCK, there has been considerable divergence in the conceptualization and interpretation of PCK that makes specifying the construct being measured most challenging. However, there are also common understandings of PCK on which most scholars agree. The purpose of the PCK Summit was to provide a forum for scholars to synthesize those shared understandings of PCK through communicating and analyzing their views. Consensus constructed during the Summit should serve as a foundation on which researchers can build to advance PCK research.

Similarly, to develop measures of PCK, one should start with a model of PCK that best reflects consensus about the construct. Given that, we adopted the pentagon model of PCK (Park & Oliver, 2008a) to guide our PCK measure development, since it is grounded in common conceptions of PCK drawn from a comprehensive literature review and further refined through empirical tests. As shown in Figure 8.1, PCK is defined as an integration of the five components represented in the model. Reflection serves as a dynamic force that facilitates and strengthens their coherent interactions through complementary and ongoing readjustment so that a resulting construct of PCK is more than the sum of the integrated components.

With the pentagon model, we also conceptualize two dimensions of PCK: teachers' understanding and enactment. Because PCK is constituted by what teachers know, what teachers do, and the reasons for their actions (Baxter & Lederman, 1999), both cognitive and enacting aspects of PCK need to be assessed. In this regard, we designed two types of measures to assess both dimensions: (1) survey-type measure (paper-and-pencil type measure to assess the understanding dimension); and (2) rubric-type measure (observation-and interview-based measure to assess the enactment dimension).

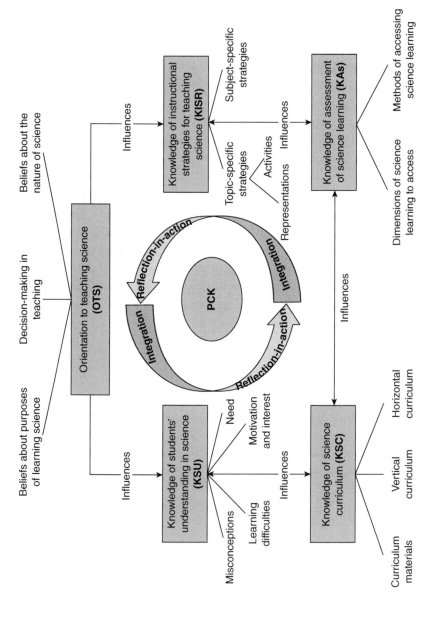

FIGURE 8.1 Pentagon model of PCK for teaching science (Park & Chen, 2012)

Influence of the PCK Summit on the conceptualization of PCK

One of the issues intensively discussed during the Summit was whether PCK is canonical, personal, or both. Engaging in that question led us to reconsider our approaches to address the unique nature of PCK, that is, topic specificity, context specificity, and idiosyncrasy. Given the nature of PCK, it would be ideal to develop different PCK measures for different topics for different teachers in different contexts. However, such an approach is unrealistic and makes the PCK measurement meaningless because comparisons are not possible. Our contemplation on this issue throughout the Summit resulted in differentiating two aspects of PCK for teaching a particular topic: indispensable PCK and idiosyncratic PCK (see Figure 8.2). Indispensable PCK refers to the parts of PCK that can be applied to any teacher in any teaching context for teaching a given topic, whereas idiosyncratic PCK refers to the parts of PCK that are unique to individual teachers and contexts. Our PCK measures mainly target measuring the indispensable PCK, even though we also consider idiosyncratic PCK to some degree in interpreting measurement results since the boundary between them is often blurred.

Then, what makes PCK indispensable? We suggest there are two major sources contributing to indispensable PCK: canonical science and learning theory (see Figure 8.3). Considering that the big ideas of a particular science topic stemming from canonical science are universal regardless of educational and cultural settings, it is expected that there is a knowledge base required for teaching those big ideas in common across any contexts and any teachers. Such a knowledge base constitutes indispensable PCK. The other source for indispensable PCK is alignment with contemporary learning theories. PCK is knowledge necessary for effective teaching of a subject, and effective teaching occurs only when instructional practices

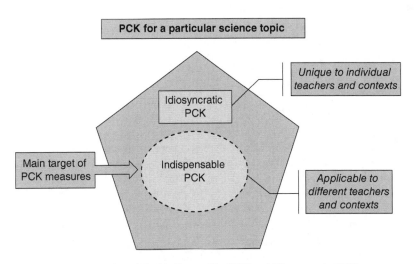

FIGURE 8.2 Conceptual model of indispensable PCK and idiosyncratic PCK

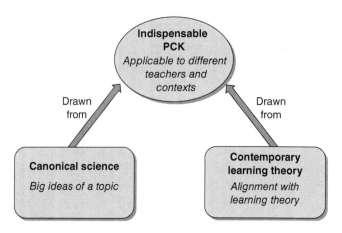

FIGURE 8.3 Major sources for indispensable PCK

are well aligned with how students learn (Hand, 2008). Understanding learning theory and applying such understandings to teaching approaches are another important foundation that shapes indispensable PCK. In sum, our measures are designed to assess indispensable PCK grounded in canonical science and learning theory that should cross boundaries between contexts and individuals.

Measuring PCK necessitates a normative stance in which some forms of PCK are more highly regarded than others. In other words, it is necessary to clarify norms for determining what counts as 'quality' PCK. The conceptualization of indispensable PCK guided us to include the degree of alignment with learning theory and focus on big ideas for the scoring criteria in addition to the soundness of pedagogical reasoning (Shulman, 1986) and the embeddedness of the five PCK components (Park, Suh, Seo, & Vo, 2013).

Design of the PCK measures

We designed two different measures, survey-type and rubric-type, to assess the understanding and enactment dimensions of PCK, respectively. The complementary combination of these two measures helps draw stronger inferences through data triangulation, balance the limitations of either type in isolation, and subsequently assess individual teachers' PCK in a more comprehensive way. In this regard, in designing our PCK measures, we presumed that individual teachers' PCK scores would be determined by the sum of the scores on both measures.

To consider the topic specificity of PCK, both measures center on a specific topic—photosynthesis. Photosynthesis was selected because it comprises a significant portion of the high school biology curriculum and because a significant amount of research exists on the learning and teaching of photosynthesis that would be useful for our PCK measure development. Acknowledging the complexity of PCK and the exploratory nature of our work, we decided to measure only two key components of PCK—knowledge of student understanding (KSU) and knowledge of instructional strategies and representations (KISR)—rather than attempting to measure all five components. The two components were chosen because they have been supported as the most critical components of PCK by both conceptual and empirical studies (e.g., Loughran, Berry, & Mulhall, 2006; Park & Chen, 2012; Shulman, 1986). The context specificity of PCK was taken into consideration in two ways in designing our PCK measures. First, we used classroom scenarios with succinct yet sufficient contextual information to create survey items. Second, the rubric-type measure was constructed in a way that enabled scorers to consider the given context in which the teacher was working when scoring the teacher's PCK.

Development of the survey-type measure

The survey-type measure (called PCK survey hereafter) has been through two major rounds of development, revision, and validation.

First round of PCK survey development

The first version of the PCK survey was a paper-and-pencil type test consisting of 11 multiple-choice items grounded in classroom scenarios. To write survey items, we first identified core concepts associated with big ideas in photosynthesis that students at grades 9–10 should know by analyzing: (1) National Science Education Standards (NRC, 1996); (2) ten selected states' science content standards; and (3) curricular materials for teaching photosynthesis, including textbooks and teachers' manuals. Identified core concepts were sent to two experienced biology teachers for review and subsequent modifications were made accordingly. Next, survey items were drafted centering on the core concepts and the two focus PCK components—KSU and KISR—referring to relevant literature, classroom observations and interviews with seven teachers, curriculum materials, and student work samples. Draft items were revised multiple times through weekly research team discussions and consultation with teachers, and finally the best 11 items were selected for the first PCK survey. The survey was mailed out to 659 biology teachers in a mid-west state of the US and 84 surveys (12.7 percent) were returned. The reliability of the survey estimated by internal consistency calculated by Cronbach's α was 0.449 that indicated unacceptable reliability and suggested significant revisions of the items (Park et al., 2011).

Second round of PCK survey development

Analysis of the collected survey data suggested a number of modifications to improve its validity and reliability. First, a generalizability analysis (Brennan,

1992) to disentangle multiple sources of measurement error revealed that the small number of items was the main reason for the low reliability. Since the items were classroom-scenario based, one item was at least half a page long. Although more than 50 items were drafted, only 11 items were included in the first survey so as not to discourage teachers' participation. To balance the number of items and the length of the survey, in the second round, we used both dichotomous and open-ended questions and increased the total number of items to 30 with a similar length to the first survey.

In modifying existing items and developing new items for the second round survey, we conducted multiple rounds of concurrent think-aloud interviews with five teachers and five scientists to see if respondents used a target PCK component intended to be tapped by each item. The reason for including scientists was to examine if the items measured PCK—not content knowledge—assuming that scientists would use more content knowledge due to a lack of PCK and consequently have difficulties responding to the PCK survey. The scientists interviewed were graduate students in biology who did not have any teaching assistant experience. All audio-taped think-aloud interviews were transcribed and coded using a pre-established set of codes consisting of Grossman's (1990) four knowledge bases for teaching and five PCK components in the pentagon model. Based on analysis results, items that did not measure the PCK component that they were supposed to measure were identified and revised. The revised items were then included in the next round of think-aloud interviews and modified again as necessary. The same procedure was repeated until the final 30 items were completed.

Thirty questions for the second round survey were based on six classroom scenarios. For each classroom scenario, the first three or four items were dichotomous questions to ask respondents to identify student learning difficulties or misconceptions in the given scenario. A following open-ended question asked them to reason out why students often have such learning difficulties or misconceptions that they identified in the previous dichotomous questions. The final open-ended question asked for a description of the teaching strategies they used/would like to use to deal with those learning difficulties or misconceptions and explain why such strategies worked/would work.

Development of the rubric-type measure

The rubric-type measure (called PCK rubric hereafter) was used to measure the enactment dimension of PCK. In other words, the PCK rubric was designed to indirectly gauge teachers' PCK revealed in their teaching practice (as reflected in observations) and their reasons for actions (as reflected in interviews). The rubric consists of a set of criteria for the two key PCK components being measured along a four-point rating scale. Once a draft of the rubric was completed, it was tested with more than 45 videotaped classroom observations of, and interviews with, five teachers and then revised accordingly. The finalized PCK rubric comprises nine elements intended to represent KSU and KISR across three different instructional stages: planning, implementation, and reflection (see Park et al., 2011 for the PCK rubric).

Administration, analysis, and validation of the PCK measures

PCK survey

While the first round PCK survey was administered by mailing it to participants, the second round PCK survey was administered through an online survey using Qualtrics, which enabled us to design the survey so that respondents could only move forward if they answered the given question. This feature was important as the second survey included open-ended questions that respondents might leave blank, which would lower the number of valid, complete surveys. Also, we expected an online survey might stimulate respondents' thorough responses to open-ended questions more than a paper-and-pencil survey because computers tend to engage and motivate production of higher quality written work (Goldberg, Russell, & Cook, 2003). Although online surveys yield higher completeness, the response rate is often lower than paper-and-pencil surveys (Kongsved, Basnov, Holm-Christensen, & Hjollund, 2007) therefore we also provided monetary compensation to participants ($5 Amazon e-gift certificate) to encourage participation.

About 2,000 secondary science teachers in a mid-west state of the US were invited to participate in the survey via emails. Eighty-five teachers completed the entire survey, while 254 teachers completed only parts of the survey. The test scores collected from 85 teachers indicated an acceptable level of reliability determined by internal consistency (Cronbach's $\alpha = 0.836$). The content-related evidence was gathered through consultation with six experts: one professor in each of biology, science education, and assessment; and, three experienced biology teachers. Construct-related evidence was collected through two approaches. First, analysis of think-aloud interviews with six teachers demonstrated that the second round survey items assessed the targeted sub-knowledge components of PCK. Second, exploratory factor analysis indicated that all but three items corresponded to the two theoretical components of PCK originally specified (Park et al., 2013).

PCK rubric

The PCK rubric achieved a high level of inter-rater reliability (i.e., $r = 0.958$, $p < 0.01$) and an acceptable degree of internal consistency across the nine elements as estimated by Cronbach's α (Park et al., 2011). The content validity of the PCK rubric was established by expert consultation. Construct-related evidence was collected through a confirmatory factor analysis for the two pre-defined PCK components that suggest that the PCK rubric appropriately measures KSU and KISR.

Dilemmas emerging from developing PCK measures

Theoretical dilemmas

A persistent dilemma in measuring PCK stems from the lack of an agreed-upon definition of PCK. Without its clear definition, the construct of PCK has been conceptualized in varied ways that subsequently make it difficult to cultivate and build on existing consensus to advance our understanding of PCK. Since sound measurement begins with clear construct conceptualizations based on strong theoretical foundations (Wilson, 2005), this deficiency of an established conceptualization poses a uniquely formidable challenge to scholars, that is, the necessity of simultaneously defining and measuring PCK.

In this regard, efforts to define and measure PCK should be considered as a necessary part of an iterative process through which one informs the other. On the one hand, well-defined conceptualizations of the construct are essential to design, develop, and refine PCK measures, especially in determining what is to be assessed and how, and theorizing important assumptions about the behaviors of the measures. On the other hand, measures of PCK are needed to further explore and validate the construct because problems arising from measurement processes and validity evidence can contribute to a better understanding of the construct itself. Further to this, more opportunities are likely suggested that can systematically engage scholars in productive discussions about how to make the concept of PCK more clear, operational, and valid. Those discussions will lend credibility to the resulting consensus at theoretical, conceptual, and methodological levels. The PCK Summit is an exemplary model of such effort.

Methodological dilemmas

Setting aside the theoretical issues, there is another important set of methodological dilemmas that challenged us. First of all, there are problems inherently involved in self-report and observation-based measures. Data collected through self-report methods such as our PCK survey are limited by participants' willingness and capability to share information. Considering that PCK is often subconscious and tacit, the teachers' lack of awareness of their PCK and practice could limit their responses. Lack of clarification opportunities while answering the PCK survey might also lead them to interpret the questions differently than we intended. All of those issues threaten the validity of the measure. However, it does not mean that self-report methods should not be used for measuring PCK. We think that a self-report type of measure is appropriate and necessary to measure PCK with a large sample of teachers, with the balance being a relatively efficient use of time and labor. The imperative is that researchers must carefully consider those limitations and measurement errors that may arise from self-report measures while analyzing and interpreting results.

Similarly, observation-based measures such as the PCK rubric can provide only limited access to a teacher's PCK because it is not possible to observe all aspects of a teacher's PCK. Although teachers' actions are a more accurate representation of what they know than a range of self-report measures (Van Driel, Beijaard, & Verloop, 2001), data from observations inevitably contains inferences because evaluators' subjectivity can come into play in making a judgment of what is observed in the situation. Furthermore, what teachers do is not always a direct reflection of what they know. With this in mind, we designed the PCK rubric to be used with a combination of observation and interview data to gain more reliable and fuller estimates of individual teachers' PCK, because interviews can provide access to the context of teachers' actions and meanings associated with the actions that we might not identify from observations alone (Seidman, 1998). Taken singly, either type of PCK measure has limitations, but using these two complementary measures reduces these limitations.

Most challenging to us was to find sound methodological approaches that take into consideration the topic-specific, context-specific, and person-specific nature of PCK. Considering the topic specificity, the PCK survey focused on a topic of photosynthesis and was not intended to measure PCK for any other science topics. That being said, it is ideal to develop different PCK surveys for different topics but that would be costly, time-consuming, and presumably unrealistic. Furthermore, what counts for a topic is still open to debate among researchers. Given the PCK rubric takes a generic form, a criticism we encountered was how the rubric addresses the topic-specific nature of PCK. We believe that the topic specificity is inevitably embedded in it because scoring with the rubric requires observation and interview data that is inherently specific to a particular topic (Park et al., 2011).

PCK is also specific to context and person (Park & Oliver 2008a). These features were taken into consideration in our work, especially in scoring open-ended questions of the PCK survey. Instead of setting up a single desirable answer for each question, our scoring focused on whether individual teachers' pedagogical reasoning was logical given the context, how much the reasoning was grounded in the five components of the pentagon model, and how much their ideas were aligned with contemporary learning theories. With respect to the PCK rubric, scorers are expected to consider the given topic, context, and teacher as much as possible in scoring each criterion of the rubric. To this end, we placed a great emphasis on scorers' qualification and training to establish the credibility of the PCK measurement.

Practical dilemmas

Due to the complexity of the construct, we advocate the use of multiple measures to assess teachers' PCK. However, this approach engenders a critical practical issue: It is time and labor intensive, and expensive to develop, administer, and score compared to the use of a single measure. This practical constraint could be handled using a computer-based test system. Using a computer-based measure can reduce the time spent on scoring because objective test items including multiple-choice and true–false items can be scored automatically by a computer. Furthermore, a computer-based test allows flexibility with test administration schedules and lowers the cost for shipping and distributing test materials (Wang, Jiao, Young, Brooks, & Olson, 2007).

An important practical issue associated with the PCK rubric is determining the appropriate number of observations and interviews to be used to measure the PCK of individual teachers. A teacher's PCK may not be evident to a scorer within the confines of one teaching experience; an extended period of time may be needed for the PCK to unfold. However, it might be unrealistic to observe all classes teaching a particular topic to measure a teacher's PCK particularly for large-scale studies. If we choose to select a certain number of classes (e.g., three lessons teaching photosynthesis for each teacher) for practicability, a question then arises as to how those lessons are selected. Should we observe a number of consecutive lessons to see connections among the lessons that may combine to culminate into more complex learning experiences? Or should we select a number of discrete lessons (e.g., beginning, middle, and end of the topic) to see the overall progression of instruction of a topic? Those questions need to be carefully examined to establish standardized measurement procedure and guidelines for reliable, operational, and fair assessment.

Finally, given the important role of scorers in the use of our PCK measures, the recruitment and training of quality scorers is critical to successful applications of the measures. To develop a systematic approach to the training, we have developed a scoring manual that includes the objectives of the assessment, scoring criteria that address each objective, a detailed description of standardized scoring procedures, and examples along the scoring scale. Besides a week-long training session, our scorers (who have all been doctoral students) were engaged in a weekly research seminar on PCK to advance their understanding of PCK and related research methodology. A new scorer was mentored by an experienced scorer using an apprenticeship model. In addition to the quality of scorers, the number of scorers impacts the reliability of scores. We suggest that more than two scorers should be assigned to each item, even though it is more expensive and requires more time for training. Also, calibration discussions among scorers on a regular basis will help establish the reliability of scores.

Directions for future research

For the PCK measures to be useful for causal effects and mechanism research, further validation efforts are necessary. We suggest four validity arguments to be examined in the future. First, the relationship between the PCK composite score (sum of PCK rubric and PCK survey scores) and another established measure of PCK needs to be examined to establish criterion validity evidence. Although there are not many measures of PCK, several instruments exist that have been widely used and validated for capturing and assessing teachers' PCK such as CoRes and PaP-eRs (Loughran et al., 2006). By comparing teachers' scores on our PCK measure and other measures, we will gain evidence to support the view that our instruments measure what they are supposed to measure.

Second, there is theoretical and empirical support that PCK and content knowledge are separate constructs even though they are interrelated (Krauss et al., 2008). Teachers' scores on our PCK measures should be compared with their scores on a content knowledge test on photosynthesis to collect evidence that indicates that our measures assess PCK not content knowledge. Third, it is essential to compare teachers' PCK composite scores from our measures and the quality of their teaching practices. This comparison will provide supporting evidence that PCK is a major factor that enables teachers to create effective learning environments. Last, since our PCK measures are designed to gauge indispensable PCK, it is critical to examine if the measures produce similar evidence for reliability and validity in other countries.

Once our measures are sufficiently validated, our research effort will continue to test important theoretical assumptions about PCK using the measures. For example, teaching experience has been considered as a key influencing factor since PCK is developed through classroom practices (Van Driel et al., 2001). This assumption can be empirically examined by comparing scores on the PCK measures between pre-service and experienced teachers. Also, statistical analyses of teachers' PCK scores and their years of teaching can provide insights into this assumption. Another assumption calling for empirical investigation is that PCK distinguishes teachers from content specialists (Shulman, 1987). A study to explore how differently science teachers and scientists perform on the PCK survey and/or PCK rubric can provide empirical supporting evidence for this theoretical conjecture. The foremost notion is that PCK impacts student learning. Examining how teachers' PCK scores on our measures relate to their students' achievement on standardized tests, or to other variables associated with student learning, will make a significant addition to our understanding of PCK.

We acknowledge the need for empirical studies that examine the content, structure, and nature of indispensable PCK. Those studies will provide useful information of what knowledge is indispensable and what is not and such understanding is essential to improve science teacher education. Although our PCK measures focus on indispensable PCK, we believe that idiosyncratic PCK is a critical means by which teachers express their professionalism. Idiosyncratic PCK represents how much a teacher is responsive to students in a given situation within a given context through adapting and tailoring instructional materials and strategies that become a unique aspect of PCK specialized only for that particular teacher. More research to portray idiosyncratic PCK will contribute to a better understanding of teacher professionalism.

Throughout our attempt to assess PCK, we have engaged in not only a measure development process but also a conceptualization process that required a strong theoretical foundation and a systematic thinking approach. We hope that the measure development procedures and conceptualization processes we employed can serve as a prototype for other researchers to make replicability possible. Through replicated research, we can accumulate enduring knowledge and develop the capacity to achieve consensus in the field. By doing so, research on PCK might move forward to answer causal effects and mechanism questions, begin to disentangle the complexity of teaching and learning, and further impact educational practices and policies.

Acknowledgement

Figure 8.1: Reproduced with permission from Park, S. & Chen, Y., "Mapping out the integration of the components of pedagogical content knowledge (PCK): Examples from high school biology classrooms," Figure 1, *Journal of Research in Science Teaching*, Copyright © 2012 Wiley Periodicals, Inc.

References

Baumert, J., Kunter, M., Blum, W., Brunner, M., Voss, T., Jordan, A., . . . Tsai, Y-M. (2010). Teachers' mathematical knowledge, cognitive activation in the classroom, and student progress. *American Educational Research Journal, 47*(1), 133–180.

Baxter, J. A., & Lederman, N. G. (1999). Assessment and measurement of pedagogical content knowledge. In J. Gess-Newsome & N. G. Lederman (Eds.), *Examining pedagogical content knowledge: The construct and its implications for science education* (pp.147–161). Dordrecht, the Netherlands: Kluwer Academic Publishers.

Brennan, R. L. (1992). Generalizability theory. *Educational Measurement: Issues and Practice, (winter)*, 27–34.

Fenstermacher, G. D., & Richardson, V. (2005). On making determinations of quality in teaching. *Teachers College Record, 107*(1), 186–213.

Goldberg, A., Russell, M., & Cook, A. (2003). The effect of computers on student writing: A meta-analysis of studies from 1992 to 2002. *Journal of Technology, Learning, and Assessment, 2*(1). Retrieved from http://escholarship.bc.edu/cgi/viewcontent.cgi?article=1007&context=jtla (accessed November 27, 2014).

Grossman, P. L. (1990). *The making of a teacher: Teacher knowledge and teacher education*. New York, NY: Teachers College Press.

Hand, B. (Ed.). (2008). *Science inquiry, argument and language*. Rotterdam, the Netherlands: Sense Publishers.

Kongsved, S. M., Basnov, M., Holm-Christensen, K., & Hjollund, N. H. (2007). Response rate and completeness of questionnaires: A randomized study of internet versus paper-and-pencil versions. *Journal of Medical Internet Research, 9*(3), e25.

Krauss, S., Brunner, M., Kunter, M., Baumert, J., Blum, W., Neubrand, M., & Jordan, A. (2008). Pedagogical content knowledge and content knowledge of secondary mathematics teachers. *Journal of Educational Psychology, 100*(3), 716–725.

Loughran, J., Berry, A., & Mulhall, P. (2006). *Understanding and developing science teachers' pedagogical content knowledge*. Rotterdam, the Netherlands: Sense Publishers.

National Research Council (NRC) (1996). *National science education standards*. Washington, DC: National Academies Press.

National Research Council (2002). *Scientific research in education*. Washington, DC: National Academies Press.

Park, S., & Chen, Y. (2012). Mapping out the integration of the components of pedagogical content knowledge (PCK): Examples from high school biology classrooms. *Journal of Research in Science Teaching, 49*(7), 922–941.

Park, S., Jang, J., Chen, Y-C., & Jung, J. (2011). Is pedagogical content knowledge (PCK) necessary for reformed science teaching?: Evidence from an empirical study. *Research in Science Education, 41*, 245–260.

Park, S., & Oliver, J. S. (2008a). Revisiting the conceptualisation of pedagogical content knowledge (PCK): PCK as a conceptual tool to understand teachers as professionals. *Research in Science Education, 38*(3), 261–284.

Park, S., & Oliver, J. S. (2008b). National Board Certification (NBC) as a catalyst for teachers' learning about teaching: The effects of the NBC process on candidate teachers' PCK development. *Journal of Research in Science Teaching, 45*(7), 812–834.

Park, S., Suh, J., Seo, K., & Vo, T. (2013, April). *Development and validation of a survey measure of secondary teachers' topic specific PCK*. Paper presented at the annual meeting of National Association for Research in Science Teaching, Rio Grande, Puerto Rico.

Shulman, L. S. (1986). Those who understand: Knowledge growth in teaching. *Educational Researcher, 15*(1), 4–14.

Shulman, L. S. (1987). Knowledge and teaching: Foundations of the new reform. *Harvard Educational Review, 57*(1), 1–22.

Seidman, I. (1998). *Interviewing as qualitative research: A guide for researchers in education and the social sciences* (2nd ed.). New York, NY: Teachers College Press.

Van Driel, J. H., Beijaard, D., & Verloop, N. (2001). Professional development and reform in science education: The role of teachers' practical knowledge. *Journal of Research in Science Teaching, 38*, 137–158.

Wang, S., Jiao, H., Young, M. J., Brooks, T. E., & Olson, J. (2007). A meta-analysis of testing mode effects in Grade K–12 mathematics tests. *Educational and Psychological Measurement, 67*, 219–238.

Wilson, M. (2005). *Constructing measures: An item response modeling approach*. Mahwah, NJ: Lawrence Erlbaum Associates.

9

TOWARD A MORE COMPREHENSIVE WAY TO CAPTURE PCK IN ITS COMPLEXITY

Ineke Henze

DELFT UNIVERSITY OF TECHNOLOGY

Jan H. Van Driel

LEIDEN UNIVERSITY

Introduction

Since 1998, we have been working on a series of studies concerning the development of pre-service science teachers' PCK in the context of initial teacher education, and on the development of in-service science teachers' PCK in the context of educational innovation. Most of these studies were conducted in the context of a broader research program at Leiden University, which focused on teacher knowledge. Teacher knowledge is conceptualized as including a large variety of cognitions, from conscious and well-balanced opinions to unconscious and un-reflected intuitions (Verloop, Van Driel, & Meijer, 2001). This knowledge is seen as person- and context-bound, action-oriented, and, to a large extent, tacit. The development of PCK is understood as a constructivist and non-linear process: New information is built upon prior knowledge (and beliefs) from different domains and upon experiences from practice, including interactions with students and colleagues (Clarke & Hollingsworth, 2002). From more recent socio-cultural and situative perspectives, learning is seen as a process of participating in socio-cultural practices that structure and shape cognitive activity (Lave & Wenger, 1991). From this view, teacher knowledge is assumed to be integrally and inherently situated in the everyday world of teachers. Moreover, this knowledge is seen as not only residing in the individual, but also distributed among people and their environments, including the objects, books, tools, and the communities of which they are a part (Greeno, Collins, & Resnick, 1996).

From these perspectives, PCK is seen as a form of teachers' professional knowledge, which refers to a transformation of subject-matter knowledge so that it can be used effectively and flexibly in the communication process between teachers and learners during classroom practice. Fundamental in our definition of PCK is the notion that teachers' knowledge of strategies to teach a certain topic is related to, if not based on, their knowledge of how students learn that topic, and their understanding that students' learning may vary according to the learning abilities of the student, student interest, context, and so on (Van Driel, de Vos, & Verloop, 1998). We see PCK as flexible, that is, it develops over time based on teachers' experiences of teaching a topic repeatedly. Specific interventions, in teacher education or professional development programs, can contribute to enhancing teachers' PCK. Our main aim for studying teachers' PCK is to understand how and why teachers teach subject matter the way they do and, in particular, how their teaching approach is related to or focused on promoting student learning. In this context, we have sought to understand the nature of science teachers' PCK, how it develops over time, and how it relates to science teachers' beliefs and other knowledge components, in particular, general pedagogical knowledge and subject-matter knowledge. Achieving such understanding is vital to the development of effective pre-service and in-service teacher education and professionalization programs.

Because a single instrument cannot capture the complexity of PCK, various instruments and procedures have been developed and used to investigate this knowledge in a valid and reliable manner (Kagan, 1990). In our work over the past 15 years, we have used a variety of tools to investigate the PCK of pre-service and in-service science teachers. These studies were usually qualitative in nature and, consequently, small scale, each including five to fifteen teachers. In terms of data collection, we focused on questioning teachers when they were planning or reflecting on teaching, using in-depth interview techniques. In addition, we also collected written materials, for instance, their lesson plans, action research plans, and action research reports. These materials were often used to triangulate interview data. Until recently, our methods were, in a sense, limited as our studies aimed to display the PCK expressed by teachers in verbal or written form.

Participating in the PCK Summit, among others, has made us more aware of these and other challenges. In particular, we benefitted from discussions on the relationship between knowledge, as expressed by teachers, verbally and on paper, and teachers' enactment of their knowledge in practice. This has inspired us to further explore theories and methodologies from a wider range of disciplines, including cognitive and educational psychology. In this chapter, we will first reflect on some of our earlier studies on PCK, with attention to the methods we have used. After acknowledging some of the benefits and limitations of these studies, we will broaden our scope, and after a brief review of the literature on the relationship between knowing and acting, we will discuss the most recent PCK study by one of us. Reflecting on this study, we conclude this chapter with a discussion of other approaches and techniques, which, combined in the design of future studies, have the potential to capture PCK in its complexity.

Studies on PCK development of in-service science teachers based on teachers' self-reports

PCK development in the context of the introduction of Public Understanding of Science

Henze (2006) studied a group of nine in-service science teachers during three years, while they were implementing a new syllabus in the Netherlands, called Public Understanding of Science, in their classrooms. There was no professional development or intervention during this period. In this context, the author aimed to identify the content and structure of the PCK for a specific topic—Models of the Solar System and the Universe. PCK development was investigated and described in terms of relations between four different elements derived from the Magnusson, Krajcik, & Borko (1999, p. 99) model: (a) knowledge about instructional strategies; (b) knowledge about students' understanding; (c) knowledge about assessment of students; and (d) knowledge about the goals and objectives of the topic in the curriculum. Unlike Magnusson et al. (1999), Henze believes that teachers' general beliefs about learning and teaching science (orientations toward teaching science) should not be considered an element of teachers' PCK, but rather an influencing factor on their knowledge and beliefs about learning and teaching specific subject matter. For this reason, orientations toward the teaching of science were not investigated.

Data collection consisted of semi-structured interviews to investigate the teachers' PCK of Models of the Solar System and the Universe. The interviews were conducted among the teachers in three subsequent academic years, each year shortly after they had finished the lessons on this topic. The interview questions were developed based on a study of the relevant literature on PCK as well as models and modeling in science and astronomy education. Some of these questions can be found in Table 9.1, each related to a specific element of PCK.

Henze found substantial differences in PCK among the teachers in her study even though they were teaching the same curriculum and using the same textbook. These differences appear to stem from a range of factors including different teaching preferences and pedagogical perspectives. On closer inspection, however, Henze identified commonalities in the PCK of the teachers and in the way it developed over time. In particular, two qualitatively different varieties of PCK emerged from the analyses (Henze, Van Driel, & Verloop, 2008). Type A was described as oriented toward model *content*, while Type B was typified as oriented toward model *content*, model *production*, and thinking about the *nature* of models. In terms of Hodson's (1992) typology: Type A was similar to teaching science as an "established body of knowledge," while Type B reflected the goal of teaching "the experience of science as a method of generating and validating such knowledge" (Hodson, 1992, p. 545).

TABLE 9.1 General phrasings of the interview questions

PCK elements	Questions about teaching Models of the Solar System and the Universe
a. Knowledge about instructional strategies	1. In what activities, and in what sequence, did your students participate in the context of this chapter? Please explain your answer. 2. What was (were) your role(s) as a teacher, in the context of this chapter? Explain your answer.
b. Knowledge about students' understanding	3. Did your students need any specific previous knowledge in the context of this chapter? Explain your answer. 4. What was successful for your students? Explain your answer. 5. What difficulties did you see? Explain your answer.
c. Knowledge about ways to assess students	6. On what, and how, did you assess your students in the context of this chapter? Explain your answer. 7. Did your students reach the learning goals with regard to this chapter? How do you know? Explain your answer.
d. Knowledge about goals and objectives of the topic in the curriculum	8. What was (were) your main objective(s) in teaching the topic of Models of the Solar System and the Universe? Explain your answer.

The results also indicated that these two types of PCK developed in qualitatively different ways in terms of relations among the four PCK elements. With regard to Type A, in particular, "knowledge about instructional strategies" further developed over the years (element a). PCK development was found to be constrained by teachers' limited subject-matter knowledge, their mainly positivist view on models and modeling, and teacher-directed pedagogical perspectives. In contrast, with regard to PCK development of teachers representing Type B, Henze et al. (2008) concluded that the development of the different PCK elements was mutually related. Moreover, PCK development was guided by their more comprehensive subject-matter knowledge, a more relativist view on models and modeling in science, and pedagogical knowledge and beliefs that are more student-directed than teacher-directed.

The methods and instruments in this study appeared useful for tracing the development of PCK of the participating teachers. However, since data collection relied heavily on teachers' oral articulations during individual interviews shortly after having conducted a lesson series, the study was limited. In fact, what Henze et al. reported was teachers' perspectives on their PCK, which to some extent were validated with artifacts from their teaching such as lesson plans, authentic lesson materials (including assignments and tests for students), and students' products.

PCK development in the context of a professional development program

In a more recent study, Wongsopawiro (2012) studied the development of PCK of experienced science and mathematics teachers who participated in a professional development program, which consisted of a two-week summer course, followed by a one-year action research project. During the summer course, teachers attended workshops about specific aspects of science teaching, as well as doing action research in their own classrooms. Teachers chose a topic from their curriculum for their own action research and studied literature on the teaching of that topic. They were asked to reflect upon their earlier teaching of this topic and to provide reasons why they now intended to use different instructional methods. By the end of the summer course, they had come up with a plan to teach this topic (i.e., lesson plans) and to study their own teaching through action research, including research questions and methods for assessing their projects. In the following academic year, this plan was carried out in practice. During that year they had four meetings with the university staff. The academic staff acted as facilitators and peers (i.e., school colleagues) served as critical friends in this professional development program. Teachers kept electronic journals and logs, and collected student materials throughout the year. At the end of the year, they wrote a report about their project and were interviewed by the researcher. The study included three cohorts of teachers from consecutive years.

This project concerned an in-depth exploration of science teachers' PCK (n = 12) in relation to their purposes and concerns of teaching science. The latter, in particular, have not received much attention in research on PCK to date. Teachers' action research reports and interviews were analyzed, resulting in representations of teachers' PCK in terms of their concerns, their purposes of science teaching (Hodson, 1992), and PCK elements according to Magnusson et al. (1999)—similar to Henze (2006). Three categories of teachers' concerns were distinguished: (i) low scores of their students on science content tests; (ii) students showing poor science skills; and (iii) students being uninterested in science. Each of these concerns was found to be related to a specific purpose, that is, focusing on learning science content, learning to do science, and learning and appreciating science content, respectively. Furthermore, the content of teachers' PCK elements was found to be consistent with their concerns and purposes for teaching science, leading to the identification of three different types of PCK, which focused on knowledge of: (I) teaching science *content* using various strategies; (II) teaching science process *skills*; and (III) teaching science through enhancing students' *motivation*. This typology is different from the one that Henze (2006) found. Motivating students, which is central in type III, is absent in Hodson's (1992) typology of science teaching goals. Furthermore, it became clear that the PCK that was found in this study was strongly influenced by teachers' specific context. The choice of a topic for their action research project was largely inspired by teachers' current concerns, and this choice impacted on the PCK that teachers expressed and developed during the project. It was concluded that teachers' previous experiences and concerns should be taken into account when studying their PCK.

Finally, what and how individual science teachers (n = 12) learned from taking part in the professional development program, in terms of development of their PCK, was explored. For this purpose, Clarke and Hollingsworth's (2002) Interconnected Model of Teacher Professional Growth was used as an analytic framework. The study focused on identifying possible pathways of change that indicate the development of science teachers' PCK. Three data sources were used: (1) the teachers' action research reports; (2) the teachers' reflective journals about their professional learning processes, as written sources; and (3) the final interview (oral source). It was found that, for all teachers, the summer course had triggered a development of PCK. In particular, teachers who conducted a literature review and participated in peer discussions acquired a better understanding of the use of instructional strategies and assessment methods, such as the use of micro-based computer labs to increase students' science skills and the use of students' journals to assess their students' knowledge. As for the ways PCK developed, different pathways for each teacher were found. However, two distinct pathways that lead to changes in PCK could be distinguished, which differed in complexity. The more complex pathway included teachers' analysis of evidence of students' learning. These teachers were able to explain what they had learned (i.e., about student learning) from such analyses and to conclude whether their instructional strategy had been effective or not and whether it needed to be adapted in future teaching cycles. It was concluded that a focus on classroom outcomes is important for the simultaneous development of PCK and classroom practice.

Like Henze (2006), Wongsopawiro (2012) mainly collected data from teachers, who expressed their ideas about teaching and learning subject matter in oral and written form. The action research format in this study prompted teachers to collect data themselves, in their own classes, from their own students. As outlined above, the way teachers collected and analyzed these data appeared to influence the development of their PCK, in terms of relating their increasing knowledge of student learning to their expanding knowledge of instructional strategies. Also, collecting and reflecting on classroom data was seen as a way to trigger teachers to express their PCK (Justi & Van Driel, 2005). However, the Wongsopawiro (2012) study was limited in the sense that it did not include data from classroom teaching.

Investigating PCK in relation to classroom teaching

Introduction

The basic idea underlying our PCK research is that reciprocity exists between the whole of teachers' cognitions (in the broad sense) and their activities, and that, consequently, it makes sense to investigate teachers' knowledge (Verloop, Van Driel, & Meijer, 2001). Historically, our research on PCK may be situated as follows. In the 1960s and 1970s, a great deal of education research was aimed at developing a knowledge base for teaching and, where possible, translating it into recommendations for teacher education (Reynolds, 1989). This knowledge base was to be shared by teachers and, ideally, form the basis for their behavior (Hoyle & John, 1995). This 'process-product' approach has been criticized, mainly because the quest for 'effective' variables in teaching behavior led to a fragmented and mechanistic view of teaching, in which the complexity of the teaching enterprise was not acknowledged (Doyle, 1990). Since the 1980s, research on teaching has shifted from investigating only teachers' behavior to also examining the teachers' knowledge and beliefs underlying that behavior. The change in focus was reinforced by developments in cognitive psychology that were based on the fundamental assumption that one's cognitions and actions are mutually related and, likewise, that teachers' cognitions are important determinants of their classroom behavior (e.g., Clark & Peterson, 1986). Therefore, to understand teachers' practice it is necessary to study their underlying knowledge and beliefs (i.e., practical knowledge; Meijer, 1999).

However, it soon became clear that teachers in practice sometimes do things other than what they planned. With regard to this gap between knowledge and action, 'decision-making' is often considered as a bridging mechanism (Bishop & Whitfield, 1972; Borko, Roberts, & Shavelson, 2008). Bishop and Whitfield (1972) distinguish in this respect between pre- and within-lesson decisions, and also between long- and short-term decisions. Decisions made prior to teaching (i.e., planning decisions) are seen as more deliberated than 'on-the-spot' decisions. Decisions made during teaching (i.e., 'interactive decisions') are mostly unconscious and would be closely related to a teacher's actual behavior. For Bishop and Whitfield, each teacher develops individual decision-making frameworks or schema (i.e., 'routines' or 'scripts') for making those decisions. Moreover, decision-making appears to be influenced by both personal factors (such as beliefs and values) and situational factors.

Diverging from one's original plans or not bringing intentions into practice can also be studied from the perspective of 'psychological barriers' to turn certain knowledge into action. Knowing what to do is not always enough to act on it. In daily life, for example, we know much more about healthy eating and exercising than we usually put in practice. This 'under-performing' is normal and as it should be. However, sometimes the lag in the transfer of knowledge to action becomes too much of a gap. Based on research in organizational psychology, Pfeffer and Sutton (2013) have identified a number of key factors that contribute to this 'knowing–doing' gap. Among these key factors are inhibitions by fear, taboos—or other social barriers—that prevent and forbid action, lack of structure for action, and personal items predisposing from taking action. The discrepancy between a teacher's intentions and actual behavior in the classroom is known in literature as the "problem of enactment" (Kennedy, 1999).

In our PCK research, up to now, we have focused on knowledge and beliefs outside the actual and immediate context of a teacher's actions in the classroom. In line with the above, the results of those studies provide an incomplete picture of a teacher's PCK because it is not clear what goes on in the teacher's mind during teaching. We think that it is necessary to reconsider the investigation of PCK so that components that are more distant from teacher's behavior *and* those that are closely related are all included.

A case study focusing on a teacher's PCK and classroom teaching

In recent years, the relationship between expressions of teachers' PCK and the enactment of this PCK in classroom teaching has attracted more attention. In particular, scholars (Baumert et al., 2010; Gess-Newsome et al., 2011) conducted large-scale studies of science teachers' PCK, measured with questionnaires or tests, in relation to observations of their teaching and to the scores of their students on standardized tests. However, these studies leave us with questions as to whether and how PCK actually informs classroom teaching, and in what ways this can be noticed or made visible. We argue that qualitative in-depth research on the relationship between PCK and classroom teaching is needed to better understand the concept of PCK and its development.

Barendsen and Henze (2012) studied a chemistry teacher's PCK and enactment of a lesson module on (Poly) Lactic Acid for Grade-9 students during the introduction of context-based chemical education (Gilbert, 2006) in the Netherlands. The aim of this case study was to explore the relationship between PCK (as formulated by the teacher) and practice (as observed in the classroom), with the ultimate goal of gaining a deeper understanding of the mechanisms through which teachers build and use their PCK in action (Schön, 1983). The teacher's PCK was captured through an interview that took place prior to his teaching of the module. This interview focused on the teacher's subjective representations of the key concepts attached to the topic of (Poly) Lactic Acid with use of the Content Representation (CoRe; Loughran, Mulhall, & Berry, 2004), which covered the four PCK elements of Magnusson's model (Magnusson et al., 1999) mentioned in Table 9.1. The interview resulted in a completed CoRe organized by the 'important ideas and concepts' which the teacher brought up. To monitor classroom interactions, the authors then developed an observation instrument in such a way that the observations could be compared with the teacher's articulated PCK. In order to construct such an instrument, they identified indicators representing the different elements of PCK. An iterative development procedure resulted in an observation form with the final observational items: instructional methods (as an indicator for PCK element a); control of choices made during the lessons (also for PCK element a); check of students' understanding during the lessons (for PCK element c); and lesson content (for PCK element d)—see Table 9.2.

TABLE 9.2 PCK elements and observational items

PCK elements	Observational items
a. Knowledge about instructional strategies	Instructional methods
	Control of choices made during the lessons
b. Knowledge about students' understanding	This aspect was not observed directly
c. Knowledge about ways to assess students during the lessons	Check of students' understanding during the lessons
d. Knowledge about goals and objectives of the topic in the curriculum	Lesson content

Each observational item was subdivided in to several categories (see Figure 9.1), which are described below.

- Starting with the 'Lesson content' part, the authors took the classical trichotomy of *Knowledge*, *Skills*, and *Attitudes*, based on Bloom's (1956) Taxonomy of Learning Domains. The *Knowledge* category was subdivided into *science concepts* (the scientific theory), *personal life* (topics from the personal environment that have scientific aspects), *society and technology* (topics from the social environment, society, and industry that have scientific aspects), and *epistemology* (nature and origin of scientific knowledge, historical models, and theories). This sub-categorization was based on recent curriculum innovations and on the Curriculum Emphasis taxonomy (i.e., positions about what the science curriculum should emphasize) by Van Driel, Bulte, and Verloop (2008).
- For the 'Instructional methods,' a typical list of teaching methods was taken and some refinements were made, especially to distinguish between the teacher's different roles during student assignments. The categories are: *Lecturing*, *Interactive instruction*, *Demo*, *Instruction for student work*, *Student work with(out) teacher assistance*, *Conclusion of student work*, *Student debate*, and *Other activities*.
- 'Control of choices made during the lessons' was introduced to register who gives direction to the actions in class with respect to lesson contents or instructional methods. Switching from teacher control to student initiative is a relevant aspect of many curriculum innovations worldwide. The Control item was subdivided in the categories *Teacher* (the teacher takes initiative) and *Student* (the student or students takes/take initiative).
- Finally, for 'Check of students' understanding during the lessons,' the authors used a simple division into *Questions* (e.g., elicitation of students' preconceptions), *Assignments* (e.g., an exercise to apply previously explained chemical concepts/theory), and *Other activities*. Because of its special layout, the observation form could capture a wide range of observations, as well as display their interrelationship.

time	lesson content						instructional method									control		check		
	knowledge																			
interval (minute)	*science concept*	*personal life*	*society*	*epistemology*	*skill*	*attitude*	*lecturing*	*interactive instruction*	*demo*	*instruction students' work*	*students' work without teacher assistance*	*students' work with teacher assistance*	*conclusion of students' work*	*debate*	*other*	*teacher*	*student*	*question*	*assignment*	*other*
																		?	!	
5							x													
6										x	x								x	
7	x												x			x				
8	x							x					x			x				
9	x							x								x				
10	x						x									x				
11	x						x									x	x			
12	x						x										x			
13	x	x					x									x				
14	x	x					x									x	x			
15	x	x					x									x				
16		x					x									x				
17		x					x									x				
18	x						x									x				
19	x						x									x				

FIGURE 9.1 Completed observation form for video-segment 2

During eight lessons (i.e., 400 minutes) classroom interactions were captured on video using two cameras, one at the front and one at the back of the classroom. For coding, segments were selected in which the teacher was clearly visible and that were of substantial length, that is, at least 10 minutes time-intervals. Six video-segments matched these criteria. They covered 240 minutes in total with intervals ranging from 15 to 52 minutes. The authors coded the selected video-segments, assigning the best fitting categories of the observation form to 1-minute intervals. Figure 9.1 shows an example of a completed observation form.

The authors added a notes sheet to the observation form to record content details. For example, the content of the topic of discussion, the content of teacher's instructions for student work, or the content of check questions and assignments, at a specific moment during the lesson.

A global frequency analysis was done, using the total number of item occurrences per video-segment. The cumulative scores (over all video-segments) of the observational items were used to identify patterns occurring *within* each observational item, as well as patterns *between* the different items. Some of these patterns are shown below.

- Within items:
  - Lesson content: The video-segments contained a mix of conceptual and contextual knowledge content, in which the conceptual content prevailed (81 percent of all Lesson content scores).
  - Instructional methods: Lecturing was predominant; student debate did not show up.
  - Control: Choices in the lessons were made by the teacher for 90 percent of the time.
- In-between items:
  - Lesson content—Instructional method—Control: During lecturing, students' initiatives to bring up contexts from personal experiences or other sources were hardly honored by the teacher.

Subsequently, a further in-depth content analysis of the observed classroom interaction was conducted using the information on the notes sheets. This qualitative analysis was aimed at confirming, refining, and explaining the found patterns, as well as discovering new patterns.

Finally, the patterns in the classroom interaction were compared to the teacher's articulated PCK as recorded in the CoRe. From this, an obvious discrepancy was noted between all PCK elements and the corresponding observations in class, both in terms of richness and overall coherence and consistency. The gap concerned the following features.

The teachers' articulated PCK could be typified as focused on the aims of context-based chemical education (Gilbert, 2006) and a student-directed perspective on learning and teaching. However, 'knowledge about ways to assess students' understanding' did not match with the other PCK elements: the teacher would prefer not to measure students' ability to connect chemical content with relevant contexts explicitly, but rather evaluate students' understanding of the key concepts of the lesson module as such. As to the relationship between the different knowledge elements, the authors typified the teacher's PCK as not fully consistent.

In contrast to the teacher's articulated PCK, the observed practice was characterized as rather traditional science education focused on conceptual knowledge. The teacher's actions in the classroom showed little variation and were quite consistent across all observed aspects of the lessons and all science topics—classroom interactions were dominated by the teacher with little room for student input.

In a final interview, the teacher was informed about the remarkable differences between the observations and his PCK articulation. His first reaction was that he recognized the main patterns found in the data. He admitted he had not been conscious of them before and he immediately started exploring possible explanations.

The teacher suggested that his dominant teacher behavior could be explained by his feeling that during classroom instruction the students were not as responsive and involved as he had hoped. He also complained about a lack of time because a physics colleague had asked him to devote some class hours to the topic of atomic models. These could point to *situational factors* in the decision framework of Bishop and Whitfield (1972), leading to the (unconscious) decision to divert from his original intentions. However, the teacher also realized now that his own teaching behavior could have been a determining factor for the students' lack of response. He started to wonder whether the observed unevenness in the teacher–student interaction had been in fact a response to stress (due to time pressure or high workload), and if so, whether this response was permanent or not. Such a response could be a *personal item predisposing from taking action* in the sense of Pfeffer and Sutton (2013).

Both theoretical perspectives (i.e., the decision framework and psychological barriers) provided insight into the discrepancy between the teacher's articulated PCK and the observed behavior in the classroom. The teacher's reflections on the results of the study were immediate, but appeared somewhat superficial. The use of additional stimulated recall techniques (Clark & Peterson, 1986; Meijer, 1999) or well-structured reflection methods (e.g., Korthagen & Kessels, 1999) could help in discovering unconscious decisions made during teaching and underlying psychological barriers (e.g., inhibitions by fear, lack of structure for action) contributing to the observed gap between the teacher's expressed PCK and classroom practice (Barendsen & Henze, 2012). Moreover, ongoing reflection on practice is a crucial factor for further development of the teacher's personal knowledge and beliefs (Clarke & Hollingsworth, 2002; Schön, 1983).

Implications for future research

Like other forms of teacher knowledge, PCK is complex and to a large extent tacit (Van Driel et al., 1998). To express PCK in words (in oral or written form), it is necessary for a teacher to be aware of this knowledge, and to have the ability to articulate it. The studies described in the section on PCK studies based on self-reports were dependent upon the teacher having this ability. Other research techniques (i.e., concept mapping and the repertory grid technique) can be valuable additions to research methods that concern the expression of PCK in spoken or written form. These techniques have been used in other of our and our colleagues' studies (Meijer, 1999; Henze, 2006). The structuring of PCK-related concepts (concept mapping) and the rating of educational activities along various construct dimensions (the repertory grid technique) are cognitive activities of a different level (Bloom, 1956), providing other kinds of representation of teachers' PCK, that is, a 'mental map' and a 'construct network' instead of an oral or written description. Compared to expressing PCK in words, the complexity and abstraction of PCK and its tacit nature are less restricting when constructing concept maps (Meijer, 1999) or rating certain elements on constructs (Henze, 2006), at least when fixed concepts (concept map) or constructs (repertory grid technique) are provided to teachers. However, it is of great importance that these concepts or these constructs are recognized by the teachers themselves. Otherwise teachers may feel that this structured research procedure hampers them in expressing their knowledge and beliefs (Meijer, 1999).

In the previous section we described a more recent study, which aimed to relate a teacher's verbal articulation of PCK to actual classroom behavior. This study revealed a rather large discrepancy between the two. The teacher's post hoc rationalizations provided some explanations for this "problem of enactment" (Kennedy, 1999). This study demonstrates that the relationship between teachers' PCK, as investigated through interviews, and their classroom practice, is far from straightforward. In their large-scale study, Gess-Newsome et al. (2011) also failed to find a correlation between PCK, measured with a test, and classroom teaching. Obviously, these findings present a challenge for future research. One option is to use stimulated recall interviews as a way to access teachers' "interactive cognitions" (Meijer, 1999), that is, the knowledge that teachers actually use *during* classroom teaching. Since teachers obviously cannot think aloud while teaching, stimulated recall is a technique that asks teachers to comment on a video of their teaching. The idea is not to ask teachers to justify what they did, but to reconstruct their thinking while they were teaching. Another way is to collect data from students. Students' perceptions of their teachers' behavior have been used successfully in research, for instance, on teachers' interpersonal behavior (Wubbels, Brekelmans, den Brok, & van Tartwijk, 2006) and on teachers' general pedagogical behavior (Van de Grift, Van der Wal, & Torenbeek, 2011). In the context of PCK research, instruments for students could be developed that focus on teachers' use of instructional strategies and their understanding of students' learning. For example, students could be asked to rate the frequency and usefulness of certain strategies used in the context of teaching a certain topic, from the perspective of how these strategies helped them to understand or appreciate this particular topic. Also, students may be asked how well they think their teacher understands their abilities to learn specific topics. Data collected with instruments like these may constitute a useful complement to observations of teaching practice, and as such may provide a better understanding of the way PCK is enacted in classroom practice. Also, data from students combined with observational data may be used to provide teachers with feedback about their practice, and may help them to become more aware of how their knowledge and intentions play out in practice. Subsequently, teachers may be stimulated and supported to reconsider both their knowledge and practice and, eventually, to improve the alignment between the two.

References

Barendsen, E. & Henze, I. (2012). *Comparing teacher PCK and teacher practice through PCK related classroom observation*. Paper presented at the NARST conference, Indianapolis, IA.

Baumert, J., Kunter, M., Blum, W., Brunner, M., Voss, T., Jordan, A., . . . Tsai, Y. M. (2010). Teachers' mathematical knowledge, cognitive activation in the classroom, and student progress. *American Educational Research Journal, 47*(1), 133–180.

Bishop, A. J., & Whitfield, R. C. (1972). *Situations in teaching*. McGraw-Hill.

Bloom, B. S. (1956). *Taxonomy of educational objectives: The classification of educational goals*. Harlow, Essex, England: Longman Group.

Borko, H., Roberts, S. A., & Shavelson, R. (2008). Teachers' decision making: From Alan J. Bishop to today. In P. Clarkson & N. Presmeg (Eds.), *Critical issues in mathematics education* (pp. 37–67). Dordrecht, the Netherlands: Springer Publishing Company.

Clark, C. M., & Peterson, P. L. (1986). Teachers' thought processes. In M. C. Wittrock (Ed.), *Handbook of research on teaching* (3rd ed., pp. 255–296). New York, NY: Macmillan Publishers Ltd.

Clarke, D. J., & Hollingsworth, H. (2002). Elaborating a model of teacher professional growth. *Teaching and Teacher Education, 18*, 947–967.

Doyle, W. (1990). Themes in teacher education research. In W. R. Houston (Ed.), *Handbook of research in teacher education* (pp. 3–23). New York, NY: Macmillan Publishers Ltd.

Gess-Newsome, J., Cardenas, S., Austin, B. A., Carlson, J., Gardner, A. L., Stuhlsatz, M. A. M., Taylor, J. A., & Wilson, C. D. (2011, April). *Impact of educative materials and transformative professional development on teachers' PCK, practice, and student achievement*. Paper presented at the Annual Meeting of the National Association for Research in Science Teaching, Orlando, FL.

Gilbert, J. K. (2006). On the nature of 'context' in chemical education. *International Journal of Science Education, 28*(9), 957–976.

Greeno, J. G., Collins, A. M., & Resnick, L. B. (1996). Cognition and learning. In D. Berliner & R. Calfee (Eds.), *Handbook of educational psychology* (pp. 15–41). New York, NY: Macmillan Publishers Ltd.

Henze, I. (2006). *Science teachers' knowledge development in the context of educational innovation*. (PhD thesis), Leiden University, the Netherlands.

Henze, I., Van Driel, J. H., & Verloop, N. (2008). Development of experienced science teachers' pedagogical content knowledge of models of the solar system and the universe. *International Journal of Science Education, 30*, 1321–1342.

Hodson, D. (1992). In search of a meaningful relationship: An exploration of some issues relating to integration in science and science education. *International Journal of Science Education, 14*, 541–562.

Hoyle, E., & John, P. D. (1995). *Professional knowledge and professional practice.* London; New York, NY: Cassell.

Justi, R., & Van Driel, J. H. (2005). The development of science teachers' knowledge on models and modelling – promoting, characterising, and understanding the process. *International Journal of Science Education, 27*, 549–573.

Kagan, D. M. (1990). Ways of evaluating teacher cognition: Inferences concerning the Goldilocks principle. *Review of Educational Research, 60*, 419–469.

Kennedy, M. M. (1999). The role of preservice teacher education. In L. Darling-Hammond & G. Sykes (Eds.), *Teaching as the learning profession: Handbook of teaching and policy* (pp. 54–86). San Francisco, CA: Jossey-Bass.

Korthagen, F. A. J., & Kessels, J. P. A. M. (1999). Linking theory and practice: Changing the pedagogy of teacher education. *Educational Researcher, 28*(4), 4–17.

Lave, J., & Wenger, E. (1991). *Situated learning: Legitimate peripheral participation.* Cambridge, UK: Cambridge University Press.

Loughran, J., Mulhall, P. & Berry, A. (2004). In search of pedagogical content knowledge for science: Developing ways of articulating and documenting professional practice. *Journal of Research in Science Teaching, 41*, 370–391.

Magnusson, S., Krajcik, J., & Borko, H. (1999). Nature, sources and development of pedagogical content knowledge. In J. Gess-Newsome & N. G. Lederman (Eds.), *Examining pedagogical content knowledge: The construct and its implications for science education* (pp. 95–132). Dordrecht, the Netherlands: Kluwer Academic Publishers.

Meijer, P. C. (1999). *Teachers' practical knowledge: Teaching reading comprehension in secondary education.* (PhD thesis). Leiden University, the Netherlands.

Pfeffer, J., & Sutton, R. I. (2013). *The knowing-doing gap: How smart companies turn knowledge into action.* Boston, MA: Harvard Business Press.

Reynolds, M. C. (Ed.). (1989). *The knowledge base for the beginning teacher.* Oxford: Pergamon Press.

Schön, D. A. (1983). *The reflective practitioner: How professionals think in action.* New York, NY: Basic Books.

Van de Grift, W. J. C. M., Van der Wal, M., & Torenbeek, M. (2011). Ontwikkeling in de pedagogisch didactische vaardigheid van leraren in het basisonderwijs. *Pedagogische Studiën, 88*, 416–432.

Van Driel, J. H., Bulte, A. M. W., & Verloop, N. (2008). Using the curriculum emphasis concept to investigate teachers' curricular beliefs in the context of educational reform. *Journal of Curriculum Studies, 40*, 107–122.

Van Driel, J. H., Verloop, N., & de Vos, W. (1998). Developing science teachers' pedagogical content knowledge. *Journal of Research in Science Teaching, 35*, 673–695.

Verloop, N., Van Driel, J. H., & Meijer, P. (2001). Teacher knowledge and the knowledge base of teaching. *International Journal of Educational Research, 35*, 441–461.

Wongsopawiro, D. (2012). *Examining science teachers' pedagogical content knowledge in the context of a professional development program.* (PhD thesis). Leiden University, the Netherlands.

Wubbels, Th., Brekelmans, M., den Brok, P. & van Tartwijk, J. (2006). An interpersonal perspective on classroom management in secondary classrooms in the Netherlands. In C. Evertson & C. Weinstein (Eds.), *Handbook of classroom management: Research, practice and contemporary issues* (pp. 1161–1191). New York, NY: Lawrence Erlbaum Associates.

10
THE PCK SUMMIT AND ITS EFFECT ON WORK IN SOUTH AFRICA

Marissa Rollnick & Elizabeth Mavhunga
MARANG CENTRE FOR MATHEMATICS AND SCIENCE EDUCATION, WITS SCHOOL OF EDUCATION, WITS UNIVERSITY

Introduction

The state of science and mathematics education in South Africa is constantly under scrutiny. The general consensus of the public, the media, and many researchers is that of an education system in crisis as South Africa consistently underperforms in international studies and in terms of its own measures (Spaull, 2013). The underperformance is not limited to comparisons with other middle-income countries but is also in relation to much less affluent close neighbors such as Zimbabwe and Botswana. Spaull further produces data to show a deficit in South African teachers in relation to content knowledge. In a report on the professional development of South African teachers written in 2011 we argued that developing teachers lay at the heart of improving science education in the country but that the focus on teachers' content knowledge was simplistic (Rollnick & Brodie in McCarthy, Bernstein, & de Villiers, 2011).

It is indeed true that the existing qualifications and abilities of many South African teachers pose a challenge to science education in the country. The historic legacy of apartheid is still with us 20 years later. The majority route for the training of black high school science teachers in the apartheid era was primarily through poorly resourced rural teacher training colleges offering three-year post-school diplomas delivered primarily through transmission teaching. Most of the recipients of these diplomas came out of a schooling system that was struggling post-1976 when large-scale unrest in the schools led to a system where communities sought to make black areas ungovernable and a large proportion of the school year was lost due to either teacher or student stay-aways.

It is into this context that our research group entered in 2001. We had been running an unusual junior postgraduate program for graduate teachers (known as an honors program) for some years that offered a combination of science education and content courses where most other programs at this level consisted purely of education courses. We were concerned that the content courses offered at this time were traditional honors courses intended for science students. The courses were abstract, unrelated to teaching and, to make matters worse, success rates in these courses were very low.

We wanted to offer a program that would address the content needs of senior teachers in the school system that would be meaningful yet manageable for them. It was at this stage that Shulman's (1986) construct of PCK became attractive to us to address the teachers' content needs in a way that was unique to teachers and provided a way to start talking about content without patronizing them. At that time, a new PhD student, who became interested in PCK, framed her study around the development of the first PCK-based content in the new honors program.

The science education research climate in South Africa

By 2001, South Africa had a vibrant science and mathematics research association that was nearly ten years old. In a review of southern African research literature covering that period, Malcolm and Alant (2004) provide some insight into the interest of researchers at that time. The authors provide the context for the research as a time of reconciliation, healing, recognition of diversity amidst a pandemic of HIV/AIDS, and managing expectations. How could research address these needs, be technically good, and worth doing?

The value of the review was that it brought into the domain of published research findings that were largely inaccessible to the international community because they were hidden in the annual proceedings of SAARMSTE (The Southern African Association for Research in Mathematics, Science and Technology Education). It revealed that until 2004, little research had been done in Southern Africa on PCK. However, there was a large body of supporting literature on research into alternate conceptions in the cognate disciplines (physics, chemistry, and biology) and teacher development which could inform research into PCK.

Influential literature and development of PCK research

Bearing in mind that our research group was seeking a method of addressing teachers' content knowledge in an empowering way, the work of Shulman (1986, 1987) provided a breakthrough for us. We were particularly interested in the connections between knowledge and practice and studies that worked with the transformation of content knowledge such as those of Geddis, Onslow, Beynon, and Oesch (1993) and Geddis and Wood (1997). Key chapters in the volume on PCK edited by Gess-Newsome and Lederman (1999) such as Gess-Newsome (1999a, 1999b) were also influential. These two chapters dealt with the relationship of PCK to content knowledge and ideas about the integration of components of PCK as opposed to transformation. Interestingly, the highly cited work of Magnusson, Krajcik, and Borko (1999) from the same volume was less influential, probably because of its placement of content knowledge outside the framework of PCK. Given the importance of content knowledge in our context, the Magnusson et al. model did not speak to us the way it spoke to other research communities.

Given the tacit nature of PCK, we were eager to find ways of making teacher knowledge explicit. We were aware of the call by Shulman (1986) for the use of case knowledge and had begun to develop cases when we were fortunate to obtain early versions of the work on CoRes and PaP-eRs by Loughran, Mulhall, and Berry (2004) which greatly influenced our understanding of how to capture and portray PCK and work with the teachers on the concept, though challenges still remained as articulated below.

Genesis of our PCK research

The first product of our research group was a conference paper exploring the initial effects of our attempts to introduce PCK in the honors program referred to above (Rhemtula & Rollnick, 2002). These attempts produced two important findings. First, we produced our first model of PCK (Rollnick, Bennett, Rhemtula, Dharsey, & Ndlovu, 2008) and second, we learned how difficult it was to introduce and use the concept of PCK with practicing teachers (Bennett, Rollnick, Dharsey, Kennedy, Ndlovu, & Rhemtula, 2005). One of the emerging issues in the study was the absence of a conceptual base for teachers' understanding of content knowledge.

The first model we produced placed PCK at the interface between knowledge and practice by considering teacher knowledge bases as articulated by Cochran, DeRuiter, and King (1993) and separating them from manifestations in the classroom. This model was later modified to include teacher beliefs (Davidowitz & Rollnick, 2011), see Figure 10.1.

The model formed the basis of several studies of teaching of specific topics including the mole and chemical equilibrium (Rollnick et al., 2008). This work highlighted two issues for us. First, we experienced difficulty asking teachers to articulate their PCK. Even when using the prompts from the CoRes as articulated by Loughran et al. (2004), interviews provided limited information about teachers' PCK. We found that, when interviewed, teachers did not easily talk about meaningful aspects of their practice. We attributed this to the tacit nature of PCK. The model also helped us see the potential of observing practice as a way to observe manifestations of PCK in practice. When we observed teachers, coding the observation using prompts from the CoRe, we were able to build CoRes based on these manifestations and make visible aspects of their knowledge that they were not explicitly aware of. Second, we held workshops where

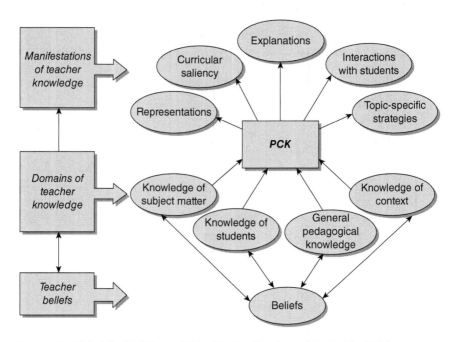

FIGURE 10.1 Model of PCK as published in Davidowitz and Rollnick (2011)

we attempted to build CoRes with teachers, but found that in order to begin meaningful engagement with them it was necessary to first brainstorm and eventually agree on a set of big ideas which were necessary precursors to the CoRe. Essentially, the workshops needed to include input on the conceptual understanding of content if they were to have any impact on practice.

Subsequent work by postgraduate students looked at the effect of subject specialization (Naidoo & Rollnick, 2008) and teacher experience on PCK in specific topics (Mohlouoa, Rollnick, & Oyoo, 2012). Unsurprisingly, in line with other studies both factors were found to have an influence on teachers' PCK in teaching particular topics.

The introduction of a new outcomes-based curriculum in the upper secondary school in South Africa in 2006 (Department of Education, 2003) produced new challenges in the form of new topics such as semiconductors, chemical systems, and electronics. There was a need for teachers to learn the new content as well as how to teach it. Since the topics were new to all teachers and textbook publishers, there were few quality resources for teaching these topics. Thus, we thought that self-studies on the teaching of new topics would be useful projects for our graduate students who were mostly high school science teachers (Nakedi, 2014; Rollnick, 2014; Rollnick, Mundalamo, & Booth, 2013). In most cases the graduate students worked in groups and grew their content knowledge alongside their PCK. All these studies made use of CoRes and PaP-eRs and provided important insights into the ways that teachers learn to teach new topics in science. The process of the self-studies also provided insight into the teachers' needs to explore both PCK and content knowledge in established topics as well.

Move to measurement

By 2009, we had involved more than ten teachers in self-studies and it became evident that baseline information was needed about teacher PCK nationally as opposed to just content knowledge data that informed the debates in the media. Our group thus applied for a grant to move into the measurement of PCK in specific topics using specially designed instruments. Given our earlier experience of the difficulties of obtaining oral information from teachers, we regarded this as a challenge. We also realized that any instrument we developed to measure PCK would need to be accompanied by a corresponding instrument exploring the content knowledge of the same topic. To do this, we would need to articulate very clearly what was being measured, as the literature of PCK highlighted the lack of agreement on its exact nature (Kind, 2009). The breakthrough was provided in a PhD study by Mavhunga (2012), which had been completed at the time of the PCK Summit. Mavhunga made three important contributions: (1) the introduction of the concept of topic-specific PCK (TSPCK) which is closely aligned to mathematical content knowledge for teaching (Ball, Thames, & Phelps, 2008); (2) an instrument to measure it for chemical equilibrium; and (3) she contributed the finding that TSPCK in a specific topic can be taught to pre-service teachers. The learned TSPCK would be similar to what Park and Oliver (2008) call planned PCK. Mavhunga's model (shown in Figure 10.2 below) places TSPCK between the teacher knowledge bases and PCK in the earlier model (Figure 10.1) and considers, after Geddis and Wood (1997), that content knowledge is transformed through five components: (1) learners' prior knowledge, including misconceptions; (2) curricular saliency; (3) what makes the topic easy or difficult to understand; (4) representations, including powerful examples and analogies; and (5) conceptual teaching strategies.

These five components have formed the basis of instruments we have developed to measure teacher TSPCK in a number of topics. By the time of the Summit, in addition to the instrument on chemical equilibrium, we had developed a second instrument for the particulate nature of matter (Pitjeng, 2014) and had begun work on an instrument for electrochemistry (Ndlovu, Mavhunga, & Rollnick, 2014). We had data that showed it was possible to improve teachers' PCK through interventions (Mavhunga & Rollnick, 2013; Pitjeng & Rollnick, 2013). Our concern at the time was to investigate the link between knowledge and practice and its effect on student outcomes.

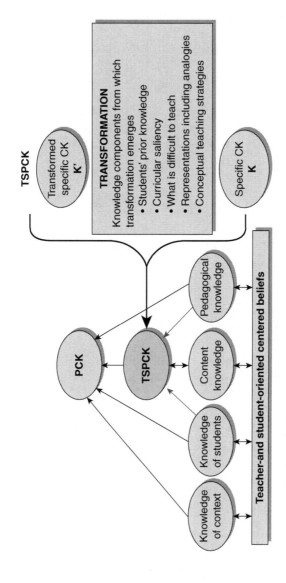

FIGURE 10.2 Mavhunga's (2012) model of TSPCK

The Summit and afterwards

The preparation prior to the Summit and the thinking and engagement that occurred during the Summit was pivotal for our group on a number of fronts. It affirmed our belief that while there was personal contextual PCK—there was a way of defining canonical PCK that was topic specific. This emerged in the consensus model produced by the Summit (see Chapter 3). Both conceptions of personal and canonical PCK separated knowledge from practice, an aspect that we had been working with, but had not adequately articulated in the past. The model provided us with new insights about possibilities for looking at learner outcomes linked to PCK. Like our models (Figures 10.1 and 10.2), the version of the model emerging from the Summit separates teacher knowledge domains from a construct referred to as topic-specific professional knowledge, which aligns to our TSPCK. Topic-specific professional knowledge then links to practice through a series of filters such as classroom context and teacher beliefs, which in turn link to student outcomes, again through a series of contextual filters. All three constructs then feed back into each other accounting for teacher learning through practice and interaction with learners. Personal PCK is incorporated into the model as part of practice. Although we are still working with our original construct of TSPCK, we are placing it in the position of topic-specific professional knowledge in the consensus model.

Post-Summit we are developing further instruments on stoichiometry, acids and bases, chemical bonding, electric circuits, and electromagnetism. Two of these are the basis of further investigations, one about the interface between knowledge and practice and another on teacher learning trajectories. Both of these studies are using adapted versions of the Summit model.

Another issue occupying our minds is the transferability of techniques taught to improve PCK from one topic to another. While we appreciated our finding on improving TSPCK of pre-service teachers in intervention-based initiatives (Mavhunga & Rollnick, 2013), we were challenged on how to build the construct across several core topics incrementally in limited time (Grossman, 2011). We have further interest in determining the transfer of learned techniques for improving TSPCK to enacted PCK in classroom contexts.

Transfer of learned TSPCK across chemistry topics

PCK is regarded as tacit knowledge gained in practice (Kind, 2009) and is thus difficult to pass on to others. Most importantly, it is topic specific (Loughran, Berry, & Mulhall, 2006) and thus needs to be learned for every topic taught. Looking for transfer sounded contradictory to the topic-specific nature of PCK. The idea of transformation of content knowledge thus became more important for us to understand apart from the construct of TSPCK that we were aiming to build. In another study (Mavhunga, 2014), we confirmed that the improvement in TSPCK through the explicit discussion of a topic through the five components of TSPCK occurs when there is successful engagement with the concepts of a topic. Thus, the mere knowledge of the components of TSPCK by themselves without the interactive engagement with content is not enough to improve TSPCK. Therefore, what is transferable to another topic is the ability to use the five TSPCK components, where successful engagement with the concepts of the new topic is still needed to improve TSPCK in the new topic. Following this understanding, we looked for transfer of the learned competence to apply the techniques for successful transformation of content across new chemistry topics. We conducted the studies with pre-service teachers in the chemistry 4th year and physics 3rd year methodology classes, respectively. We applied the treatment from Mavhunga and Rollnick (2013) to the topics of the particulate nature of matter in chemistry and kinematics in physics. We tested transfer using chemical equilibrium and several other science topics of the pre-service teachers' choice. The study had two important findings. First, it confirmed the important role of content knowledge, as the pre-service teachers were able to transfer and apply the learned techniques of transforming only to topics where they had adequate content knowledge. Second, the pre-service teachers found the component of curricular saliency (Geddis et al., 1993) most accessible and a possible leverage component in the process of transfer. Curricular saliency embraces the notion of big ideas in a topic, their sequencing, the requisite pre-knowledge, and why it is important to teach the concepts. Most importantly, it also includes knowledge of what teachers should avoid dealing with at a particular point. This finding was encouraging as it provided a potentially concrete way of incrementally building topic-specific professional knowledge across core chemistry and physics topics.

Transfer of learned TSPCK to classroom practices

A common concern about planned or learned PCK is whether it is transferable to actual enactments in classroom practices (Park & Oliver, 2008), an issue considered in the Summit consensus model (see Chapter 3). When the excellence of teaching is evaluated, the reasons behind a teacher's decisions and choices are critical insights (Jang, 2011). This means it is beneficial to influence the development of thinking in pre-service teachers that can be employed to justify teaching actions in a classroom (Shulman, 1987). Previous research across different disciplines indicates a positive relationship between developed pedagogical reasoning and decision-making in classroom practices. For example, Guzey and Roehrig (2009) found that teachers' pedagogical reasoning mirrored their pedagogical actions. Teachers' reasons for their decisions about classroom instruction are closely related to their conceptions of science, effective science teaching and instructional strategies, purposes of science teaching, and student understanding. In our quest to determine the transfer of learned TSPCK to classroom practice, we followed the teaching of two pre-service teachers. The two pre-service teachers were part of the study on improving TSPCK reported in Mavhunga and Rollnick (2013). A month after completing the intervention, two of the teachers taught the topic during their school experience. The findings from this study indicated an improved TSPCK in the topic corresponding to a 'developing' level of TSPCK demonstrated in the CoRe as planned TSPCK, and a similar level of quality was demonstrated in the classroom practices (Rollnick & Mavhunga, 2014). While this observation was limited to two teachers, similar to Guzey & Roehrig (2014) the findings, however, point to consistencies between improvements in planned and enacted TSPCK.

The next objective for the group is to find ways of linking good teacher PCK to student outcomes. Here we hope to select teachers who have scored highly on our TSPCK instruments and observe them teaching the target topic, testing their students before and after teaching.

Concluding remarks

While our attraction to the construct of PCK is driven by a specific historical context, we share with the larger science education research community the need to teach science in a more accessible and understandable manner. Conceptualizing the construct of topic-specific professional knowledge at the Summit was useful to us because we felt the need to separate the teacher knowledge needed for teaching specific topics from the broader teacher knowledge bases. Thus the process assisted us to crystallize our thoughts around our idea of TSPCK. However, our recent finding of the importance of curricular saliency in the ability to transfer techniques for transforming content between topics suggests that this component should be considered in future modifications of the conceptualization of topic-specific professional knowledge. Further, the notion of amplifiers and filters in the processes of development of topic-specific professional knowledge and in the transfer processes to teaching practices has provided us with a useful lens to cater for the various variables associated with our national context of diverse school backgrounds and teacher quality. We now have a framework to explore the next stage of our research investigating transfer of planned PCK to classroom practices on a large scale and also linking it to student performance. While we do not consider our research journey unique, we value the contribution of the work done at the Summit in steering our thoughts to three distinct areas of PCK: (1) possible ways to improve PCK in specific topics at the pre-service level; (2) the transfer of planned PCK across other topics and into classroom practices; and (3) exploration of the link between PCK and student performance. These areas are critical to leverage initiatives towards improving the teaching of science in schools. We recommend that the work of the Summit, in particular the consensus model, be considered when exploring teacher knowledge.

Acknowledgement

Figure 10.1: Reproduced by permission of The Royal Society of Chemistry.

References

Ball, D. L., Thames, M. H., & Phelps, G. (2008). Content knowledge for teaching: What makes it special? *Journal of Teacher Education, 59*, 389–407.

Bennett, J., Rollnick, M., Dharsey, N., Kennedy, D., Ndlovu, T., & Rhemtula, M. (2005). *Developing science teachers' pedagogic content knowledge (PCK): Models of practice and strategies for action.* Paper presented at the Symposium presented at the ESERA 2005 conference, Barcelona, Spain.

Cochran, K., DeRuiter, J., & King, R. (1993). Pedagogical content knowing: An integrative model for teacher preparation. *Journal of Teacher Education, 44*(4), 263–272.

Davidowitz, B., & Rollnick, M. (2011). What lies at the heart of good undergraduate teaching? A case study in organic chemistry. *Chemical Education Research and Practice, 12*, 355–366.

Department of Education. (2003). *National Curriculum Statement – Grades 10–12 Physical Sciences.* Pretoria: DOE, South Africa ISBN 1-919975-61-6.

Geddis, A. N., Onslow, B., Beynon, C., & Oesch, J. (1993). Transforming content knowledge: Learning to teach about isotopes. *Science Education, 77*, 575–591.

Geddis, A. N., & Wood, E. (1997). Transforming subject matter and managing dilemmas: A case study in teacher education. *Teaching and Teacher Education, 13*(6), 611–626.

Gess-Newsome, J. (1999a). Pedagogical content knowledge: An introduction and orientation. In J. Gess-Newsome & N. G. Lederman (Eds.), *Examining pedagogical content knowledge: The construct and its implications for science education* (pp. 3–20). Dordrecht, the Netherlands: Kluwer Academic Publishers.

Gess-Newsome, J. (1999b). Secondary teachers' knowledge and beliefs about subject matter and their impact on instruction. In J. Gess-Newsome & N. G. Lederman (Eds.), *Examining pedagogical content knowledge: The construct and its implications for science education* (pp. 51–94). Dordrecht, the Netherlands: Kluwer Academic Publishers.

Gess-Newsome, J., & Lederman, N. G. (Eds.). (1999). *Examining pedagogical content Knowledge: The construct and its implications for science education.* Dordrecht, the Netherlands: Kluwer Academic Publishers.

Grossman, P. (2011). Framework for teaching practice: A brief history of an idea. *Teachers College Record, 113*(12), 2836–2843.

Guzey, S. S., & Roehrig, G. H. (2009). Teaching science with technology: Case studies of science teachers' development of technology, pedagogy, and content knowledge. *Contemporary Issues in Technology and Teacher Education, 9*(1), 25–45.

Jang, S. J. (2011). Assessing college students' perceptions of a case teacher's pedagogical content knowledge using a newly developed instrument. *Higher Education, 61*(6), 663–678.

Kind, V. (2009). Pedagogical content knowledge in science education: Perspectives and potential for progress. *Studies in Science Education, 45*(2), 169–204.

Loughran, J. J., Berry, A., & Mulhall, P. (2006). *Understanding and developing science teachers pedagogical content knowledge.* Rotterdam, the Netherlands: Sense Publishers.

Loughran, J. J., Mulhall, P., & Berry, A. (2004). In search of pedagogical content knowledge in science: Developing ways of articulating and documenting professional practice. *Journal of Research in Science Teaching, 41*(4), 370–391.

Magnusson, S., Krajcik, J., & Borko, H. (1999). Nature sources and development of pedagogical content knowledge for science teaching. In J. Gess-Newsome & N. G. Lederman (Eds.), *Examining pedagogical content knowledge: The construct and its implications for science education* (pp. 95–132). Dordrecht, the Netherlands: Kluwer Academic Publishers.

Malcolm, C., & Alant, B. (2004). Finding direction when the ground is moving: Science education research in South Africa. *Studies in Science Education, 40,* 49–104.

Mavhunga, E. (2012). *Explicit inclusion of topic specific knowledge for teaching and the development of PCK in pre-service science teachers.* (PhD thesis). University of the Witwatersrand, Johannesburg.

Mavhunga, E. (2014). Improving PCK and CK in pre-service chemistry teachers. In H. Venkat, M. Rollnick, M. Askew, & J. Loughran (Eds.), *Exploring mathematics and science teachers' knowledge: Windows into teacher thinking* (pp. 31–48). Abingdon: Routledge.

Mavhunga, E., & Rollnick, M. (2013). Improving PCK of chemical equilibrium in pre-service teachers. *African Journal of Research in Mathematics, Science and Technology Education, 17*(1–2), 113–125. doi: http://dx.doi.org/10.1080/10288457.2013.828406

McCarthy, J., Bernstein, A., & de Villiers, R. (2011). *Value in the classroom: The quality and quantity of South Africa's teachers* (CDE in Depth Report no. 11). Retrieved from http://cdn.mg.co.za/uploads/2011/09/21/value-in-the-classroom-full-report.pdf (accessed November 12, 2014).

Mohlouoa, N. H., Rollnick, M., & Oyoo, S. (2012). *Exploring PCK in the process of teaching radioactivity: Strategies employed by Lesotho physics teachers.* Paper presented at the 20th Annual Meeting of the Southern African Association for Research in Mathematics, Science and Technology Education, Lilongwe, Malawi.

Naidoo, M., & Rollnick, M. (2008). *Learning to teach about chemical change in the new curriculum: The case of two Grade 10 teachers.* Paper presented at the 15th Annual Conference of the Southern African Association for Research in Mathematics, Science and Technology Education, Maseru, Lesotho.

Nakedi, M. (2014). Profiling chemistry teachers' changing PCK. In H. Venkat, M. Rollnick, M. Askew, & J. Loughran (Eds.), *Exploring mathematics and science teachers' knowledge: Windows into teacher thinking* (pp. 84–95). Abingdon: Routledge.

Ndlovu, M., Mavhunga, E., & Rollnick, M. (2014). The design of an instrument to measure physical sciences teachers' topic specific pedagogical content knowledge in electrochemistry. *Proceedings of the Nelson Mandela Metropolitan University, Port Elizabeth,* Vol 2, (pp. 98–105). Paper presented at the 22nd Annual Meeting of the Southern African Association for Research in Mathematics, Science and Technology Education, Port Elizabeth, South Africa.

Park, S., & Oliver, J. S. (2008). Revisiting the conceptualisation of pedagogical content knowledge (PCK): PCK as a conceptual tool to understand teachers as professionals. *Research in Science Education, 38*(3), 261–284.

Pitjeng, P. (2014). Novice unqualified graduate science teachers' topic specific pedagogical content knowledge and their beliefs about teaching. In H. Venkat, M. Rollnick, M. Askew, & J. Loughran (Eds.), *Exploring mathematics and science teachers' knowledge: Windows into teacher thinking* (pp. 65–83). Abingdon: Routledge.

Pitjeng, P., & Rollnick, M. (2013). *Ascertaining the topic specific PCK of the novice unqualified graduate teachers (NUGTs) on teaching about the particulate nature matter.* Paper presented at the European Science Education Research Association, Nicosia, Cyprus.

Rhemtula, M., & Rollnick, M. (2002). *The influence of initial aspects of a course on pedagogical content knowledge on a group of teachers and teacher educators.* Paper presented at the Tenth

Annual Meeting of the Southern African Association for Research in Mathematics, Science and Technology Education, Durban, South Africa.

Rollnick, M. (2014). Using self-study to learn new topics in chemistry – A case study of three practicing teachers. In H. Venkat, M. Rollnick, M. Askew, & J. Loughran (Eds.), *Exploring mathematics and science teachers' knowledge: Windows into teacher thinking* (pp. 147–162). Abingdon: Routledge.

Rollnick, M., Bennett, J., Rhemtula, M., Dharsey, N., & Ndlovu, T. (2008). The place of subject matter knowledge in PCK – A case study of South African teachers teaching the amount of substance and equilibrium. *International Journal of Science Education*, *30*(10), 1365–1387.

Rollnick, M., & Mavhunga, E. (2014). *The relationship of PCK knowledge to practice: A case study of two pre-service teachers teaching chemical equilibrium.* Paper presented at the Conference of the Southern African Association for Research in Mathematics, Science and Technology Education, Port Elizabeth, South Africa.

Rollnick, M., Mundalamo, F., & Booth, S. (2013). Concept maps as expressions of teachers' meaning-making while beginning to teach semiconductors. *Research in Science Education*, *43*, 1435–1454. doi: 10.1007/s11165-012-9314-1

Shulman, L. S. (1986). Those who understand: Knowledge growth in teaching. *Educational Researcher*, *15*(2), 4–14.

Shulman, L. S. (1987). Knowledge and teaching: Foundations of the new reform. *Harvard Educational Review*, *57*(1), 1–22.

Spaull, N. (2013). *South Africa's education crisis: The quality of education in South Africa 1994–2011.* Johannesburg: Centre for Development and Enterprise. Retrieved from http://www.cde.org.za/images/pdf/South%20Africas%20Education%20Crisis%20N%20Spaull%202013.pdf (accesed November 12, 2014).

11

MY PCK RESEARCH TRAJECTORY

A purple book prompts new questions

Patricia Friedrichsen

UNIVERSITY OF MISSOURI

> The questions which one asks oneself begin, at least, to illuminate the world, and become one's key to the experience of others.
> *(James Arthur Baldwin, American novelist and activist)*

Introduction

"You should read this book." My doctoral advisor, Tom Dana, handed me a new book with a purple cover. The book, *Examining pedagogical content knowledge: The construct and its implications for science education* (Gess-Newsome & Lederman, 1999), was to have a big impact on my academic career. Prior to graduate school, I taught secondary biology for ten years in a university town. As a classroom teacher, I enjoyed mentoring a steady stream of pre-service science teachers (PSTs). At the urging of several university faculty members, I left the classroom to work as a clinical instructor at the University of Nebraska, teaching elementary science methods and a biology course for elementary education majors. Even though the faculty assured me I was qualified for this new position, I knew that my classroom experience did not automatically make me a teacher educator. As I worked with my university students, I had lots of questions: What should I be teaching in my methods courses? What's the appropriate balance of content and pedagogy in a science content course for future teachers? In what ways do specialized science courses support pre-service elementary teachers' attitudes toward science? How do teacher educators help students learn to become teachers? After two years, these questions prompted a move across the country to enter a doctoral program at Penn State.

As I read the purple book, I was immediately intrigued with the construct of pedagogical content knowledge (PCK) and felt that it legitimized the wisdom gained through teaching experience. In Lee Shulman's address at the PCK Summit, he affirmed his goal of professionalizing teaching.

> So the roots of PCK were not only cognitive psychology, theory of teaching, better modes of assessment of teaching, better designs of teacher education, but it really was a policy claim about how special teachers were and that they ought to be regarded and respected.
>
> *(Shulman, 2012)*

The Magnusson, Krajcik, and Borko (1999) chapter, *Nature, sources and development of pedagogical content knowledge for science teaching*, had the greatest influence on me because it raised a lot of questions. For example, as a high school teacher, I attended many of the same professional development workshops as my colleagues and I wondered why particular teaching ideas were taken up by some teachers but not by others. Most of my secondary colleagues taught by lecture, rolling their eyes as my 10th graders designed mosquito control public service announcements during my insect unit and analyzed studbooks (pedigree records) from the local children's zoo in my genetics unit. The science teaching orientation component of the PCK model might explain the differences I saw in teachers' practice. The Magnusson et al. chapter not only raised questions, but also gave direction to my doctoral research work.

As a doctoral student, I designed my first qualitative study exploring elementary PSTs' science teaching orientations (Friedrichsen & Dana, 2003). I created a card sort of teaching scenarios illustrating each of the science teaching orientations identified by Magnusson et al. (1999). I interviewed PSTs, asking them to sort the cards and to explain their reasoning. I was immediately hooked on qualitative research, fascinated by the PSTs' rationales as they sorted the cards. But as I analyzed the data, their responses did not fit cleanly into any of the nine categories in the Magnusson et al. chapter (i.e., process, academic rigor, didactic, conceptual change, activity driven, discovery, project-based science, inquiry, and guided inquiry). I was left with more questions than answers. At the time, I attributed this unexpected finding to the PSTs' lack of teaching experience.

My questions about science teaching orientations led me to study highly regarded, experienced biology teachers for my dissertation (Friedrichsen, 2002). After observing the teachers' practice and interviewing them, I found, once again, the data did not fit into Magnusson et al.'s (1999) nine categories. The experienced teachers had complex beliefs that included goals related to general schooling, the affective domain, and subject matter. Teaching experience, prior work experience, and time constraints shaped participants' science teaching orientations. The participants' teaching orientations influenced their teaching practice as well as their choice of professional development activities. The implication of this study was that science teaching orientations would be better represented by identifying the individual teacher's central and peripheral course goals, rather than trying to make teachers fit into pre-determined categories (Friedrichsen & Dana, 2005). From this study, I saw the complexity of teachers' beliefs and its influence on teaching practice. I also became more critical of the Magnusson et al. chapter, particularly the science teaching orientation component and the PCK model.

In 2002, after graduation, I joined the faculty at the University of Missouri. Sandi Abell was the Director of the MU Science Education Center. She was an outstanding mentor and we shared common research interests around teacher education and PCK. When I joined the faculty, Sandi was in the process of designing a new alternative certification program, a post-baccalaureate master's degree to prepare secondary science and mathematics teachers. In the research literature, we referred to this program by the pseudonym A-STEP. In 2006, we received National Science Foundation funding to research PCK development in A-STEP (http://resmar2t.missouri.edu/index.html).

Researching science and mathematics teacher learning in an alternative certification project

The purpose of the research project was to examine science and mathematics teacher learning in the context of an alternative certification program. Our research team consisted of three science education researchers (Sandi Abell, Mark Volkmann, and me), three mathematics education researchers (Fran Arbaugh, Kathryn Chval, and John Lannin), and an ever-changing group of graduate students. As part of the project, I advised four graduate students' dissertations: Patrick Brown, Deanna Lankford, Aaron Sickel, and Enrique Pareja. Andrew West was a fifth science education graduate student who worked in the project.

Theoretical framework

For our theoretical framework, we drew upon the work of Shulman (1986), Grossman (1990), and Magnusson et al. (1999). Grossman's (1990) model of teacher knowledge includes three domains: subject matter knowledge (SMK), pedagogical knowledge (PK), and PCK. To further delineate PCK, we used the Magnusson et al. model with the components of science teaching orientations and knowledge of learners, curriculum, assessment, and instructional strategies. Our research questions, protocols, and data analysis were carefully aligned with our theoretical framework, with the exception of PK. We did not specifically seek to collect PK data. The overarching research question was:

- How does science and mathematics teacher knowledge (SMK and PCK) develop in an alternative certification program and what facilitates and constrains teacher learning?

Our sub-research questions were aligned with SMK and components of the Magnusson et al. PCK model. For example:

- What SMK do teachers learn and what facilitates their learning?
- What teaching orientations do they hold at various points in time?
- What do teachers learn about science/mathematics curriculum and what facilitates their learning?

For data collection, our interview protocols were aligned with our theoretical framework. There were questions designed to elicit the participant's SMK, as well as each component of the Magnusson et al. PCK model. For example, to elicit knowledge of learners, we asked a series of questions related to the learners' prior knowledge, what they might find difficult in the lesson, etc.

Also in alignment with Magnusson et al., we viewed PCK as topic specific. In analyzing our initial data, we realized much of the participants' developing knowledge was better described as either general PK or discipline-specific PCK (Davis & Krajcik, 2005). An example of discipline-level PCK would be the use of a 5E instructional model in science with the sequential phases of engagement, exploration, explanation, elaboration, and evaluation (Bybee, 1997). In order to better describe the nature of participants' general PK and discipline-level PCK, we divided these knowledge bases into sub-components, using the same sub-components from the PCK model (i.e., instructional strategies, assessment, curriculum, and learners; Friedrichsen, Abell, Pareja, Brown, Lankford, & Volkmann, 2009). For example, if PSTs learned about the existence of state education standards, we referred to this as general PK for curriculum. This knowledge is not specific to science teachers, but is knowledge that all beginning teachers in our state would develop.

Methodology

Because we were interested in teacher learning, we used qualitative case study methodology to investigate 'how' and 'why' questions, which seek to make sense of the operational links individuals make over time, rather than at a single incidence (Stake, 2005; Yin, 1994). Our primary data sources were semi-structured interview transcripts; our secondary data sources included lesson plans, videotapes of classroom teaching, field notes from classroom observations, and lesson artifacts. We collected this data from the participants at multiple points across two years, beginning as they entered the alternative certification program and continuing into their first year as classroom teachers.

To obtain a baseline of incoming teacher knowledge, we engaged participants in a lesson preparation task and follow-up interview (van der Valk & Broekman, 1999). Working individually and without any resources, participants designed two days of lesson plans to address an assigned state science standard in their discipline. In the semi-structured interview, we probed participants' rationale for their lesson plan, as well as their SMK, teaching orientation, and their knowledge of each of the PCK components: learners, instructional strategies, curriculum, and assessment. This task was repeated as an exit data collection strategy at the end of two years. Later, a manuscript reviewer criticized our use of the lesson preparation task because it lacked typical lesson planning resources and a real school context; however, we found the task provided useful information about our participants' incoming teaching knowledge.

Our primary data collection strategy for studying PCK development was referred to as the observation cycle. For four consecutive semesters, we collected data consisting of a pre-observation interview around the participant's lesson plan, classroom observation and videotaping of two consecutive days of teaching, two stimulated recall interviews, and a follow-up written reflection. As we analyzed participant data, we began to question whether a two-year data collection window was adequate to collect PCK data for beginning teachers, as most of their developing knowledge was general PK. So we continued to collect data on some individuals in their second and third years of teaching, resulting in four years of longitudinal data. We also conducted interviews with the classroom mentor teachers and the methods course instructors.

Selected PCK development studies

In this section, I highlight selected studies and dissertations in the research project and reflect on the lessons learned. The studies are organized in the following sequence: participants' prior knowledge and beliefs upon entering the program, beginning teacher PCK, and experienced teacher PCK.

Prior knowledge and beliefs

In the first summer of the project, we collected the entry lesson preparation task data and interview data from 15 science students in the first cohort. Due to Sandi's illness, I found myself as the lead author of the first research conference paper from project data. The amount of data was overwhelming given the short timeline to analyze and write the conference paper. Out of necessity, I needed to be strategic. There were two individuals in the project who, prior to entering A-STEP, had been teaching biology for one or two years under emergency state certification and had actually taught the state science standard given in the lesson preparation task. Were these two individuals different from the rest of the cohort who lacked teaching experience? This question led us to compare the data from these two teachers with two other participants who lacked teaching experience but had similar backgrounds in regard to undergraduate major, grade-point average, and a standardized teaching examination score (Friedrichsen et al., 2009). We found that all four participants had didactic teaching orientations and wrote similar lesson plans, prioritizing lectures. The two teachers had more PK than the non-teaching pair and were beginning to integrate PK components. For example, the teachers used group work because they knew students had difficulty with Mendelian genetics. Group work was a management strategy because it lessened the number of student questions they needed to answer. However, the teaching pair didn't know *why* students struggled with this topic. Beyond Punnett squares (which all four used based on their experience learning genetics in high school), the two beginning teachers had not developed topic-specific PCK from their teaching experience.

From this study, I learned the importance of asking critical questions of a large dataset. If we had analyzed all 15 participants' entry task data, we would have focused on looking at similarities across the participants, rather than differences between sub-populations. A pragmatic question resulted in a better understanding of what individuals learn from teaching experience alone when they lack a teacher education framework for reflecting on their experiences. As state policies permit teacher certification with minimal or no additional coursework, more of these comparison studies are needed.

Beginning teacher knowledge and beliefs

In this section, I highlight three dissertation studies that examined the participants' PCK development, beginning in the first semester of the A-STEP program.

Critical role of science teaching orientations.

In the A-STEP program, Patrick Brown and I co-taught a methods course in which we emphasized the use of a variety of student-centered instructional strategies. Patrick began to wonder how our students used these instructional strategies in their internships. Patrick pursued this question in his dissertation by studying four individuals during their two-semester teaching internship, analyzing data from their entry lesson preparation task and two observation cycles (Brown, 2008). Initially, Patrick focused only on the participants' knowledge of learners and the sequence of the instructional strategies they used in their lessons. He found that while the participants developed knowledge of students' learning difficulties and requirements for learning, they consistently sequenced their instruction to give priority to transmitting information (i.e., lecturing). To understand this lack of integration, he needed to analyze their science teaching orientation data. The participants entered A-STEP with didactic teaching orientations, and these beliefs were robust and resistant to change in the program. Their teaching orientations greatly influenced what they learned from the methods courses and their internship (Brown, Friedrichsen, & Abell, 2012).

I would like to highlight four important insights from this study. First, my working definition of PCK shifted from teachers' declarative knowledge to teachers' instructional decisions and practice. Second, I re-learned the lesson of the importance of teacher beliefs. Patrick wanted to avoid delving into the messiness of the participants' teaching beliefs; however, we were unable to explain the teachers' practice until we examined their science teaching orientation data. Third, we needed to pay more attention to the influence of the internship context, particularly the role of the mentor teacher in the intern's learning. Our field notes and mentor teacher interviews were inadequate data sources. In our already lengthy interviews, we needed to probe more deeply into the participants' perception of their teaching context and the influence of their mentor teacher. Fourth, although there is a great need for longitudinal studies in PCK development, the design of this study was problematic for reviewers. In this one-year study, the participants taught different biology topics in each observation cycle. Although we collected topic-specific PCK data, we generalized across the two semesters to understand the teachers' PCK development. In making this decision, reviewers argued that we lost the topic-specific nature of PCK.

Teacher beliefs vs. PCK model

Based on our experience with Patrick Brown's study, my research team decided to observe the participants, whenever possible, teaching the same topic each year. However, this decision created a logistical nightmare as our participants were becoming geographically dispersed beyond our state borders. We studied one beginning biology teacher, Alice, teaching a 5E natural selection unit during her internship and in the first two years at her new school (Sickel & Friedrichsen, in press). Alice entered the A-STEP program with a discovery teaching orientation and embraced the 5E instructional model because of the exploration phase. Over the next three years, Alice's science teaching orientation remained stable. As a full-time teacher, in the second and third years, Alice modified her 5E unit based on her perceptions of her new school context. She believed her students struggled with inquiry-based learning and that parents did not support inquiry teaching; consequently, she became more teacher-directed and omitted the elaboration phase. Although Alice attributed her modifications to the school context, we asserted Alice's beliefs about teaching and learning had a greater influence on her practice when those beliefs were strongly held. Alice's discovery-oriented beliefs aligned with the exploration phase of the 5E model, and she increased the number of exploration activities in years two and three, while omitting the elaboration phase which she believed was redundant and unnecessary since students would discover the scientific explanation during the explorations.

As a researcher, I gained several insights from this study. We had a better window on PCK development when we observed teachers teaching the same topic over several years. Despite the scheduling challenges, I continue to advocate for this longitudinal data collection strategy. Second, although this was conceived as a PCK study in which data was collected in alignment with the Magnusson et al.

(1999) PCK model, we didn't use PCK as a theoretical framework in the final manuscript (Sickel & Friedrichsen, in press). In earlier drafts, when Aaron told Alice's story using a PCK framework, the storyline got lost amidst the various PCK subcomponents (e.g., curriculum, learners, instruction, and assessment). So we decided to tell Alice's story by focusing on her beliefs, which provided coherence to the story. Initially, we tried to stay away from the messiness of beliefs, but we needed to focus on Alice's beliefs in order to explain changes in her teaching practice.

Conceptual change and PCK

Over time, I became frustrated using the Magnusson et al. PCK model in PCK development studies because the model lacked explanatory power. My graduate students and I began exploring different learning theories to couple with the PCK framework. Aaron Sickel explored using a sociocultural perspective (Lave, 1988; Wertsch, 1985a, 1985b); however, we lacked rich data for understanding how the particular school context shaped teachers' learning. For his dissertation study, Enrique Pareja applied conceptual change theory (Chi, 1992; Posner, Strike, Hewson, & Gertzog, 1982; Vosniadu, 1994) to PCK in a three-year longitudinal study of four beginning biology teachers' PCK of learners and assessment (Pareja, 2014). Initially, participants thought their students were passive learners with no prior knowledge. Over time, the participants developed co-existing reform-based conceptions of student learning; however, based on their teaching experiences, they found these new conceptions to be only partially applicable to their teaching experience, so they never prioritized reform-based conceptions in their schema. Participants' teaching experience and their own experiences as learners supported their initial conceptions of students as passive learners. In regard to assessment, participants expanded their conceptions of assessment over time but never formed a cohesive, integrated view of assessment. State and school assessment requirements took priority over what they learned in the A-STEP program. Participants' conceptions of assessment changed over time but were always grounded in coherency with their school's policies. Competing conceptions were evident in the interviews, and participants' reconciled competing conceptions based on congruency with their teaching context.

It is challenging to retrofit an additional theoretical framework to an existing dataset. In the project, we collected data during a three-day snapshot of each semester. We focused more on participants' declarative knowledge and their decision-making process related to their practice during two specific lessons, rather than probing competing conceptions or identifying instances over the semester that caused their conceptions to be challenged. In spite of those challenges, Enrique's study offered insights into participants' competing conceptions and the role of the school context.

These three studies revealed beginning teachers' beliefs were fairly resistant to change and that beliefs played a significant role in shaping PCK development.

Although individual PCK development was idiosyncratic, in general, participants expanded their knowledge of learners, instructional strategies, and assessment; however, the influence of the teaching context was greater than the influence of the A-STEP program. Exploring participants' beliefs helped Patrick and Aaron explain their participants' PCK development, while the addition of conceptual change theory allowed Enrique to explain similar findings.

Experienced teacher PCK

What does highly developed PCK look like? Based on the contrast between beginning teachers' practice and the A-STEP program goals, I began to ask questions about reform-oriented, experienced teachers' PCK. On a pragmatic level, what was an achievable end target for PCK development? Two graduate students working in the project, Deanna Lankford and Andrew West, explored these questions in their dissertation studies of experienced teachers who served as mentors in the A-STEP program (Lankford, 2010; West, 2010). In this section, I highlight Deanna's study.

Using project data collection strategies, Deanna studied six experienced biology mentor teachers' PCK for teaching diffusion and osmosis (Lankford, 2010). She found that the teachers had highly developed and integrated PCK components. The teachers planned their instruction using an implicit 5E instructional sequence; students explored the phenomenon prior to the teacher helping students construct a scientific explanation. From prior teaching experience and extensive use of formative assessment, teachers identified topic-specific student learning difficulties (e.g., confusing terminology such as hypertonic and hypotonic), which informed their instructional strategies. For example, the teachers omitted unnecessary terminology or delayed the introduction of confusing vocabulary until after students had demonstrated a conceptual understanding. The teachers used multiple representations sequenced from concrete (e.g., wilting lettuce) to more abstract (e.g., dialysis tubing). Throughout the unit, teachers monitored student understanding by asking students to predict the direction of water movement in different representations, and used this information to inform their instruction. The teachers also made explicit connections to the horizontal curriculum, connecting osmosis with cell membranes, photosynthesis, human physiology, etc. The teachers identified teaching experience, professional development, reflection, and work with colleagues as the sources of their highly integrated PCK for teaching diffusion and osmosis.

In reflecting on this study, we selected mentor teachers who were highly regarded by colleagues and administrators. We did not collect student data confirming the teachers' effectiveness in teaching diffusion and osmosis. PCK research would be strengthened if we connected teachers' PCK to student learning. Outside this research project, one of my graduate students, Emily Walter, studied a college instructor's PCK for teaching macro-evolution (Walter, 2013).

She was able to link student outcomes to the instructor's PCK, as students showed significant gains in measures of conceptual understanding and acceptance of evolution. In the study, she also compared the instructor's use of instructional strategies to students' perceptions of the most effective strategies in supporting their acceptance of evolution.

Challenges

In the earlier sections, I highlighted several key research studies in the larger research project and the insights gained from this work. In this section, I focus on some of the bigger challenges in the project, including working in a large qualitative PCK project in which we observed more PK than PCK development, the difficulty in qualitatively assessing SMK, and challenges associated with using the Magnusson et al. (1999) PCK model.

Large qualitative project and limited PCK development

In total, we collected two years of longitudinal data from 43 science and mathematics teachers, spanning their year-long teaching internship and their first year of teaching. The data collection process was time-consuming and could not have been accomplished without the help of many graduate students. We generally employed six graduate students a year on the project. Our data collection strategies resulted in a huge amount of qualitative data. During data analysis, we focused on a fine grain level, often analyzing small groups of participants in the project. This level of analysis allowed us to see the idiosyncratic nature of PCK; however, this approach made it difficult to see the forest for the trees. What did we learn, in general, about PCK development across all the participants over time? This question is more difficult to answer. Overall, I learned beginning teachers developed more PK than topic-specific PCK. This observation led us to question whether our two-year window of data collection was adequate to document beginning teachers' PCK development. As a result, we selected approximately six to eight teachers and continued to collect longitudinal data for Years 3 and 4.

Difficulty in qualitatively assessing SMK

In introducing the construct of PCK, Shulman spoke of the missing paradigm of SMK in teacher research (Shulman, 1986). Shulman introduced the construct of PCK, in part, to address the lack of research attention on the content of lessons; however, SMK can still get lost in PCK studies. In our interview protocols, we asked a set of general questions to assess the participant's SMK. What do you know now about the topic that you're teaching that you didn't know last year? If you could sit down with a content expert in this topic, what questions would you ask? In our project, the participants were teaching a wide array of topics in biology, physics, chemistry, and earth science. Interviewers needed to have strong SMK for every topic in every science domain to be effective interviewers. We tried to match interviewer content expertise with the participant's teaching assignment. All members of my research team were former high school biology teachers and were knowledgeable about the biology topics taught by our participants. However, several issues arose during interviews. It was difficult to ask participants probing questions about their SMK. In many cases, they didn't know what they didn't know and they weren't confident in discussing the general SMK questions. Additionally, a trust violation emerged if I pushed participants too far to expose their misconceptions or lack of understanding about the topic. Although our research team attempted to assess participants' SMK, this is an area where we failed to get adequate data because we relied on general SMK interview questions. To truly capture SMK knowledge, we needed validated content assessments for each topic taught by the participants, which were not available.

Magnusson, Borko, and Krajcik PCK model

In this section, I explore several challenges we encountered related to the use of the Magnusson et al. (1999) PCK model. The first issue relates to the taxonomic nature of the model. The second issue relates to aspects of the model that sit in tension with the highly integrated nature of experienced teachers' PCK.

Taxonomy vs. theoretical framework

There is an inherent tension in the use of models in that a model both guides and constrains one's thinking. We used the Magnusson et al. model to frame our research questions, interview protocols, and data analysis. Veal and MaKinster (1999) referred to various PCK models as taxonomies. The strength of the Magnusson model is derived from this characteristic in that it provides a general map, identifying categories of knowledge to pay attention to (i.e., instructional strategies, assessment, curriculum, learners). We found the model useful in designing our data collection protocols and in our initial data analysis. However, as we further analyzed our data, the model did not lend itself to representing PCK development nor did it help us explain our findings. After using the Magnusson et al. PCK model for many years, I have come to think of it more as taxonomy of teacher knowledge and less as a theoretical framework because it lacks explanatory power. The power and usefulness of the Magnusson et al. model would be strengthened if it were combined with an explicit learning theory.

Representing highly integrated PCK of experienced teachers

Another limitation of the Magnusson PCK model is that the model represents knowledge (e.g., curriculum, assessment) as separate silos; however, during data collection we found that teachers do not organize their knowledge in these categories. Our experienced mentor teachers' knowledge was episodic—relating past experiences to their current planning and teaching decisions. So, while the model identifies types of knowledge, it does not easily lend itself to representing experienced teachers' integrated knowledge. We found it time-consuming and artificial to de-construct experienced teachers' episodic knowledge into the PCK model components, and then to put it back together by adding dense connections among the PCK components to represent the integrated nature. At one point, we explored counting the number of connections among the PCK components based on analysis of interview transcripts (Sickel, 2012), similar to the work of Park and Chen (2012). However, we wondered if the number of connections among PCK components was merely an artifact related to the verbosity or succinctness of the participant's responses during the interview. At some point, one begins to wonder whether the model is an artificially constraining conceptualization for experienced teacher PCK.

Influence of the PCK Summit

The structure of the PCK Summit was designed to foster sharing of ideas and working toward consensus. As an individual, this structure allowed me to interact with other PCK researchers in a collaborative environment and, as a result, I formed new professional relationships and deepened existing ones. For the group as a whole, the PCK Summit was an important step in opening a collaborative dialogue among a large group of PCK researchers. This dialogue is a necessary first step in moving toward consensus on a PCK model, terminology, and definitions. We cannot make progress in a field that lacks a common conceptualization of the construct being studied. For many participants, this productive dialogue has continued as we planned PCK Summit-related sessions at the 2013 and 2014 National Association of Research in Science Teaching Conference (NARST), the 2103 European Science Education Research Association Conference (ESERA), and the 2014 Australasian Science Education Research Association Conference (ASERA). After the Summit, Amanda Berry, Rebecca Cooper, Rebecca Schneider, and I continued our PCK development discussions by exploring the promises and challenges of PCK learning progressions (see Chapter 15). Most of all, the Summit renewed my interest in PCK research. Spending a week talking with other PCK researchers was intellectually stimulating and invigorating. The death of my colleague and mentor, Sandi Abell, and the disbanding of our PCK research group (through retirements and shifts to administrative positions) created a void. I have come to understand, that for me, research is a social process and the PCK Summit helped me connect with other PCK researchers.

Future directions

Returning to Baldwin's quote at the beginning of the chapter, my questions continue to focus on understanding the experiences of teachers. Over time, my questions have increased in number and, hopefully, in refinement. In what ways are teachers learning in their school context? How do professional learning communities support teacher learning? What data collection methods best capture teacher learning? Are snapshots of teacher practice (e.g., videotaped lessons and stimulated recall interviews) the most effective data collection strategies? What role do quantitative assessments, such as rubrics, play in studying PCK development? How do we best represent teacher learning across the continuum from pre-service to teacher leaders? How do local school structures, as well as state and national policies, impact teacher learning and practice? How do teachers interpret the *Next Generation Science Standards* (NGSS Lead States, 2013)? What supports do teachers need to implement the new standards? These questions require much more attention to school context and the multilayered systems in which teachers work. In the research project described in this chapter, we stepped into teachers' lives for three days a semester, observing and asking questions as a way of attempting to understand their PCK. Based on this experience, my research is shifting to long-term collaborations working *with* teachers in schools, learning together, and co-constructing our knowledge of teaching.

It has been a great pleasure and honor to work with outstanding graduate students over the years. They have pushed my thinking by asking new questions. Without fail, my graduate students always referred to the Gess-Newsome and Lederman (1999) book as the "Purple PCK Book." The title of this chapter is a tribute to their contributions to my learning. So the book with a purple cover, *Examining pedagogical content knowledge: The construct and its implications for science education* (Gess-Newsome & Lederman, 1999), provoked a great number of questions and greatly influenced my research. The PCK Summit renewed my interest in PCK and fostered new collaborations, including exploring new questions related to PCK learning progressions (Schneider & Plasman, 2011). I hope this new book, *Re-examining pedagogical content knowledge in science education*, has a similar effect on its readers, stimulating new questions about PCK.

Acknowledgement

The majority of the work described in this chapter was supported by a National Science Foundation grant number 0202847. Any opinions, findings, and conclusions or recommendations expressed in this material are those of the author and do not necessarily reflect the views of the National Science Foundation.

References

Brown, P. (2008). *Investigating teacher knowledge of learners and learning and sequence of instruction in an alternative certification program.* (Doctoral dissertation). University of Missouri, Columbia, MO. Retrieved from https://mospace.umsystem.edu/xmlui/handle/10355/5601 (accessed November 13, 2014).

Brown, P., Friedrichsen, P., & Abell, S. (2012). The development of secondary biology teachers PCK. *Journal of Science Teacher Education, 24,* 133–155.

Bybee, R. W. (1997). *Achieving scientific literacy: From purposes to practices.* Portsmouth, NH: Heinemann Educational Books, Inc.

Chi, M. (1992). Conceptual change within and across ontological categories: Examples from learning and discovery in science. In R. Giere (Ed.), *Cognitive models of science: Minnesota studies in the philosophy of science* (pp. 129–186). Minneapolis, MN: University of Minnesota Press.

Davis, E. A., & Krajcik, J. S. (2005). Designing educative curriculum materials to promote teacher learning. *Educational Researcher, 34,* 3–14.

Friedrichsen, P. J. (2002). *A substantive-level theory of highly regarded secondary biology teachers' science teaching orientations.* (Doctoral dissertation). The Pennsylvania State University. Available from ProQuest Dissertations and Theses database. (UMI No. 3060018)

Friedrichsen, P., Abell, S., Pareja, E., Brown, P., Lankford, D., & Volkmann, M. (2009). Does teaching experience matter? Examining biology teachers' prior knowledge for teaching in an alternative certification program. *Journal of Research in Science Teaching, 46,* 357–383.

Friedrichsen, P., & Dana, T. (2003). Using a card sorting task to elicit and clarify science teaching orientations. *Journal of Science Teacher Education, 14,* 291–301.

Friedrichsen, P., & Dana, T. (2005). A substantive-level theory of highly regarded secondary biology teachers' science teaching orientations. *Journal of Research in Science Teaching, 42,* 218–244.

Gess-Newsome, J., & Lederman, N. G. (Eds.). (1999). *Examining pedagogical content knowledge: The construct and its implications for science education.* Dordrecht, the Netherlands: Kluwer Academic Publishers.

Grossman, P. (1990). *The making of a teacher: Teacher knowledge and teacher education.* New York, NY: Teachers College Press.

Lankford, D. (2010). *Examining the pedagogical content knowledge and practice of experienced secondary biology teachers for teaching diffusion and osmosis.* (Doctoral dissertation). University of Missouri, Columbia, MO. Retrieved from https://mospace.umsystem.edu/xmlui/handle/10355/8345 (accessed November 13, 2014).

Lave, J. (1988). *Cognition in practice: Mind, mathematics, and culture in everyday life.* Cambridge, UK: Cambridge University Press.

Magnusson, S., Krajcik, J., & Borko, H. (1999). Nature, sources and development of pedagogical content knowledge for science teaching. In J. Gess-Newsome & N. G. Lederman (Eds.), *Examining pedagogical content knowledge: The construct and its implications for science education* (pp. 95–132). Dordrecht, the Netherlands: Kluwer Academic Publishers.

NGSS Lead States. (2013). *Next Generation Science Standards: For States, By States.* Washington, DC: National Academies Press.

Pareja, E. (2014). *The development of PCK in a post-baccalaureate certification program: A longitudinal study of the development of teacher knowledge of students as learners and assessment.* (Unpublished doctoral dissertation). University of Missouri, Columbia, MO.

Park, S., & Chen, Y.-C. (2012). Mapping out the integration of the components of pedagogical content knowledge (PCK): Examples from high school biology classrooms. *Journal of Research in Science Teaching, 49*, 922–941. doi: 10.1002/tea.21022

Posner, G. J., Strike, K. A., Hewson, P. W., & Gertzog, W. A. (1982). Accomodation of a scientific conception: Toward a theory of conceptual change. *Science Education, 66*, 211–227.

Schneider, R., & Plasman, K. (2011). Science teacher learning progressions: A review of science teachers' pedagogical content knowledge development. *Review of Educational Research, 81*, 530–565.

Shulman, L. S. (1986). Those who understand: Knowledge growth in teaching. *Educational Researcher, 15*, 4–14.

Shulman, L. S. (2012). *Keynote address at International PCK Summit*. Retrieved from http://pcksummit.bscs.org/node/68 (accessed November 27, 2014).

Sickel, A. (2012). *Examining beginning biology teachers' knowledge, beliefs, and practice for teaching natural selection*. (Unpublished dissertation). University of Missouri, Columbia, MO.

Sickel, A., & Friedrichsen, P. (in press) Beliefs, practical knowledge, and context: A longitudinal study of a beginning biology teacher's 5E Unit. *School Science and Mathematics*.

Stake, R. E. (2005). Qualitative studies. In N. Denzin & Y. Lincoln (Eds.), *Handbook of qualitative research* (3rd ed., pp. 443–446). Thousand Oaks, CA: Sage Publications, Inc.

van der Valk, A. E., & Broekman, H. (1999). The lesson preparation method: A way of investigating pre-service teachers' pedagogical content knowledge. *European Journal of Teacher Education, 22*, 11–22.

Veal, W. R., & MaKinster, J. G. (1999). Pedagogical content knowledge taxonomies. *Electronic Journal of Science Education, 3*(4). Retrieved from http://ejse.southwestern.edu/article/viewArticle/7615/5382 (accessed July 14, 2014).

Vosniadu, S. (1994). Capturing and modelling the process of conceptual change. *Learning and Instruction, 4*, 45–69.

Walter, E. (2013). *The influence of pedagogical content knowledge (PCK) for teaching macroevolution on student outcomes in a general education biology course*. (Doctoral dissertation). University of Missouri, Columbia, MO. Retrieved from https://mospace.umsystem.edu/xmlui/handle/10355/37821 (accessed November 13, 2014).

Wertsch, J. V. (1985a). *Culture, communication, and cognition: Vygotskian perspectives*. Cambridge, UK: Cambridge University Press.

Wertsch, J. V. (1985b). *Vygotsky and the social formation of mind*. Cambridge, MA: Harvard University Press.

West, A. (2010). *The development of veteran 9th-grade physics teachers' knowledge for using representations to teach the topic of energy transformation* (Unpublished doctoral dissertation). University of Missouri, Columbia, MO.

Yin, R. (1994). *Case study research: Design and methods*. (2nd ed.). Newbury Park, CA: Sage Publications, Inc.

12
PEDAGOGICAL CONTENT KNOWLEDGE RECONSIDERED

A teacher educator's perspective

Rebecca M. Schneider
THE UNIVERSITY OF TOLEDO

Introduction

Creating high-quality, ambitious teacher education is complex work that requires teacher educators think carefully about what and how teachers learn and continue to learn. Teacher educators are concerned with the initial preparation and continued education of effective teachers who can use what they know when working on authentic problems of teaching. To do this work well, teacher educators both design and study programs intended for teacher learning.

This stance often leads teacher educators to consider pedagogical content knowledge (PCK) as a tool to guide their thinking about what teachers need to learn. PCK is attractive to teacher educators because it is described as the knowledge that enables teachers to make content accessible to their students (Carter, 1990; Shulman, 1986). And PCK does appear to hold promise as a heuristic for teacher knowledge to untangle the complexities of what teachers know about teaching science and how such knowledge changes over time (Schneider & Plasman, 2011). It turns out, however, that PCK is not yet clearly described and, thus, how PCK might inform the design of opportunities for teacher learning is not entirely clear. As an interesting, yet still debated construct, PCK was the focus of a week-long summit. One outcome of the many conversations was the recognition that different viewpoints resulted in different ways to describe PCK. A teacher educator's perspective was one of these viewpoints.

In this chapter, I reflect on PCK from a science teacher educator's perspective. For PCK to be a suitable guide for designing and studying learning opportunities for science teachers, it appears to be necessary to reconsider the construct from a teacher educator's perspective. This means thinking about how teachers learn, what teachers think about what they do, and what tools teacher educators need to guide their work. Thinking about PCK from a teacher educator's perspective raises interesting questions such as how this view might influence the way we define or organize PCK, frame our curriculum and instruction for teachers, and structure how we document or research teachers' progress. In this chapter, I explore how a teacher educator's perspective might change how PCK is conceived and used.

Framing a teacher educator's perspective

A teacher educator's perspective is, naturally, formed by engaging in teacher education. Science teacher educators think about what and how teachers learn in order to create opportunities for learning about teaching science. Teacher educators are recognized by many as a community (Gallagher, Griffin, Parker, Kitchen, & Figg, 2011; Trent, 2012) with a unique knowledge base (Abell, Rogers, Hanuscin, Lee, & Gagnon, 2009; Smith, 2000) and practice (Berry & Van Driel, 2012). As a community, teacher educators develop and use their knowledge of teachers as learners as they design programs, guide teachers' thinking, and study teachers' progress.

This work leads teacher educators to ask questions about the impact of instruction on teacher learning. Knowledge communities are defined by the questions they ask and how they pursue answers (Shulman, 1987). Teacher educators ask: What do teachers learn when supported by opportunities intended to be educative? Teaching is a practice, so it is important to understand teachers' pedagogical reasoning and action (Shulman, 1987). Thus, teacher educators also ask: What do teachers think about what they do? These questions are focused on the link between instruction and thinking about actions. Seeking answers to these questions leads teacher educators to examine teachers' plans, enactments, and reflections in light of opportunities for their learning and their school context. Teacher education should provide educative experiences, experiences that change a teacher's ability to participate in the community of science teachers (Dewey, 1938). Teacher educators seek answers to these questions for the purpose of designing and refining teachers' educative experiences. A teacher educator's interest in PCK is based on its value in explaining teachers' ideas that are likely impacted by instruction and, in turn, impact a teacher's instructional practice.

Learning progressions for science teachers

A framework to organize our thinking about what teachers learn about teaching science over time and with instruction is the notion of learning progressions. Learning progressions are thought of as the successively more sophisticated ways of thinking about ideas that follow one another over a broad span of time (Heritage, 2008). Growth is continuous and coherent, achieved in an incremental sequence moving from novice to expert performance, and mediated by instruction. The idea that educative experiences would encourage learners to build on their ideas over time has its roots in Dewey's (1938) principle of continuity, where the order of events matter with the past influencing the present and future; and Bruner's (1960) spiral curriculum, where ideas are revisited in more depth, building understanding over time. Learning progression is a framework for thinking about teachers becoming successively more sophisticated in their thinking as they spend time in the classroom and are supported by opportunities for learning.

Ambitious teacher education informed by this idea would aim to purposefully progress teachers' learning. Programs should take a holistic, practice-based approach for learning to teach (Hollins, 2011). Such programs would focus on knowledge, skills, and understanding—beyond what is described in standards for teachers—with articulation among courses and field experiences. Program experiences should be designed to be educative, in that they build upon who teachers are as they come to the program and contribute to their development in the future (Dewey, 1938). In addition, teachers need continuous instruction for learning about teaching; learning to teach is considered a career-long endeavor (Ball & Cohen, 1999; Borko, 2004; Feiman-Nemser, 2008). Thinking about learning progressions for teachers encourages teacher educators to think about educative experiences for pre-service, new, and continuing teachers as a coherent curriculum.

A learning progression framework within holistic teacher education leads teacher educators to unpack the ways in which teachers' ideas become more sophisticated. This, in turn, leads us to look for a heuristic for teacher knowledge. Science teacher PCK is a promising construct for this role. Learning progression research is recommended as beneficial for improving curriculum based on a better understanding of learners' (in this case, teachers') progress in relationship to instruction (Corcoran, Mosher, & Rogat, 2009). To do this work in teacher education, a description of what ideas should be developed is needed. In a recent review of twenty-five years of research, PCK was used to untangle the complexities of teachers' thinking about their science teaching to suggest trajectories (Schneider & Plasman, 2011). Although these trajectories are only as reliable as the data on which they are based, including how PCK was described at the time, and that improved teacher education will likely shift these trajectories, it was possible to use this construct to do this work.

A learning progressions framework also leads us to consider the target for learning progress. "Growth is not enough; we must specify the direction in which growth takes place" (Dewey, 1938, p. 36). Although some researchers are using standards as goals for student learning, others caution that learning progression research that examines students' ideas is needed first to uncover what are reasonable goals (Shavelson, 2009; Sikorski & Hammer, 2010). Ambitious teacher education aims beyond standards so that teachers will be able to use what they know in working on authentic problems of teaching. For teachers, it is important to have a notion of expertise that requires sophisticated thinking. Creating educative experiences intended to progress teachers' thinking over long periods of time is consistent with teachers developing as adaptive experts who evolve their core competencies and expand the breadth and depth of their expertise (Bransford, Derry, Berliner, & Hammerness, 2007). Adaptive expertise requires relatively sophisticated ways of thinking about teaching to make intelligent, flexible, and adaptive decisions that are responsive (Bransford et al., 2007; Dewey, 1929). From a teacher educator's perspective, PCK needs to be useful in describing learning progress in ways that will help us prepare teachers for novel situations that cannot be predicted or comprehensively covered in teacher education.

Research that describes learning progressions for teachers will help teacher educators in planning for and determining teachers' progress. A better understanding of what teachers think about what they do at multiple steps along the way to expertise will assist teacher educators in creating a coherent curriculum for pre-service, new, and continuing teachers. Moreover, empirical descriptions will refine our expectations for teachers at each career phase. In addition, work to unpack trajectories for the components of PCK might be helpful in diagnosing teachers' ideas. One outcome of the work on science teacher learning progressions mentioned above was that in some cases, multiple trajectories were identified (Schneider & Plasman, 2011). Although both pathways led to expertise, one was consistent with ideas about adaptive thinking while the alternative was more consistent with routine thinking. It is possible that well-described trajectories could assist teacher educators in diagnosing early whether teachers are on a productive path and adjust instruction appropriately. However, the work to describe pathways of teacher learning will rely on how we think about PCK.

Thinking about PCK

Ambitious teacher education aims to prepare effective teachers who can use what they know when working on authentic problems of teaching. Teacher education needs to make the relevant aspects of PCK accessible to teachers in the situations where they will learn and apply these ideas. Teachers think about teaching in cases or stories (Merseth, 1991; Putnam & Borko, 2000; Shulman, 1986). This type of thinking requires teachers to access multiple ideas simultaneously within a scenario. PCK needs to be useful in determining educative scenarios and guiding teachers' thinking. Teacher educators need a description of PCK that allows them to both unpack progress and construct cases. However, this thinking leads to new questions. These are questions about the structure and organization of PCK for teacher education such as: Is our description of PCK sophisticated enough to aid us in uncovering progress across broad spans of time? Have we unpacked components of PCK that will be helpful in describing how teachers are thinking about what they are doing? Do we have components that can be integrated within experiences intended for teacher learning? Empirical work is also needed here to improve our description of PCK.

A teacher educator's view on PCK

Coming to the PCK Summit, I brought ideas about teacher learning and program design, learning progressions for teachers, and working ideas about PCK from my work designing and studying experiences intended to be educative for teachers. Across the week, conversations about the nature of PCK, how to measure it, and how to use it, uncovered a variety of ideas that we discussed. Discussion subgroups formed, including a group focused on how to develop PCK (i.e., teacher education). I participated most often in this group.

Several ideas from the Summit are important to mention here. I noted them at the time and they have contributed to my thinking and this chapter. Two ideas in particular are interesting when considered together. Early in the week John Settlage, as teacher educator, raised the question of what is the value of PCK. He described a love–hate relationship, being attracted to PCK but then not being sure what use to make of it. He challenged all of us to think about how PCK might be useful, generative, influential, or usefully wrong, during our week together. Also early in the week in his keynote address, Lee Shulman pointed out that it is possible to have equally legitimate and conflicting structures for PCK. He used BSCS biology as an example (see BSCS Biology an ecological approach, a human approach, and a molecular approach; http://bscs.org/). All three versions are legitimate but based on different frameworks of thinking with different structures. BSCS did not reconcile the conflict and published all three versions. Perhaps a teacher educator's framework for PCK is a legitimate but different structure that takes a development of PCK approach. This approach would need to answer John's question, what is the value of PCK for teacher educators?

Lee Shulman also raised the question of why doesn't teacher education have a fully developed signature pedagogy like other professions. Like nurses who learn to think like nurses or lawyers who learn to think like lawyers, how do teachers learn to think like teachers? This thinking brings to mind the premise that teachers need to learn to think, know, feel, and act like a teacher (Feiman-Nemser, 2008). PCK is only one piece of a larger picture of becoming a teacher that includes pedagogy, knowledge for (developed outside the classroom), knowledge of (developed inside the classroom), identity, judgment, and adaptive expertise. Shulman's question also brings to mind that we do not have a curriculum for teachers across their careers. During the Summit, the idea of learning progressions for teachers gathered quite a bit of attention. Teacher educators liked the idea but then they had questions. Many of these questions lead back to how we think about PCK. With these questions in mind, I describe my teacher educator's view of PCK.

Knowledge of science teaching

Within a practice-based approach to teacher education, PCK is an attractive construct for thinking about what teachers need to learn to support students' content learning. PCK is described as the knowledge of teaching used and developed within practice (Feiman-Nemser, 2008). It is what teachers know about how to make their subject matter accessible to students (Carter, 1990). Part of the attractiveness of PCK is that it is a domain-specific, yet, professional knowledge thought to be important for content teachers (in this case, science) beyond their specific classroom. In contrast to practical knowledge (knowledge of classrooms and the complexities of teaching), PCK is more formal and built on the profession's collective wisdom (Carter, 1990; Munby, Russell, & Martin, 2001). PCK is directly linked to classroom practice but is not as personal or as situated in classroom events as practical knowledge and thus may describe the ideas that enable teachers to develop the type of expertise that is adaptive to multiple settings. In this way, PCK makes sense as an element of formal teacher education.

To be useful in teacher education, PCK need to be theoretical enough to inform instruction for multiple teachers working in real classrooms with different students on a variety of topics, yet, particular enough to be applied in specific situations. Singer-Gabella (2012) argues that scholarship in practice requires a productive tension between the theoretical and the particular. In this sense, teacher educators need a description of PCK that is between general pedagogical ideas and specific content ideas. It makes sense in a discussion of a knowledge construct to be clear about the underlying theory of knowledge (Settlage, 2013). As described above, in my view teacher learning means to develop sophisticated thinking that will enable them to make adaptive decisions that are responsive to authentic problems of teaching. In this view, knowledge is not a commodity and it does not seem helpful to think about PCK too narrowly. Although PCK is knowledge that manifests itself in topics, how we structure PCK for our use seems to be unique by domain. Knowledge of how to make science accessible to students is different than knowledge of how to make mathematics, for example, accessible to students (Shulman, 1999). The facets of PCK are described differently by mathematics, language arts, and social studies educators (Depaepe, Verschaffel, & Kelchtermans, 2013; Grossman, Schoenfeld, & Lee, 2005; Gudmundsdottir & Shulman, 1987). It is also difficult to imagine an accumulation of ideas as a trajectory toward sophisticated thinking. It makes sense to think about PCK as knowledge teachers develop and demonstrate within topics while at the same time as a tool for teacher educators that transcends topics to guide our thinking about teacher learning.

Recognizing that it is not practical to teach PCK for every topic that teachers may be asked to teach with students who have various experiences and backgrounds, thinking during the Summit turned to the notion of high leverage or generative topics. This seems like a productive way to begin to think about cases for teacher learning. The idea is that, through the study of a purposefully chosen set of topics, teachers will be able to transfer the PCK they develop to other topics. The challenge for practice-based teacher education is to align these particular topics with the school calendar. These would not be cases of content but, rather, cases of teaching content with learners in a particular setting. It is also important to keep in mind that the tasks for teacher learning—planning, enacting, and reflecting—are all important aspects of teachers' work with students, each requiring teachers to draw on ideas in an integrated fashion. For PCK to become a useful guide for designing teacher education, we need to understand how teachers link pedagogical content ideas as they work on tasks intended for their learning.

A working model of PCK

In the interest of creating well-designed teacher education from pre-service preparation onward, I am thinking about how to intentionally progress teacher learning. Part of this work has been to create program experiences that explicitly emphasize a theoretical understanding of teaching science in connection with the practice of teaching science. The iterative design and study of programs has included a teacher educator's examination of PCK as a knowledge construct. This work is an opportunity to examine how PCK might be used to guide science teacher educators and program designers.

My work to examine PCK has two interrelated themes based on an interest in how PCK might be used to guide the design of learning experiences for science teachers. One research purpose is to describe science teacher learning progressions. The over-arching question is: How does science teachers' thinking progress over time with experiences focused on PCK and classrooms? The second research purpose is to understand what ideas science teachers consider together within tasks for teacher learning. The question asked here is: What aspects of PCK do science teachers learn and use together as they participate in experiences focused on PCK and classrooms? To pursue these questions, I am using PCK as a guide for examining artifacts of teaching tasks (i.e., plans, enactments, and reflections). Initially components were identified from the literature on science teacher PCK (Park & Oliver, 2008; Schneider & Plasman, 2011). However, to better capture the thinking illustrated in teachers' work, the components of PCK were reorganized and further defined. This, in turn, refined how tasks were structured. Although presented individually here for the reader, it is important to keep in mind that analysis and development are ongoing and interrelated.

A working model for PCK is presented in Table 12.1. Many pieces are similar to other descriptions for PCK, since the ideas have their roots in those descriptions. Here, though, the organization and descriptions are based on thinking about use more so than sources. This includes using the term facets, rather than components, to emphasize the cohesive or case-based nature of PCK during planning, enactment, and reflection. Facets are organized and expanded based on pre-service science teachers' descriptions of their reasoning and current ideas about teaching science. Figure 12.1 illustrates that pre-service teachers frequently think about instructional strategies and student thinking together and that both of these are thought about under the umbrella of frameworks. They also tended to think about orientations along with curriculum as another grouping. For science teachers, thinking about engaging students with natural phenomena is core to teaching science across all topics. Science phenomena experiences and assessments are grouped as strategies since teachers thought about these together within lessons. Frameworks for science teaching include both inquiry and discourse. Discourse is a relatively recent consideration for PCK but is central to thinking about students learning science. Inquiry and discourse were used as broader ideas within which to think about student thinking and instructional strategies. Teachers tended to think about science curriculum along with the purpose and goals for teaching science. Teachers were thinking about *how* to think about curriculum including materials prepared for both teacher and student thinking.

Program design informed by PCK

My work designing and studying science teacher education has been focused on graduate teacher education. Guided by the ideas described above for ambitious teacher education, theory about teaching is integrated with the practice of teaching in the classroom. Teachers entering these programs have completed their undergraduate study of science, hence, an examination of their content knowledge was not an issue taken up in this work. Research regarding PCK has been concentrated in the pre-service program. Initial findings are informing program refinement and are being applied to new and continuing teacher education.

The Licensure and Master's Program (LAMP) is a one-year, graduate, pre-service program designed to follow the K-12 school calendar and structured around four cycles of plan, enact, reflect. This program is in its fifth year. The LAMP mentoring program is in its second year and is a continuation of the pre-service program for LAMP graduates in their first three years of teaching. The program for continuing teachers is not as tightly linked to the pre-service and new teacher stages but the approach to ambitious teacher education is continued. This is an 18-month master's program in partnership with the graduate science faculty to qualify teachers to teach first-year college science to their high school students. This program is in its first year.

Thinking about planning

The tasks given to teachers to support their learning—planning instruction, enacting lessons with students, and reflecting on enactments—are the tasks of teaching. Each requires teachers to draw on ideas in an integrated fashion. Initial research, however, shows that teachers draw on different aspects of PCK during each task (see Figure 12.2). To illustrate how PCK might inform instructional

TABLE 12.1 A working model of science teacher PCK

Facets	Facets include . . .
Orientations to teaching science	Teachers' ideas about . . . • nature of learning and teaching science • *goals* of teaching science • *purpose* of teaching science
Science *curriculum* prepared for teacher and student thinking	Teachers' ideas about . . . • *scope* of science (ideas that are important and worth learning) • *standards* (how to think about as guides for planning and teaching) • curricular *resources* (how and when to use for self and students) • *sequence* of science (organizing science ideas for learning)

Frameworks for science teaching	Teachers' ideas about . . .
	• *inquiry* science learning environments (such as the use of questions)
	  ○ how and when to develop
	  ○ how science is characterized
	  ○ how student thinking is made visible and supported
	• *discourse* in science (oral and written such as argumentation or technical writing)
	  ○ how and when to develop
	  ○ how science is characterized
	  ○ how student thinking is made visible and supported

Student thinking about science	Teachers' ideas about . . . • students' *initial* science ideas and experiences • *development* of science ideas (including process and sequence) • how students *express* science ideas (including demonstration of understanding, questions, and responses) • *challenging* science ideas for students (including why the ideas are challenging) • appropriate *level* of science understanding

Instructional strategies for science topics	Teachers' ideas about . . .
	• science *phenomena* experiences
	  ○ how and when to use (including safety)
	  ○ how science is presented
	  ○ how student thinking is made visible or supported
	• *assessment* of science learning
	  ○ how and when to use
	  ○ how science is presented
	  ○ how student thinking is made visible or supported

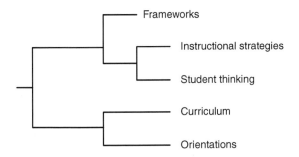

FIGURE 12.1 PCK facets grouped by how they are described by pre-service teachers

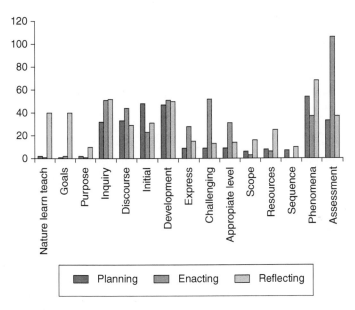

FIGURE 12.2 Frequency of attention to aspects of PCK described by pre-service teachers within planning, teaching, and reflecting

design, I describe how thinking about planning is structured across pre-service, new, and continuing teacher education. The design work guided by PCK is similar for enacting and reflecting.

Planning is a complex teaching task closely related to what happens in classrooms. Planning is a theoretical and design-oriented view of making curricular and instructional decisions. Planning is knowledge-based and a strategic and purposeful approach to instruction (Calderhead, 1996; Clark & Peterson, 1986). Planning is a nonlinear process to design instruction where teachers visualize instruction from multiple facets and levels. Planning requires sophisticated thinking. What teachers think about what they do is made visible in their plans and, in particular, their planning rationales.

A sample of the working model for teaching about planning is presented in Table 12.2. The suggested PCK ideas to emphasize during planning are informed by the initial learning trajectories and grouping of ideas identified for pre-service teachers as well as the trajectories suggested across career phases (Schneider & Plasman, 2011). Because the pre-service program is more mature and was the primary source of data, ideas become increasingly propositional toward the continuing teachers' column. Thinking was also guided by the descriptions in Table 12.1 and the goal of focusing teachers' thinking on successively complex issues of planning. For example, pre-service teachers tended to focus on science phenomena along with developing students' science ideas or science phenomena in conjunction with initial science ideas and experiences during planning. Thus, it will be beneficial to guide teachers to think about how to demonstrate phenomena and guide students' attention at the same time as guiding teachers to think about how to gather and make sense of students' ideas and experiences beyond identifying right or wrong ideas. Another example is that pre-service teachers only begin to notice, mostly during enactment, how some science ideas are challenging for students. This implies that new teachers may be ready to think about why ideas are challenging during planning. It makes sense that specifications for teacher learning such as these could be a guide for what could be assessed in plans, rather than enactments or reflections, and what would be appropriate descriptions of teachers' progress. This type of design work moves teacher education beyond the idiosyncratic to purposeful improvement (Dewey, 1929).

Progressing teacher education

It is important to keep in mind that many of the ideas presented in this model of PCK-based teacher education are propositional. This is the nature of design work. I can imagine that this model can feel underspecified. The detail needed to create evaluations of teacher knowledge in particular topics is missing. The model is more useful for the scale it was intended—broad spans of teacher education appropriate for all the possible teaching situations teachers may and do encounter. It is not unusual for models to reduce complexity in order to highlight important features. Yet, even though we cannot predict all the situations, the need to anchor teachers' thinking in core cases of teaching science is a valid point. This program design model needs an underlying set of high-impact cases for teachers to plan, enact, and reflect within that are grounded in important science ideas. In the end, the test will be whether the model helps to explain teacher learning.

Throughout this chapter I pose many questions to guide our thinking about PCK that are not easy to answer. Understanding how to support learning about teaching is not a simple problem. One more question is: What is the nature of the connection between teachers' developing PCK and students' science learning?

TABLE 12.2 A sample from a working model of science teacher education focused on PCK in planning

	Pre-service science teachers		New science teachers		Continuing science teachers
	Early	Later	Early	Later	
Planning task Facets and time horizon	Explore how students think about science Plan a set of connected lessons emphasizing inquiry with a performance assessment	Explore how student talk supports science thinking Plan a unit emphasizing student talk with a unit assessment plan	Explore how students make sense of science phenomena through talk Plan support for student sense-making talk about science	Explore multiple ways students express ideas in tasks and discussion Plan task-based discussions and tailored instruction	Explore student science thinking across broad spans of time Plan sequence of ideas and instruction for the school year
Orientations Guiding question	What does it mean to teach science? (teachers notice orientations most often during reflection)		What is possible for me, as a teacher, to do to learn about my students' science ideas and make better instructional decisions?		In what ways does instruction support students in developing sophisticated thinking?
Curriculum Guide teachers to think about . . .	Scope Identifying scientific concept and process idea set How ideas are worthwhile and meaningful	Scope Identifying a nature of science idea Resources Tools to visualize units, lessons, daily plan structure Selecting resources that support inquiry	Resources Using ideas such as images of teaching to inform their teaching	Scope Ideas that are worthwhile and meaningful Standards Selecting science ideas for achievement data	Sequence Sequencing ideas across grade levels Standards How standards were identified and develop ideas across schooling

(continued)

TABLE 12.2 *(continued)*

	Pre-service science teachers		New science teachers		Continuing science teachers
	Early	Later	Early	Later	
Framework Guide teachers to think about . . .	Inquiry★ How questions to investigate present science	Discourse How questions frame how students write and talk about ideas	Inquiry How student questions illustrate their ideas and can be investigated	Discourse How student contribution to discussion can be structure around tasks	Inquiry★ with discourse How student contributions to discussions can be purposefully sequenced Transitioning students to guided inquiry
Student thinking Guide teachers to think about . . .	Development★ Types of questions that guide thinking Initial★ Gathering and making sense of student ideas and experience beyond right or wrong	Development★ How explaining ideas supports thinking How scientific explanations support scientific thinking★★ Initial How conversation uncovers students' initial ideas and experiences	Challenging★★ Why some ideas are challenging Express How students express ideas when making claims and justifications	Express How students demonstrate understanding in their own language before they use academic or scientific language	Challenging★★ Why some ideas are challenging Appropriate level What ideas students will develop now and in the future
Strategy Guide teachers to think about . . .	Science phenomena★ Demonstrating phenomena and guiding student attention Linking phenomena and student data gathering	Science assessment How different strands of science can be assessed (teachers notice most often during enactment)	Science phenomena Supporting student experiences with inaccessible or challenging aspects of phenomena	Science assessment★ Using discussion and artifacts such as drawings as documentable evidence of student learning	Science phenomena★ Embedding phenomena experiences in student interest and community

★Areas teachers focus on during planning.
★★Areas of opportunity to emphasize during planning.

PCK may be one tool to help teacher educators untangle the complex process of learning to teach. But it is only helpful in the long run if it makes a difference for students. Because what teachers learn depends on instruction, and instruction for teachers depends on understanding their learning, exploring these questions will take time for iterative cycles of program design and research. Without this type of research, however, we may not be able to really answer, what is the value of PCK for teacher educators.

Acknowledgements

Kellie Plasman is a doctoral student at the University of Toledo. Her contribution has been instrumental in our research efforts.
Jenny Denyer is an associate professor of language arts and an expert in teacher education. Her contribution has been invaluable in designing the LAMP program.
   LAMP was developed with many faculty and administrative partners at the University of Toledo (http://www.utoledo.edu/education/lamp/accelerated/index.html). LAMP was selected for the Woodrow Wilson Ohio teaching fellows program for science and mathematics teacher education. Woodrow Wilson supports the LAMP new teacher mentoring program.

References

Abell, S. K., Rogers, M. A. P., Hanuscin, D. L., Lee, M. H., & Gagnon, M. J. (2009). Preparing the next generation of science teacher educators: A model for developing PCK for teaching science teachers. *Journal of Science Teacher Education, 20*(1), 77–93.

Ball, D. L., & Cohen, D. K. (1999). Developing practice, developing practitioners: Toward a practice-based theory of professional education. In G. Sykes & L. Darling-Hammond (Eds.), *Teaching as the learning profession: Handbook of policy and practice* (pp. 3–32). San Francisco, CA: Jossey-Bass.

Berry, A., & Van Driel, J. H. (2012). Teaching about teaching science: Aims, strategies, and backgrounds of science teacher educators. *Journal of Teacher Education, 64*(2), 117–128.

Borko, H. (2004). Professional development and teacher learning: Mapping the terrain. *Educational Researcher, 33*(8), 3–15.

Bransford, J. D., Derry, S., Berliner, D. C., & Hammerness, K. (2007). Theories of learning and the roles in teaching. In L. Darling-Hammond & J. D. Bransford (Eds.), *Preparing teachers for a changing world* (pp. 40–87). San Francisco, CA: Jossey-Bass.

Bruner, J. (1960). *The process of education.* Cambridge, MA: Harvard University Press.

Calderhead, J. (1996). Teachers: Beliefs and knowledge. In D. C. Berliner & R. C. Calfee (Eds.), *Handbook of educational psychology* (pp. 709–725). New York, NY: Macmillan Publishers Ltd.

Carter, K. (1990). Teachers' knowledge and learning to teach. In W. R. Houston (Ed.), *Handbook of research on teacher education* (pp. 291–310). New York, NY: Macmillan Publishers Ltd.

Clark, C. M., & Peterson, P. L. (1986). Teachers' thought processes. In M. C. Wittrock (Ed.), *Handbook of research on teaching* (3rd ed., pp. 255–296). New York, NY: Macmillan Publishers Ltd.

Corcoran, T., Mosher, F. A., & Rogat, A. (2009). *Learning progressions in science: An evidence-based approach to reform*. New York, NY: Center on Continuous Instructional Improvement.

Depaepe, F., Verschaffel, L., & Kelchtermans, G. (2013). Pedagogical content knowledge: A systematic review of the way in which the concept has pervaded mathematics education research. *Teaching and Teacher Education, 34*, 12–25.

Dewey, J. (1929). *The sources of a science of education*. New York, NY: Liveright.

Dewey, J. (1938). *Experience and education*. New York, NY: Touchstone.

Feiman-Nemser, S. (2008). Teacher learning: How do teachers learn to teach? In M. Cochran-Smith, S. Feiman-Nemser, D. J. McIntyre, & K. Demers (Eds.), *Handbook of research on teacher education: Enduring questions in changing contexts* (pp. 697–705). New York, NY: Routledge.

Gallagher, T., Griffin, S., Parker, D. C., Kitchen, J., & Figg, C. (2011). Establishing and sustaining teacher educator professional development in a self-study community of practice: Pre-tenure teacher educators developing professionally. *Teaching and Teacher Education, 27*, 880–890.

Grossman, P., Schoenfeld, A. H., & Lee, C. (2005). Teaching subject matter. In L. Darling-Hammond & J. D. Bransford (Eds.), *Preparing teachers for a changing world: What teachers should learn and be able to do*. San Francisco, CA: Jossey-Bass.

Gudmundsdottir, S., & Shulman, L. (1987). Pedagogical content knowledge in social studies. *Scandinavian Journal of Educational Research, 31*, 59–70.

Heritage, M. (2008). *Learning progressions: Supporting instruction and formative assessment*. Washington, DC: National Center for Research on Evaluation, Standards, and Student Testing (CRESST).

Hollins, E. (2011). Teacher preparation for quality teaching. *Journal of Teacher Education, 62*(4), 395–407.

Merseth, K. K. (1991). *The case for cases in teacher education*. Washington, DC: American Association for Higher Education.

Munby, H., Russell, T., & Martin, A. (2001). Teachers' knowledge and how it develops. In V. Richardson (Ed.), *Handbook of research on teaching* (4th ed., pp. 807–904). Washington, DC: American Educational Research Association.

Park, S., & Oliver, J. S. (2008). Revisiting the conceptualization of pedagogical content knowledge (PCK): PCK as a conceptual tool to understand teachers as professionals. *Research in Science Education, 38*(3), 261–284.

Putnam, R. T., & Borko, H. (2000). What do new views of knowledge and thinking have to say about research on teacher learning? *Educational Researcher, 29*(1), 4–15.

Schneider, R. M., & Plasman, K. (2011). Science teacher learning progressions: A review of science teachers' pedagogical content knowledge development. *Review of Educational Research, 81*(4), 530–565.

Settlage, J. (2013). On acknowledging PCK's shortcomings. *Journal of Science Teacher Education, 24*, 1–12.

Shavelson, R. (2009). *Reflections on learning progressions*. Paper presented at the Learning Progressions in Science (LeaPS), Iowa City, IA.

Shulman, L. S. (1986). Those who understand: Knowledge growth in teaching. *Educational Researcher, 15*, 4–14.

Shulman, L. S. (1987). Knowledge and teaching: Foundations of the new reform. *Harvard Educational Review, 57*(1), 1–22.

Shulman, L. S. (1999). Foreword. In J. Gess-Newsome & N. G. Lederman (Eds.), *Examining pedagogical content knowledge: The construct and its implications for science education* (Vol. 6, pp. ix–xii). Boston, MA: Kluwer Academic Publishers.

Sikorski, T.-R., & Hammer, D. (2010). A critique of how learning progressions research conceptualizes sophistication and progress. In K. Gomez, L. Lyons, & J. Radinsky (Eds.), *Learning in the disciplines: Proceedings of the 9th International Conference of the Learning Sciences* (pp. 1032–1039). Chicago, IL: International Society of the Learning Sciences.

Singer-Gabella. (2012). Toward scholarship in practice. *Teachers College Record, 114*(8), 1–30.

Smith, D. (2000). Content and pedagogical content knowledge for elementary science teacher educators: Knowing our students. *Journal of Science Teacher Education, 11*(1), 27–46.

Trent, J. (2012). Multiple boundary-crossing experiences of beginning teacher educators. *Journal of Teacher Education, 64*(3), 262–275.

13

ON THE BEAUTY OF KNOWING THEN NOT KNOWING

Pinning down the elusive qualities of PCK

Vanessa Kind

DURHAM UNIVERSITY, UK

I met PCK about ten years ago. I was an experienced teacher educator, and thought I knew how to do the job: recruit the best possible graduates on to our teacher education program; give input on key topics; supervise teaching practices; set and mark essays on relevant aspects of science education theory and practice; and help those completing successfully find a teaching position. A sneaking suspicion that there could be more to it led to 'discovering' PCK: At last, a framework that provided a constructive way of thinking about teachers' knowledge! Shulman's teacher knowledge base (1986, 1987) seemed a panacea for educating teachers. I began collecting data to investigate further. Initially I probed preservice teachers' (PSTs) content knowledge, how this develops, and the impact of content knowledge on self-confidence (Kind, 2009a). Extensive reading about PCK led to a review paper (Kind, 2009b). Next, I worked on what PSTs' PCK might look like, using vignettes (Kind, 2014). I carried out this activity within a Shulman-based paradigm without thinking critically about PCK as a construct. My participation in the PCK Summit prompted a rethink. This chapter sets out the issues I began to discover, and shows my steps toward resolution to date.

Shulman's PCK model: Functional but flawed

Shulman (1986, 1987) proposed that PCK comprises two components: knowledge labeled as *representations*, from this point referred to as *instructional strategies*, and knowledge of students' subject matter *learning difficulties*. Instructional strategies comprise illustrations, analogies, explanations, and demonstrations teachers use to make content knowledge about a subject comprehensible to students. Learning difficulties comprise two sub-components—knowledge about students' misconceptions, that is, their naïve ideas gained through interpretation of prior learning experiences, or preconceived ideas about a topic; and knowledge of any other potential barriers students may experience in learning content knowledge, such as how concepts interrelate and strategies to help solve problems. This description identifies PCK as a separate sub-component that signifies specialist knowledge held by a teacher within a broader teacher knowledge base, within which Shulman (1987) identified seven components.

An implication arising from Shulman's PCK model is that instructional strategies exist to make specific content knowledge accessible to students. To become an expert (or at least effective) teacher, these must be learned together with information about any difficulties students may experience in learning a topic. Shulman might argue this specialist knowledge equates to the case knowledge held by a doctor or lawyer, as this is specific to teachers, marking them out as possessors of knowledge that is relevant and targeted to their profession. This body of information could be termed common or canonical PCK, applicable across a range of educational settings and situations. In learning to teach, instructional strategies and knowledge of students' difficulties could be learned separately, as the model does not indicate the nature of any connections between the two. In practice, though, student difficulties associated with learning a topic, such as misconceptions, possible misunderstandings arising from the constraints of an analogy or illustration and any impact of non-scientific prior knowledge must affect a teacher's instructional strategy choice, its use, and application. Therefore, the model offers a plausible means of identifying aspects of teacher knowledge relevant to teacher education.

Closer inspection of Shulman's proposals reveals a number of operational flaws. First, the description offers a static, unchanging representation of teacher knowledge (Banks, Leach, & Moon, 2005; Cochran, deRuiter, & King, 1993). Although contradictory to Shulman's original intentions, which were engaged with professionalizing teaching, the notion that a body of knowledge about instructional strategies and students' difficulties exists and can be learned could be interpreted as turning teaching from a skilled profession based on exercising judgment to a technical exercise with limited opportunities for consideration of choice and/or independence. Also, the means of development of such knowledge is unclear, leading to a perception that progression toward expertise as a teacher is problematic to define. There is no requirement within the model, for example, that student learning *outcomes* should be considered, only that a teacher learns about instructional strategies that *might* generate these. Thus, the model gives no indication about appropriate instructional strategies or how these could be judged effective for generating student learning. Third, learning in schools is generally regarded as multifactorial (Rutter, Maughan, Mortimore, & Ouston, 1979): Context, environment, curriculum, individual student preferences, abilities, behaviors, and motivations all play a part in determining the impact of a teacher's efforts. A successful teacher works within and/or establishes conditions in which learning occurs. The most appropriate instructional strategy and/or detailed knowledge of students' learning difficulties will generate little impact without consideration of these factors. Minimizing PCK to two components at the expense of all other factors could be regarded as an over-simplification of a complex situation. Finally, Shulman himself noted (PCK Summit Guest Lecture, October 20, 2012) that his model lacks recognition of non-cognitive attributes, such as self-efficacy and self-confidence. These are important in learning to teach, as teachers must be resilient, reflective, and able to handle feedback in establishing good quality practice.

Shulman's model also harbors theoretical difficulties. Bromme (1995), for example, notes a complete lack of theoretical background, and that Shulman defines his components in vague terms. A constructivist perspective can be implied as an under-pinning framework, as connections between instructional strategies and knowledge of students' difficulties may be seen as a means to ensure teachers scaffold student learning sensibly and prompt any necessary conceptual change (Anderson & Smith, 1987). However, this was not stated explicitly in Shulman's original proposal. The fact is that PCK could be all things to all people or mean nothing to anyone. Any instructional strategy or knowledge about a student learning difficulty in any educational setting could constitute PCK.

Since Shulman made these initial proposals, researchers have gathered extensive evidence and made proposals about PCK resulting in a range of models (Kind, 2009b) that variously include knowledge about content, general pedagogy, curriculum, learners, schools/context of education, assessment, and orientations (also known as teacher beliefs or purposes). PCK is clearly an attractive framework for describing teacher behaviors. However, despite this activity and popularity, PCK has yet to feed into or impact teacher education policy and practice at a significant level. For example, PCK is not mentioned in teacher effectiveness research (Darling-Hammond & Bransford, 2005; Hattie, 2012; HayMcBer, 2000; Kidwell, 2013; Ko, Sammons & Bakkum, 2013; Turner-Bisset, 2001) published in 'the post-Shulman' era, that is, following publication of Shulman's (1986, 1987) papers introducing PCK as a knowledge base component. Nor is PCK mentioned in national teacher standards documents or science education frameworks (e.g., Australian Institute for Teaching and School Leadership, 2014; Department for Education, 2011; National Research Council, 2011), even though individual PCK components such as subject knowledge, assessment, instructional strategies, and school context *do* feature. Contributory factors for this low level of impact include those for undertaking the Summit: recognition in the field that PCK lacks definition and is poorly conceptualized.

PCK models presented at the Summit

PCK models presented at the Summit varied, exhibiting differences in the number and range of components considered part of PCK. Table 13.1 summarizes these, using a similar structure and approach to Kind (2009b). Shulman's (1987) proposals are highlighted in grey. Thus, Table 13.1 shows the extent to which researchers embrace or differ from his starting point. A component shown as 'P' indicates this was part of a research group's PCK model; '0' denotes no reference to this component; 'K' indicates a research group explicitly placed the component outside PCK, but within a teacher's knowledge base. The analysis is based on participants' pre-Summit position papers (see http://pcksummit.bscs. org). Table 13.1 indicates that all agreed tacitly that PCK is more complex than Shulman proposed, although most accept his initial suggestion. An exception is Hill, who presented a model for Mathematical Knowledge for Teaching, not PCK, discussed later. The models can be grouped into categories: Those based on the PCK model proposed by Magnusson, Krajcik and Borko (1999), and those based on alternative theoretical perspectives. Each group is considered separately.

Models based on Magnusson, Krajcik, and Borko (1999)

Six Summit teams (Banilower & Smith; Freidrichsen, Lannin, & Sickel; Kind; Padilla & Garritz; Park & Suh; Van Driel & Henze) used models based on the PCK structure proposed by Magnusson et al. (1999; see Figure 13.1).

Specific components identified within these researchers' PCK models are noted 'P' in Table 13.1. Magnusson et al. comment that they see PCK as "the transformation of several types of knowledge for teaching (including subject matter knowledge) . . . and . . . represents a unique domain of teacher knowledge" (p. 85).

Their model follows Shulman's line of thought, identifying subject matter or content knowledge (SM/CK) as a distinct knowledge base category, and defining PCK as the special knowledge used by a teacher to transform his/her SM/CK to benefit students. Besides instructional strategies and knowledge of students' difficulties, Magnusson et al. include science teaching orientations, knowledge of assessment, and curricular knowledge.

Teaching orientation emerges as a PCK component from Grossman's (1990) work. She observed contrasting purposes for teaching in her study of six teachers teaching English Literature. One teacher wanted to ensure students could "make connections between the text and their own lives" (Grossman, p. 8), while another wanted his students to learn how to analyze and understand a text. Grossman argued these differing goals influenced teachers' choices of instructional strategies, so contributed to PCK. She defined purposes as "the overarching conceptions of teaching a subject [that] are reflected in teachers' goals for teaching particular subject matter" (p. 8).

Magnusson et al. (1999) accepted this, but changed her term to orientations, proposing nine contrasting examples including "Discovery," "Conceptual change," "Process," "Didactic," and "Inquiry" (p. 100). A teacher may switch orientation, adopting any one for different reasons: A Didactic orientation may imply fact transmission, while Discovery aims for students finding out science

TABLE 13.1 PCK models represented at the Summit

Summit participants	Representations/ instructional strategies	Students' subject-specific learning difficulties	Purposes/ orientations/ nature of science	Curriculum knowledge	Assessment	Subject matter/ content knowledge	General pedagogical knowledge	Context for learning	Knowledge of the learner	Author-specific terminology
Banilower & Smith	P	P	0	0	P	K	K	0	P	Sequencing ideas; canonical/ idiosyncratic PCK
Friedrichsen, Lannin, & Sickel	P	P	P	P	P	0	0	0	0	Topic- and discipline-specific Episodic
Kind	P	P	P	P	P	K	0	0	0	Transformative
Padilla & Garritz	P	P	P	P	P	0	0	0	0	Transformative
Park & Suh	P	P	P	P	P	0	0	K	0	Connections important; integrative Tacit, topic-specific
Van Driel & Henze	P	P	P	P	P	K	K	0	0	Relationships between components are important

Schneider	P	P	P	P	P	O	O	O	O	
Berry, Cooper, & Loughran	P	O	O	P	O	O	O	O	O	Tacit or collective Constructivist Topic-specific
Kirschner, Borowski, & Fischer	P	P	O	K	O	P	K	O	O	
Daehler et al.	P	P	O	O	O	P	K	O	O	Tacit or explicit
Rollnick & Mavhunga	O	P	K	O	O	P	P	P	O	Topic-specific
Gess-Newsome	P	O	O	O	O	P	O	P	O	Topic-specific
Hill	O	K	O	O	O	K	O	O	O	Mathematical knowledge for teaching
Consensus model	P	P	K	K	K	K	K	P	O	Topic-specific

Legend: 0 = not mentioned, K = Knowledge base component, P = PCK component, Grey panel: PCK sub-components proposed by Shulman (1986, 1987)

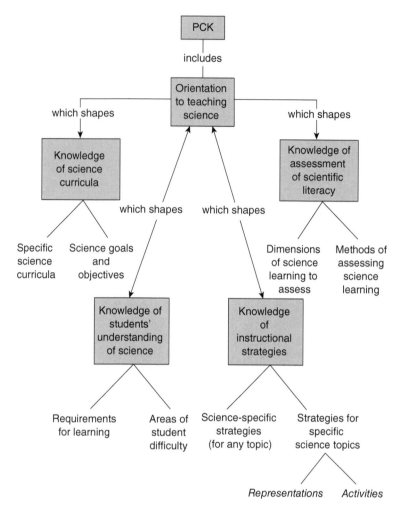

FIGURE 13.1 Magnusson, Krajcik, and Borko's (1999) model for pedagogical content knowledge

concepts as independent learners. Hence, an orientation impacts instructional strategy choice, and thus PCK.

The inclusion of curricular knowledge also originates from Grossman (1990). She observed English teachers requiring and using "horizontal and vertical" (p. 8) curricula in their teaching: A teacher exhibiting curriculum knowledge would know which books were needed when teaching a specific age range (horizontal) and would use awareness of books studied in earlier and later years (vertical) to best effect. Magnusson et al. argue that curricular knowledge "distinguishes the content specialist from the pedagogue – a hallmark of pedagogical content knowledge" (p. 103).

Magnusson et al. follow Tamir's (1988) proposal in adding assessment knowledge. He defined this component as comprising knowledge of dimensions of science learning that are important to assess, and knowledge of methods for assessing learning. Teachers plan lessons with the science that will be examined or tested in mind, and adjust instructional strategies accordingly. Also, teachers must assess students to find out what has been learned and how learning is progressing. In the UK, this formative assessment for learning or AfL (Black, Harrison, Lee, Marshall, & Wiliam, 2003) is integral to teachers' instructional strategies, so again impacts PCK.

At this stage in my work, I accepted the Magnusson et al. (1999) model. I found it helpful in considering the knowledge PSTs need to develop. Like Friedrichsen, Lannin, and Sickel, I saw strength in the model offering a general map of areas that need attention. From my teacher education standpoint, all components seemed obvious prerequisites for effective teaching. Summit teams differed in their application of the Magnusson et al. model. For example, Banilower and Smith state only that their model is adapted from Magnusson et al. Their view is that a teacher creates PCK when combining subject matter knowledge with pedagogical knowledge and knowledge of learner, generating sequencing of ideas, instructional strategies, assessment, and knowledge of students' understandings. Park and Oliver interpret the five sub-components of PCK in their "pentagon model" (2008). They situate this within a learning environment with limitations imposed by context, cultural, and social features.

Is PCK integrative or transformative?

Gess-Newsome (1999) picked up Shulman's notion that PCK represents a transformation of all the knowledge needed to be a teacher, including subject matter, pedagogical, and contextual knowledge, into a unique form of knowledge that impacts teaching practice (p. 10). Referring to this as the "transformative" model, Gess-Newsome (1999) defined PCK at one extreme of a spectrum as the transformation of subject matter, pedagogical, and contextual knowledge to create new knowledge for the purposes of instructing students. The transformative model is analogous to a chemical compound, which resists easy separation of its component parts: Gess-Newsome describes them as being "inextricably combined into a new form of knowledge, PCK" (p. 11). In a transformative model, SMK is separate from PCK, while PCK itself is a unique type of knowledge. A teacher uses SMK in creating PCK. At the opposite end of a PCK spectrum Gess-Newsome identifies an "integrative" model, in which a teacher selects knowledge from three domains—subject matter, pedagogy, and context—combining these as necessary in order to teach. An integrative model does not recognize PCK as a separate knowledge component; instead, teacher knowledge as a whole embraces SMK, pedagogy, and context.

Gess-Newsome uses the analogy of a chemical mixture to illustrate integrative PCK, as components retain their individual identities, but are indistinguishable on a macroscopic level. Thus, in an integrative model, SMK is part of PCK, because PCK itself summarizes a teacher's knowledge base, so does not 'exist' as a separate type of knowledge.

Summit participants adopting or adapting the Magnusson et al. (1999) model interpreted transformative/integrative stances differently. Prior to the Summit, I believed PCK to be transformative, a view shared explicitly by Padilla and Garritz, and Van Driel and Henze. I interpreted SMK as representing a teacher's academic expertise in a subject. I distinguished this from curriculum knowledge, which I understood as the distillation of subject knowledge for teaching purposes. One team, Park and Suh, took the opposite stance, adopting Magnusson et al.'s sub-components, but regarding PCK as an integration of these in their "pentagon" model. They perceived strong PCK to comprise all components connected in coherent ways, enabling the whole structure to function as a scaffold for student learning. Banilower and Smith expressed uncertainty about whether or not PCK is integrative or transformative. They reported instances of being able to identify content knowledge and pedagogical knowledge in PCK, supporting an integrative model. At other times, Banilower and Smith report seeing PCK as distinct from the knowledge bases contributing to it, suggesting a transformative nature. Friedrichsen et al. saw no connections between PCK model components at all, but described these as "separate silos." Friedrichsen et al. rejected the model as a portrayal of experienced teachers' integrated knowledge. This lack of interconnectedness was also identified by Van Driel and Henze, who note that Magnusson et al. do not propose connections between PCK sub-components in their model.

Magnusson et al. based PCK models: Summary and outcomes

Pre-Summit, Magnusson et al.'s (1999) model was adapted/adopted as a representation of PCK by six Summit research groups, indicating a dominance of this view within the field. However, although researchers agreed generally on PCK components (Table 13.1), variation and deviations were apparent. Research groups used different terminology to describe the same component and understood the nature of some components differently. For example, a definition for 'science teaching orientations' was left open; and whether or not 'instructional strategies,' includes inquiry-based learning was not discussed. I found, however, that rather than developing entrenched positions, colleagues sought to listen, understand, and learn from contrasting viewpoints. This led, in my own case, to questioning my rigid, uncritical thinking about the Magnusson et al. model. As a next step, I considered the integrative/transformative debate further.

The role of subject matter or content knowledge in PCK: Taking integration further

Whether or not PCK includes a teacher's SMK or CK lies at the heart of the integrative/transformative debate. Pre-Summit, I was clear that SMK/CK was a separate component, as indicated above. My earlier work on teachers' CK (Kind, 2009a) suggested PSTs struggled initially to make decisions about how to select appropriate content knowledge for teaching from the wealth of academic scientific knowledge they held. Knowledge about an unfamiliar science topic (usually physics in the case of a biology graduate) could be learned in sufficient depth to teach it to lower high school students. I report (Kind, 2009a) contrasting, counter-intuitive outcomes: Pre-service science teachers' lessons on their non-specialist sciences exhibited appropriate instructional strategy choices more often than in lessons on within-field topics. Conversely, within-field lessons were less effective, as PSTs did not consistently choose instructional strategies that supported student learning. This finding seemed inconsistent with PCK involving integration of SMK. My evidence suggested SMK was purposefully selected by PSTs (within-field lessons) or learned as necessary (out-of-field lessons). I thus rejected PCK models that promoted SMK integration. Table 13.1 shows some Summit colleagues held opposite views to mine. Kirschner, Borowski, and Fischer; Daehler, Heller, Little, Sheingold, and Shinohara; Rollnick and Mavhunga; and Gess-Newsome's papers all indicated that SMK (or CK) are part of PCK. This thinking aligns with Marks (1990), Fernandez-Balboa and Stiehl (1995) and Koballa, Gräber, Coleman, and Kemp (1999). These researchers' interpretations of PCK are reviewed briefly.

Marks's (1990) PCK model emerged from data collected from eight primary mathematics teachers. In his model, instructional strategies are "instructional processes" and learning difficulties rephrased "students' understanding." Marks adds "media for instruction," meaning knowledge about texts and materials, a component similar to curricular knowledge. Marks includes SMK within PCK because this reflects his participants' views. In describing PCK, teachers' personal understandings of mathematical concepts were taken for granted. Rather than describing their teaching as *transforming* mathematical knowledge, they emphasized pedagogical practices they termed "justifications," "important ideas," "prerequisite knowledge," and knowledge of "typical school math problems" (p. 5). Marks argues accordingly that SMK and PCK were not clearly distinguished teacher knowledge base components.

Fernández-Balboa and Stiehl (1995) collected data from university lecturers, who seemed to roll SMK into their teaching practices when describing their work, as did Marks's teacher sample. These data led to the proposal that PCK comprises knowledge about subject matter; knowledge about students; instructional strategies; the teaching context; and the teaching purposes (p. 293). Including *context* is relatively unusual in PCK models. The authors justify this by noting "contextual barriers" contribute to characteristic university teaching practices. These include handling large class sizes, specific time limits, scarcity of appropriate resources, students' attitudes, and tenure and promotion issues. Fernández-Balboa and Stiehl contend that lecturers' effectiveness depends on "the specific beliefs and knowledge that guide their decisions and actions" (p. 305), so context influences PCK.

Koballa et al. (1999) support inclusion of SMK within PCK on the basis of their data collected from trainee chemistry teachers preparing to teach 16–19-year-olds in German gymnasium schools. Their PCK model is a "nested" (p. 276) structure in which chemistry knowledge gained from university and school lies at the center of teachers' PCK. Koballa et al. add *general pedagogy*, a factor they call "multi-dimensional knowledge" (p. 278) to their set of PCK components.

These models share similarities with integrative PCK models presented at the Summit. For example, Daehler et al. refer to teachers organizing instruction around accurate, precise, and coherent understandings of specific content, as well as content-specific classroom activities. Daehler et al.'s views are wrapped within a context of developing teacher professional development materials. The context role mirrors Fernandez-Balboa and Stiehl's position. Meanwhile, Kirschner et al. distinguish between CK, PCK, and pedagogical knowledge (PK), but comment that all three dimensions are required and that PCK assessment items include varying amounts of content or pedagogical knowledge. They explicitly include teachers' knowledge about concepts and experiments within PCK for physics teaching. Their combination of CK, PCK, and PK seems similar to Koballa et al.'s (1999) position.

The relative merits of transformative and integrative models bear consideration. Abd El-Khalick (2006), for example, argues integrative models lack explanatory power, as no mechanism is suggested that shows how interaction between SMK, pedagogy, and contextual factors results in PCK. Banks et al. (2005) propose a solution, suggesting that a teacher's "personal subject construct," could be responsible. This combines experiences from teaching with other factors held by the teacher, such as purposes and orientations. Mixing these with subject, pedagogical, and school knowledge constitutes PCK. However, none of the PCK Summit researchers seemed to identify with these proposals.

In defending my pre-Summit position, transformative models imply one or more mechanisms exist in a teacher's brain that 'convert' SMK/CK to PCK, use SMK in creating PCK, and/or adapt SMK for school use. The possible existence of a cognitive process prompting transformation seemed consistent with my earlier findings (Kind, 2009a). These showed that PSTs received significant support from experienced teachers for preparing out-of-field lessons, by-passing the need for PSTs to process information for themselves. Contrastingly, a tacit assumption that within-field lessons should be prepared unaided led to difficulties selecting appropriate SMK/CK and instructional strategies. Thus, in a PST, a transforming 'mechanism' seemed more likely than an 'integration' process. My thinking was that if we could describe experienced teachers' PCK and find out how this develops, then this could be taught explicitly to PSTs. A difficulty was that no precise mechanism had been found. More perplexing was that experienced teachers, such as those investigated by Marks, do not seem to transform subject matter in deciding how to teach. I reasoned that Gess-Newsome's continuum perhaps represented contrasting positions between novice (pre-service) teachers who transform their (often recently acquired) subject knowledge expertise, and experienced teachers for whom academic subject knowledge is dominated by curriculum and assessment requirements. Arzi and White (2008) found curriculum knowledge becomes a main driver for teacher activity over time, while up-to-date subject knowledge atrophies. I struggled to reconcile these positions. I revisited my data post-Summit, finding content knowledge embedded in PSTs' PCK statements (Kind, 2014). This diminished my need to find a transforming mechanism and led me to acknowledge that the distinction between transformative and integrative PCK models was irrelevant.

Models based on alternative theoretical perspectives

This section discusses two alternative theoretical perspectives: Rollnick and Mavhunga, and Schneider, who take different stances on PCK to those discussed above.

Rollnick and Mavhunga: Topic-specific PCK

Rollnick and Mavhunga argue PCK is topic-specific (Table 13.1). Their PCK views are grounded in four knowledge domains suggested by Cochran et al. (1993). These are: student context, student knowledge, subject matter knowledge, and pedagogical knowledge. Rollnick and Mavhunga note the SMK–PCK link is crucial, as this acts as the "pathway" to transform any given topic. Perhaps this represents a mechanism noted above. Before examining this possibility, however, the background to this PCK proposal is discussed in more detail.

Cochran et al. (1993) adopt a strongly psychological perspective on PCK. Their stance is rooted in critique that the term 'knowledge' in PCK is "too static and inconsistent" (p. 266). They adopt "knowing" (which they abbreviate to 'Kg,' hence 'PCKg') as a dynamic word capturing their perceptions that teachers construct PCK on the basis of understanding students' needs. Cochran et al. describe themselves as "radical constructivists," arguing that teachers would devise instructional strategies actively, in response to understanding their students: "Increasingly strong PCKg enables teachers to use their understandings to create teaching strategies for teaching specific content in a discipline in a way that enables specific students to construct useful understandings in a given context" (p. 266).

These authors suggest that a teacher's PCK, or "PCKg," develops with time as he/she becomes increasingly aware of students' needs. Rather than being separate, SMK lies within PCK, as this knowledge is used to help decide how best to handle students in a class. The authors include "Student characteristics" in PCK, defining these as "a teacher's understanding of abilities, learning strategies, ages, development, motivation and prior conceptions of the subject" (p. 266). This corresponds to and expands Shulman's "learning difficulties." Notably, differently from Shulman or Magnusson-et-al-based models, Cochran et al. (1993) place knowledge of instructional strategies outside PCK, as Shulman implies these are 'pre-learned' techniques. This helps address criticism raised earlier in the chapter that canonical instructional strategies equate to a technical approach to teaching devoid of genuine professionalism.

Thus, Cochran et al. (1993) propose that a teacher's PCKg combines SMK, pedagogical knowledge, and awareness of the environment in which they work. They argue a teacher's environment is influenced by political, social, cultural, and physical factors, any or all of which may impact PCK. Their definition emphasizes general pedagogy, rather than subject-specific representations and strategies. The authors stress that "integration of the four components comprises PCKg" (p. 268), and that teacher education should promote its acquisition by offering simultaneous experience of the four components. This is achieved through provision of classroom-based teaching practice. Picking up Bromme's (1995) point that PCK lacks a theoretical background, Cochran et al. (1993) offer one, as their proposal is based on constructivism. This may resonate with current science teachers, drilled in constructivist principles applied to students' conceptual learning. Anderson and Smith (1987) note that teachers focused on achieving conceptual change from non-scientific to scientific understanding are high performing, as they practice awareness of student knowledge, and design and develop practices that promote learning. Applying Cochran et al.'s (1993) model would lead to teacher education encouraging PSTs to construct personal knowledge about 'how to teach,' avoiding the integration/transformation debate discussed above.

Rollnick and Mavhunga call their model of PCK "Topic-specific," or TSPCK. They diverge slightly from Cochran et al.'s original proposals, placing less explicit emphasis on a teacher's environment and relatively more on the SMK–PCK link. A feature unique to Rollnick and Mavhunga's model is interpretation of curriculum knowledge as "curricular saliency," a term originating in Geddis, Onslow, Beynon, and Oesch (1993). This reflects understanding a teacher has of the place and value of a topic within the curriculum, which influences how and how long to spend teaching it.

Schneider: PCK connects with learning progressions

Schneider connects PCK to learning progressions. This leads to a learning trajectory that describes PCK development. Using Magnusson et al.'s (1999) PCK components, Schneider identified the qualities of a "well-started beginner." Such a teacher is characterized by thinking about science in relation to phenomena (content knowledge); ideas that challenge students (curriculum knowledge); creating inquiry-learning environments that include opportunities for data collection (instructional strategy); and talking with students to understand initial ideas and prior experiences to help them make connections between science topics (knowledge of students' learning difficulties). Schneider claims progress toward describing learning trajectories that illuminate stages in a pre-service teacher's development.

This model shares similarities with Veal and MaKinster's (1999) proposals. These authors suggest PCK is based on a hierarchical structure or taxonomy. This proposal hints at progression toward higher levels. For example, the taxonomy "attempts to represent a hierarchical process by which prospective secondary science teachers obtain different knowledge bases contributing to their PCK development" (p. 6).

Four levels of knowledge are presented, "General" PCK is lowest. This includes understanding pedagogical concepts applicable to a wide range of subjects. This aligns with Schneider's "well-started beginner." Above this lie subject-specific PCK strategies (broadly equivalent to Magnusson et al.'s (1999) "orientations" and Grossman's (1990) "purposes"). The two higher levels introduce "domain-" and "topic-specific" PCK. The authors define "domain-specific" as a teacher's understanding about how to teach a specific area within a subject. For example, a teacher may choose a titration experiment when teaching about moles, volume, and concentration in chemistry. "Topic-specific" PCK is Veal and MaKinster's highest PCK level. They argue that distinctions between science teachers with different SMK backgrounds play out at this level. For example, a science teacher with a physics background may explain chemical concepts differently from a chemist. Veal and MaKinster propose a teacher's SMK arises from intellectual training, is specific to their specialist topic or field, and is integrated into their PCK.

The hierarchy is proposed from theoretical, not empirical perspectives. In contrast to Schneider's inductive process, Veal and MaKinster (1999) do not claim teachers learn PCK in this organized, taxonomic fashion. The description is nonetheless helpful, as PCK components for science teaching may have a hierarchical dimension. For example, teachers with strong SMK in biology and physics may have similar lowest level general PCK and may acquire similar domain-specific PCK. Their different science backgrounds may mean that acquiring similar topic-specific PCK is more difficult, relying on intensive input to overcome missing knowledge about scientific ideas (Kind, 2009a). Kirschner, Borowski, and Fischer found strong correlations between PCK and CK quality. Although stopping short of a hierarchy or taxonomic presentation, there are suggestions here that developing CK and PCK may impact each other positively, moving teachers toward higher level practices.

Pinning down PCK's elusive qualities

Inevitably for a varied field, the Summit featured a range of PCK interpretations. Through discussion, consensus began to emerge. Figure 13.2 represents the consensus model, achieved by comparing and sharing through active discussion the many viewpoints discussed above.

The consensus model resembles a complex version of all the models discussed above combined together. Nothing is omitted. Student outcomes are added to acknowledge PCK as an active, rather than static knowledge that influences and impacts beyond its internal components. The consensus model places science teaching orientations and beliefs in a specific 'amplifier' or 'filter' role that mediates teachers' actions and choices. Similarly, student behaviors, beliefs, and prior knowledge amplify or filter the impact of teachers' PCK on learning outcomes.

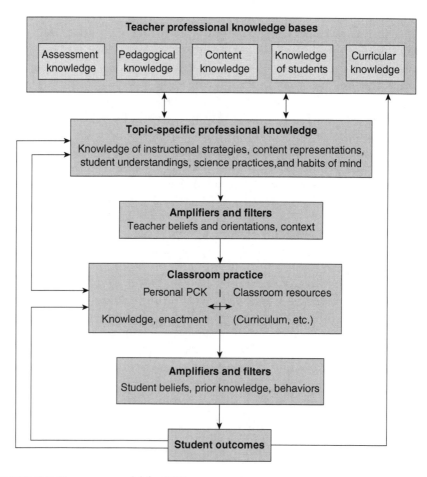

FIGURE 13.2 Consensus model for PCK

The notion of transformative or integrative PCK is dropped in favor of a broad range of possible components that interact. Topic specificity is introduced, adding a smaller grain size to provide focus.

The consensus model addresses some weaknesses of Shulman's original (1987) proposals. The move to topic-specific professional knowledge reduces the dominance of generalized canonical PCK, implying that teachers' instructional strategy choices within a given contextual environment are theirs to make as professionals, rather than learned from a technical exercise. Broadening the component range makes PCK an embracing, holistic statement of teachers' professional practices. At the Summit, Berry, Cooper, and Loughran acknowledged this position; they did not advocate for PCK components beyond "curricular" and "instructional" decision-making, aiming to capture a complete picture of teachers' practices.

However, despite its attractions, critique leveled at Shulman's proposals applies. The consensus model lacks theoretical basis. Design by a committee does not give theoretical credence to satisfy external critics. The model is complex, with connecting arrows and component layers. Nothing indicates what these arrows are or mean. Thus, mechanisms connecting the model's components remain undescribed, vague, and thus open to debate. Finally, although all Summit participants were empirical researchers, there is no evidence this model genuinely represents teachers' PCK.

A final viewpoint to mention is Hill's: That in fact, only a teacher's subject matter knowledge and knowledge of students' learning difficulties are essential for teaching practice. Her model, of mathematical knowledge for teaching, is advantageous, as by generating a narrow construct, more reliable methods for testing and development can be designed, which may yield evidence that simplifies and focuses the teacher education process.

I regarded participation in the PCK Summit as a privileged opportunity to reflect deeply on a topic that I had come to know, after a fashion, and believe in as a research agenda. What I thought I knew about PCK was challenged. Post-Summit, I have become much more skeptical and critical of PCK models, but also see the need to agree in order to progress the field. The consensus model offers a way forward, as an all-encompassing structure that permits any researcher to work effectively under its protection. However, testing this is the next challenge. The elusive qualities of PCK are not quite tamed yet.

Acknowledgement

Figure 13.1: "Figure 2: Components of pedagogical content knowledge for science teaching" (p. 99) is reprinted with kind permission from Springer Science and Business Media. Originally published in Magnusson, S., Krajcik, J., & Borko, H. (1999), "Nature, sources, and development of pedagogical content knowledge for science teaching," in J. Gess-Newsome & N. G. Lederman (Eds.), *Examining pedagogical content knowledge: The construct and its implications for science education* (pp. 95–132). Dordrecht: Kluwer.

References

Abd El-Khalick, F. (2006) Pre-service and experienced biology teachers' global and specific subject matter structures: Implications for conceptions of pedagogical content knowledge. *Eurasia Journal of Mathematics, Science and Technology Education, 2*(1), 1–29. Retrieved from http://www.ejmste.com/012006/d1.pdf (accessed November 28, 2014).

Anderson, C. W., & Smith, E. L. (1987). Teaching science. In V. Richardson-Koehler (Ed.), *Educators' handbook: A research perspective* (pp. 84–111). London: Longman.

Arzi, H. J., & White, R. T. (2008). Changes in teachers' knowledge of subject matter: Results of a longitudinal study. *Science Education, 92*(2), 221–251.

Australian Institute for Teaching and School Leadership (2014). *Australian Professional Standards for Teachers*. Retrieved from http://www.ceo.aitsl.edu.au/blog/professional-standards-0 (accessed July 15, 2014).

Banks, F., Leach, J., & Moon, B. (2005). Extract from—New understandings of teachers' pedagogic knowledge. *The Curriculum Journal, 16*(3), 331–340.

Black, P., Harrison, C., Lee, C., Marshall, B., & Wiliam, D. (2003). *Assessment for learning: Putting it into practice*. Buckingham, UK: Open University Press.

Bromme, R. (1995). What exactly is pedagogical content knowledge? Critical remarks regarding a fruitful research programme. *Didaktik and/or curriculum. IPN Schriftenreihe, 147*, 205–216.

Cochran, K. F., DeRuiter, J. A., & King, R. A. (1993). Pedagogical content knowledge: An integrative model for teacher preparation. *Journal of Teacher Education, 44*(4), 263–271.

Darling-Hammond, L., & Bransford, J. (2007). *Preparing teachers for a changing world: What teachers should learn and be able to do*. New York, NY: Wiley.

Department for Education (2011). *Teachers' standards*. London: The Stationery Office. Retrieved from https://www.gov.uk/government/uploads/system/uploads/attachment_data/file/301107/Teachers__Standards.pdf (accessed July 15, 2014).

Fernandez-Balboa, J.-M., & Stiehl, J. (1995).The generic nature of pedagogical content knowledge among college professors. *Teaching and Teacher Education, 11*(3), 293–306.

Geddis, A. N., Onslow, B., Beynon, C., & Oesch, J. (1993). Transforming content knowledge: Learning to teach about isotopes. *Science Education, 77*(6), 575–591.

Gess-Newsome, J. (1999). Pedagogical content knowledge: An introduction and orientation. In J. Gess-Newsome & N. G. Lederman (Eds.), *Examining pedagogical content knowledge*, (pp. 3–17). Dordrecht, the Netherlands: Kluwer Academic Publishers.

Grossman, P. L. (1990). *The making of a teacher: Teacher knowledge and teacher education*. New York, NY: Teachers College Press.

Hattie, J. (2012). *Visible learning for teachers*. London: Sage Publications.

Hay McBer, (2000). *Research into teacher effectiveness: A model of teacher effectiveness*. (Research Department for Education and Employment Report No. 216). Norwich, UK: Her Majesty's Stationery Office.

Kidwell, K. (2013). *Characteristics of highly effective teaching and learning*. Retrieved from http://education.ky.gov/curriculum/docs/pages/characteristics-of-highly-effective-teaching-and-learning-(chetl).aspx (accessed July 15, 2014).

Kind, V. (2009a). A conflict in your head: An exploration of trainee science teachers' subject matter knowledge development and its impact on teacher self-confidence. *International Journal of Science Education, 31*, 1529–1562.

Kind, V. (2009b). Pedagogical content knowledge in science education: Perspectives and potential for progress. *Studies in Science Education, 45*(2), 169–204.

Kind, V. (2014). Pre-service science teachers' science teaching orientations and beliefs about science. Accepted for publication in *Science Education*.

Ko, J., Sammons, P., & Bakkum, L. (2013). *Effective teaching: A review of research and evidence*. Reading, UK: CfBT Education Trust.

Koballa, T. R., Gräber, W., Coleman, D., & Kemp, A. C. (1999). Prospective teachers' conceptions of the knowledge base for teaching chemistry at the gymnasium. *Journal of Science Teacher Education, 10*(4), 269–286.

Magnusson, S., Krajcik, J., & Borko, H. (1999). Nature, sources, and development of pedagogical content knowledge for science teaching. In J. Gess-Newsome & N. G. Lederman (Eds.), *Examining pedagogical content knowledge: The construct and its implications for science education* (pp. 95–132). Dordrecht, the Netherlands: Kluwer Academic Publishers.

Marks, R. (1990). Pedagogical content knowledge: From a mathematical case to a modified conception. *Journal of Teacher Education, 41*(3), 3–11.

National Research Council (2011). *A framework for K-12 science education – practices, crosscutting concepts, and core ideas*. Washington, DC: National Research Council.

Park, S., & Oliver, J. S. (2008). Revisiting the conceptualisation of pedagogical content knowledge (PCK): PCK as a conceptual tool to understand teachers as professionals. *Research in Science Education, 38*(3), 261–284.

Rutter, M., Maughan, B., Mortimore, P., & Ouston, J. (1979). *Fifteen thousand hours: Secondary schools and their effects on children*. London: Open Books Publishing Limited.

Shulman, L. S. (1986). Those who understand: Knowledge growth in teaching. *Educational Researcher, 15*(2), 4–14.

Shulman, L. S. (1987). Knowledge and teaching: Foundations of the new reform. *Harvard Educational Review, 57*(1), 1–22.

Tamir, P. (1983). Inquiry and the science teacher. *Science Education, 67*(5), 657–672.

Turner-Bisset, R. (2001). *Expert teaching: Knowledge and pedagogy to lead the profession*. London: David Fulton.

Veal, W. R., & MaKinster, J.G. (1999). Pedagogical content knowledge taxonomies. *Electronic Journal of Science Education*. Retrieved from http://unr.edu/homepage/crowther/ejse/vealmak.html (accessed July 15, 2014).

PART III

Pedagogical content knowledge
Emerging themes

14
EXAMINING PCK RESEARCH IN THE CONTEXT OF CURRENT POLICY INITIATIVES

Aaron J. Sickel
UNIVERSITY OF WESTERN SYDNEY

Eric R. Banilower*
HORIZON RESEARCH, INC.

Janet Carlson*
STANFORD UNIVERSITY

Jan H. Van Driel*
LEIDEN UNIVERSITY

Teacher education goals, standards, and policies were once considered to be mostly under the purview of university programs. However, with the advent of international tests, articulation of standards both for student achievement and teacher performance, and calls for more accountability, education policy is increasingly established by a wide range of stakeholders that extend beyond the traditional education community. These stakeholders are asking many questions related to who is qualified to teach a particular subject area; what types of knowledge, skills, and supports are needed for teachers to be highly effective; and what are the most appropriate ways to assess teacher quality? Despite these questions, recent research on teacher learning has not focused strongly on current policy issues (Sleeter, 2014).

It has long been proposed that pedagogical content knowledge (PCK) represents the professional knowledge base for teaching subject matter (Shulman, 1987). The construct has helped science education researchers understand how knowledge for teaching science is different than knowledge of science or knowledge for teaching other disciplines, and has helped frame the curriculum of teacher education programs. To date, much of the research has focused on different methods for documenting teachers' PCK and various approaches to developing it, but little effort has been devoted to considering the implications of this research in the context of current policy initiatives that are affecting education systems.

The 2012 PCK Summit challenged participants to not only consider their current work, but also discuss emerging issues for future PCK research. Due to a collective interest in the policy contexts that frame our work in research and teacher education, the authors of this chapter volunteered to participate in a dedicated forum on exploring how PCK research connects to policy. This chapter represents the outcome of those initial discussions and subsequent examination of policy issues and recent PCK research.

The purpose of this chapter is to explore connections between PCK research and policy areas related to science teacher development. To accomplish this, it is necessary to explain our view of PCK. We ascribe to Loughran, Berry, and Mulhall's (2012) definition of PCK as "the knowledge that teachers develop over time, and through experience, about how to teach particular content in particular ways in order to lead to enhanced student understanding" (p. 9). In the following sections, we consider four major policy areas: (1) pre-service teacher education; (2) curriculum reform; (3) professional development; and (4) teacher evaluation. For each area, we define examples of current policy issues, discuss policy implications based on recent research, and posit future research questions.

Science teacher education

Policy trends in science teacher education

Many countries are currently facing a shortage of qualified science teachers, which leads policymakers to wonder what the attributes of successful teacher candidates are and how they can be prepared. Most programs for science teacher preparation around the world (see Abell, 2000) recognize the importance of subject matter knowledge, general pedagogical knowledge, and PCK in preparing high-quality science teachers. Most programs also value the authority of learning from experience (Russell & Martin, 2007), and thus include substantial internships offering pre-service teachers opportunities to practice science teaching in authentic classrooms. However, programs around the world vary widely in terms of the relative emphasis placed on these common components, on program length, on academic level, and on organization. In some countries, for example, science teacher education takes place in a two-year program in higher education colleges, in some countries it consists of a four-year university program, whereas in others, it is offered as a one-year postgraduate course.

From the perspective of developing PCK, it is particularly interesting to look at how programs incorporate 'methods courses' in relation to science content courses on the one hand, and to field experiences on the other hand. Looking at the organization of programs, various formats can be distinguished:

- Some programs organize the learning of science content, and learning to teach science in a parallel mode, whereas in other programs (i.e., postgraduate courses) subject matter courses are completed prior to entering the teacher education program (e.g., bachelor's degree in a science content area).
- Most programs incorporate school-based experiences parallel with institution-based methods courses, aiming to situate pre-service teachers' experiences with teaching science in classrooms, with opportunities to learn from research on teaching science, teacher educators' expertise, and the experiences of other pre-service teachers. However, in some countries, pre-service teachers take institution-based methods courses for a semester or more, before they actually go into classrooms.
- Methods courses are sometimes organized at the level of the disciplines (e.g., chemistry, physics), but in some programs at the level of general science. The latter could make it difficult to help pre-service teachers develop topic-specific PCK when compared to a discipline-specific format.

Existing PCK research relevant to policy issues in teacher education

Research on PCK has demonstrated some of the benefits or problems with each of the abovementioned formats. It has been found that programs are most successful when they purposefully facilitate the simultaneous development of pre-service teachers' subject matter knowledge and PCK. For instance, Nelson and Davis (2012) incorporated a unit on student-generated scientific models in a methods course. The program was successful in developing pre-service teachers' ability to evaluate these models by increasing their understanding of the science represented in the models, as well as their knowledge of scientific models and modeling. At the same time, pre-service teachers learned to adopt criterion-based approaches to evaluating students' scientific models. The latter was seen as indicative of their emerging PCK about scientific models and modeling. Similarly, Nilsson and Van Driel (2011) promoted elementary pre-service teachers' subject matter knowledge, PCK, and interest in teaching physics, through a design where pre-service teachers performed and discussed school experiments in small groups, discussed video-recordings of these sessions with a physics teacher and a teacher educator, and concluded with a session during which the physics teacher addressed questions about the physics content underlying the experiments.

Studies on postgraduate programs typically report how pre-service teachers develop PCK on the basis of their subject matter knowledge. A vital aspect of such programs is making pre-service teachers aware that their own subject matter knowledge is much more sophisticated than that of their students, and that science concepts or procedures that are evident to them may be highly problematic for their students (De Jong, Van Driel, & Verloop, 2005). In this context, it is crucial that pre-service teachers are confronted with students' authentic reasoning about science, analyze students' reasoning, and reflect on it in relation to their classroom teaching experiences. To achieve this, pre-service teachers may collect student data through action-research (Justi & Van Driel, 2005). When a program successfully increases pre-service teachers' awareness of student learning of science, their PCK may develop in terms of integrating their science teaching orientations, and their knowledge of science learners and of instructional strategies (Brown, Friedrichsen, & Abell, 2013).

Future research

Two areas in science teacher education can be identified where research on PCK is needed. First, PCK research related to selecting science teacher candidates is lacking. Because the development of PCK requires teaching experience (e.g., Grossman, 1990), it is unlikely that science teacher candidates have developed much PCK before they enter a teacher preparation program. Therefore, it does not seem reasonable to include assessments of science teacher candidates' PCK as part of a procedure aimed to assess their capability to become high-quality science teachers. However, a crucial aspect of PCK is teachers' orientation toward students' learning of science, and their ability to adapt their instruction to the needs of individual students (Van Driel & Berry, 2010). In other words, sensitivity to student learning, flexibility or adaptivity to specific situations or contexts, and reflectivity, may be considered as precursors to the development of PCK. Existing procedures for highly selective teacher education programs often include an assessment of these generic characteristics—for instance, candidates' interpersonal and communications skills, and willingness to learn (Barber & Mourshed, 2007). Accreditation organizations, such as the Council for Accreditation of Educator Preparation (CAEP) in the US, require programs to provide evidence that candidates develop professional dispositions related to habits and moral commitments of teaching (CAEP, 2013). Future research could focus on the predictive value of disposition assessments with respect to PCK development.

Second, because PCK is included in accreditation procedures as a knowledge base that teachers need to develop, it would seem logical that teacher candidates' PCK be assessed at the end of pre-service teacher education. However, there are few examples of assessments that include PCK, compared to tests of content knowledge and general pedagogy. Research and development is needed on the implementation of such instruments and procedures as part of the examination at the exit point of teacher education.

Curriculum reform

Policy trends in curriculum reform

For a variety of reasons, including the analysis of international assessment data and attempts to increase global economic competitiveness, many nations are engaging in curriculum reform. We see these reform efforts as both updated curricular goals and revised or new curriculum materials. The Next Generation Science Standards (NGSS) in the US serve as one significant example of curricular goals designed to articulate what is to be taught and learned about science at certain points from kindergarten through 12th grade.

Curriculum materials provide support to teachers about how to teach to particular curricular goals. This support can include the structure and flow for specific content, recommended instructional strategies, and suggested experiences for the learners. We see curriculum materials, which greatly influence the content and pedagogy of science instruction (Weiss, Pasley, Smith, Banilower, & Heck, 2003), as an area in which PCK research has significant policy implications.

The nature of materials that support the development of PCK

When considering curriculum reform, we take the stance that 'educative curriculum materials' are a primary point of focus if materials are to play a role in improving PCK (Carlson, Davis, & Buxton, 2014). Educative curriculum materials are those designed to support teachers in developing a stronger knowledge base and more effective instructional practices (Schneider & Krajcik, 2002). Not all curriculum materials are educative and those that include educative features vary greatly in the degree to which they illustrate those features (Beyer, Delgado, Davis, & Krajcik, 2009).

Among the highly educative curriculum materials, there are a number of features that work to support the development of teachers' PCK (Carlson, Gess-Newsome, & Schneider, 2014). For example, highly educative curriculum materials that support PCK development will provide explicit text and diagrams to help teachers understand and recognize how the science ideas within a unit and across the year are connected so that they can help students explicitly link the ideas from individual lessons together. Another feature that supports PCK development is the prevalence of examples that provide the teacher with ideas for increasing the relevancy of the lesson for students. A less common but powerful support for developing PCK is the strategic use of exemplary student work. When curriculum materials include examples of actual student work from contexts that teachers relate to, it can help establish high expectations for all learners because teachers have real-life examples of how to push student thinking as it plays out in actual assignments.

In addition, educative curriculum materials also attend to the research on how students learn specific ideas, including common challenges. In attending to this research, the materials not only describe a variety of instructional strategies, but also support the teacher in learning and using those strategies. For example, the materials may provide teachers with prompts for initial questions as well as probes for follow-up questions that help unpack students' prior conceptions. Below, we describe some specific ways that curriculum materials can support the development of PCK as it relates to science content and student thinking.

Science content

Many teachers are underprepared to teach the science classes they are assigned (Banilower, Smith, Weiss, Malzahn, Campbell, & Weis, 2013). They may not have a degree in the content area and they often have not developed a deep understanding of the discipline. This lack of content knowledge impedes teachers' development of PCK and their ability to help students learn science. As curriculum reforms are implemented, we recommend that materials be developed that:

- describe the big ideas in a given content area and the relationships among those ideas;
- clearly establish how the subordinate or supporting ideas relate to those big ideas;
- present multiple representations for the teaching of a concept;
- recognize the prerequisite knowledge teachers need to teach a concept and include resources for the teachers to learn or review that knowledge. These resources can include background information in the form of text, videos, or graphics in print or online;
- articulate what students are to learn about key science ideas if they successfully complete the lessons;
- describe why it is important for students to understand these ideas to help teachers develop rationales for themselves as well as their students about why they are doing the lessons.

Student thinking

It is common in the US and many other countries that little instructional time is devoted to giving students time to make sense of the ideas they have encountered in their science activities and readings (Forbes, Biggers, & Zangori, 2013; Weiss et al., 2003). At the elementary level, this may be due to lack of instructional time in general that is set aside for science (Banilower et al., 2013), the limitations of teachers' content knowledge, or a general belief that students are not able to engage in sophisticated thinking. At the secondary level, the lack of time spent on sense-making is often rationalized as necessary so that more content can be 'covered.' In addition, when students complete lab activities, too often they are doing verification labs that are designed to reproduce known results, rather than asking questions of interest or puzzling with results and making sense of data.

When instructors and materials do not focus on sense-making, students' science experiences can be reduced to a vocabulary-driven approach to instruction or a series of fun activities that do not necessarily facilitate meaningful learning. Teachers who want to ensure that their students make sense of science ideas will need well-developed PCK for the range of science concepts they teach. To support the development of PCK, curriculum materials can:

- include explicit sense-making strategies embedded in the lessons that are varied appropriately to fit the nature of the lesson and give the students a range of opportunities;
- articulate the typical difficulties associated with learning a particular concept and include instructional strategies that explicitly address the difficulties;
- support teachers in using knowledge about students' thinking and context to influence instructional decisions;
- provide assistance to teachers so they can draw upon a repertoire of ways to ascertain students' understanding or confusion.

When developed to intentionally support teachers' PCK, curriculum materials can serve as an effective tool for supporting more consistent and coherent science instruction, supporting teachers in developing important conceptual knowledge of science, and framing science learning as a sense-making activity.

Future research

The research evidence indicating that educative materials have a role in developing and supporting teachers' PCK coupled with the relationship between teachers' PCK and their students' learning provide a foundation for considering policy implications that support the development and implementation of research-based curriculum materials. To do this well, we should consider conducting additional research that examines the link between PCK and student learning. Future research questions that can inform policy from this perspective include the following:

- How do teachers adapt their personal professional knowledge with updated curriculum materials to enhance their students' learning?
- In what ways can governing bodies advocating curriculum reform support teachers' development of PCK for teaching new curriculum?
- In what ways can current findings about PCK guide the development of educative curriculum materials for teachers? And conversely, how do educative materials actually promote the development of PCK?

Professional development

Policy trends in professional development

In-service growth opportunities are an important part of teachers' ongoing development, and a great deal of money is invested in professional development for teachers of science each year. Often, professional development is associated with the adoption of new standards, new curriculum materials, or the latest innovation (e.g., scientific inquiry, notebooking). More recently, professional learning communities (PLCs) have become common (Banilower et al., 2013) in attempts to foster ongoing, classroom-focused professional growth. Regardless of the exact purpose or format, most professional development is based on the assumption that it will lead to increased teacher knowledge and skills, which in turn will lead to improved student outcomes.

However, the recent economic crisis has led to a decrease in funding for education in many nations, including support for professional development programs. These tighter budgets have led to greater calls for evaluating the effectiveness of professional development initiatives. However, few programs have been able to generate strong evidence of their effectiveness; in fact, there are a number of voices describing the professional development system as broken and ineffective, and programs that do have evidence of effectiveness are deemed not scalable (e.g., Hill, 2009).

Existing PCK research relevant to policy issues in professional development

Much has been learned in the last several years about effective science instruction, including the importance of paying attention to student thinking throughout instruction, providing opportunities to delve deeply into substantive scientific ideas, and metacognition (Donovan & Bransford, 2005). It is also widely accepted that learning how to provide effective science instruction requires teachers to develop PCK. Because developing PCK among teachers requires a great deal of time and resources beyond what is currently possible in most pre-service preparation programs, professional development aimed at the (further) development of teachers' PCK is required. Even developing the requisite knowledge bases for PCK is a daunting task, particularly at the elementary level where teachers typically are generalists required to teach multiple subject areas. Consequently, it should come as no surprise that many do not feel well prepared to teach science (Banilower et al., 2013). Although secondary teachers tend to have more preparation in science, it cannot be assumed that they have deep knowledge of all the content they teach as many teach courses in multiple science disciplines.

There is an emerging consensus about the structures of professional development that can facilitate the development of PCK among teachers (e.g., Loucks-Horsley, Love, Stiles, Mundry, & Hewson, 2003; Wilson, 2013). The substantial professional knowledge that science teachers need to teach effectively points to the critical importance of moving away from one-and-done professional development experiences to creating a culture of in-depth, coherent, ongoing, and job-embedded professional learning. As time for professional development is typically limited, it is important that professional learning experiences for teachers are efficient and relevant, taking into account what is known from research.

For example, professional development should both model and incorporate explicit discussion of high-quality teaching, as well as the implications for transfer to the classroom. In addition, professional development programs must recognize that all teachers have different learning needs based on their backgrounds and where they are in their career trajectories. Consequently, professional learning experiences should provide opportunities for frequent classroom feedback and support structures to shape and refine instructional practice.

In many ways, effective professional development is similar to effective science teaching. It must have clear goals in mind, start from the needs of the learners, and be carefully designed using what is known from research and wisdom of practice about the teaching and learning of the content. One can extend the model of PCK to professional development, where the content is knowledge of effective teaching and learning, the pedagogy is knowledge of effective professional development practices, and the students are teachers. This extended model implies that effective professional development providers have 'PD–PCK' that includes, but goes well beyond, PCK for the particular science content (Landes & Roth, 2013).

Developing PCK among teachers at scale faces a number of challenges. One is the scope of the education system. For example, there are over one million teachers of science in grades K-12 in the US. Although there have been successful efforts to develop teachers' PCK (e.g., Daehler & Shinohara, 2001; Gess-Newsome, Taylor, Carlson, Gardner, Stuhlsatz, & Wilson, 2011), they have tended to focus on relatively small numbers of teachers. In addition, these efforts have tended to require intensive involvement of master teachers and other experts in science education. Even if it were decided to devote resources to programs aimed at developing teachers' PCK at scale, the number of professional development providers with PD–PCK would be a constraint.

Consequently, although professional development has an important role in developing teachers PCK, it is unlikely, by itself, to be sufficient for creating a large teaching force with deep PCK. Rather, other changes to the education system will likely be necessary. These changes might include modifications to pre-service programs (e.g., increasing the science course requirements for prospective elementary teachers), school organization (e.g., moving to a specialist model at the elementary level), and instructional materials (e.g., the development and adoption of educative curriculum materials).

Future research

Despite the growing body of knowledge about developing teachers' PCK, there are a number of areas in which further research is needed. One is expanding the knowledge base of PCK to more topics, including common conceptions students have and effective strategies for fostering learning. Doing so would allow for the development and testing of PCK-based professional development programs in more topic areas. Another research area is exploring cost-effective and efficient models for going to scale with high-quality professional development. For example, professional learning communities (PLC) have become very common—over half of the schools in the US, employing approximately three-quarters of the nation's science teachers, have PLCs that meet on a regular basis (Banilower et al., 2013). Given their pervasiveness, research is needed to identify the critical elements of successful PLCs, their relationship to developing PCK, and how these elements can be replicated in other schools.

Finally, teachers' classroom practice, and ultimately student learning, is affected by many factors including students' prior experiences, teachers' knowledge and beliefs, and high-stakes assessment systems. Consequently, it will be important for researchers and policymakers to remember that direct links between teachers' PCK and these outcomes may be difficult to detect. This challenge highlights the need to identify the factors inhibiting the impact of professional development on deepening teachers' PCK. Doing so will allow policymakers to consider options for changing the education system in ways that increase the value given to PCK.

Teacher evaluation

Policy trends in teacher evaluation

The accountability movement in education has led to a focus on teacher quality and new policies on in-service teacher evaluation. Marzano (2012) argues that stakeholders discuss teacher evaluation policies with two overarching purposes. The first purpose is to assess teacher effectiveness to ensure that students have access to a high-quality teacher; and the second purpose is to provide opportunities to help teachers develop and improve. In addition, there are two primary components typically used to evaluate teachers. The first component has focused on student learning measures, which typically include students' scores on a state or federal test to inform teachers' ratings (Collins & Amrein-Beardsley, 2014) The second component consists of an evaluation of teacher performance, often assessed by a school administrator, and based on classroom observations and teaching artifacts (Danielson, 2010). Below, we discuss how current PCK research could inform both components, from the perspective of each purpose of teacher evaluation.

Exploring connections between PCK research and teacher evaluation

Many stakeholders are interested in using evidence of student learning to inform teacher evaluation. It has been conjectured that science teachers with well-developed PCK have great potential to facilitate meaningful learning by their students. Recent research supports this claim. For example, a study by Sadler, Sonnert, Coyle, Cook-Smith, and Miller (2013) examined tests administered to middle school students to investigate teachers' ability to examine the misconceptions related to test items. They found that teachers who could predict popular wrong answers showed statistically significant gains in their students' test scores, suggesting that teachers' PCK related to knowledge of students' understandings is associated with student learning. Kanter and Konstantopoulos (2010) investigated the impact of teachers' content knowledge and PCK on student learning in conjunction with a project-based curriculum in biology, and reported that teachers' improved PCK was a significant predictor of improved student learning. Thus, the argument to incorporate student-learning measures in teacher evaluation policies for the purpose of assessing science teacher effectiveness is supported by recent PCK research. However, it should be noted that a multitude of variables influence student learning, many of which are outside the teacher's control (e.g., socioeconomic background, home environment; Darling-Hammond, Amrein-Beardsley, Haertel, & Rothstein, 2012). Caution should be exercised with regard to assigning too much weight to student-learning measures in a teacher's annual evaluation.

In contrast to the first purpose of teacher evaluation, it has not been clear how student-learning measures can be used for the second purpose of teacher evaluation—providing meaningful feedback for teacher improvement. Collins and Amrein-Beardsley's (2014) review of teacher evaluation in the US noted that no state's current system articulated a plan for formative use of student-learning measures by teachers. Yet, PCK research has demonstrated that teachers can improve their knowledge by reflecting on student-learning data (Nilsson, 2014). We therefore recommend that teacher evaluation systems afford teachers access to more fine-grained data from student-learning measures to provide meaningful feedback regarding students' difficulties with particular science topics. In conjunction with this recommendation, attention must also be given to the nature and quality of the assessment itself, as many standardized tests do not provide meaningful data for formative assessment purposes.

In addition to student-learning measures, teacher evaluation policies also typically include assessments of teaching performance. Thus, from a PCK perspective, including assessments of knowledge related to teaching practice is warranted. This component is often assessed through the use of rubrics, which establish standards related to planning, instruction, and the classroom environment, as well as levels of performance across the standards (Danielson, 2010). One challenge with assessments of teacher performance is a lack of articulation regarding tools and processes that teachers can use to help them work toward high levels of performance in specific subject areas. A fruitful avenue of PCK research in science education is the use of content representations (CoRes) and professional and pedagogical experience repertoires (PaP-eRs) (Loughran, Mulhall, & Berry, 2004). While CoRes help science teachers reveal particular aspects of PCK, PaP-eRs provide representations of teaching science topics in the classroom. Several components of CoRes and PaP-eRs align with general teacher evaluation rubrics—for example, attention to specific content and using particular instructional strategies (Danielson, 2010). These instruments also focus on science teachers' knowledge of student thinking, which is an important predictor of student learning (Sadler et al., 2013). Thus, we see potential for incorporating CoRes and PaP-eRs or other related instruments in evaluation systems.

Regarding the purpose focused on teacher development, studies have documented that science teachers find CoRes and PaP-eRs to be helpful with articulating and improving their knowledge (e.g., Bertram & Loughran, 2012). However, these tools have not been used to assess teacher quality, as this was not their original purpose. Researchers could explore this possibility, noting several considerations. First, instruments such as CoRes and PaP-eRs take a significant amount of time for teachers to construct (Bertram & Loughran, 2012), and therefore research is required to determine the extent to which condensed versions or just a few exemplars can be used as indications of in-depth explications of PCK. Second, valid and reliable rubrics need to be developed to assess teachers' PCK as explicated by these instruments.

Future research

Recent PCK research supports the use of both student-learning measures and teacher knowledge/practice in teacher evaluation policies. However, student measures have been used primarily to address the purpose of assessing teacher effectiveness, with little attention to teacher improvement. Future research could explore how science teachers' reflection upon student-learning data within teacher evaluation systems provides affordances for improving PCK and enhancing student learning. Regarding assessments of teachers' knowledge and practice, current policies typically use generic criteria and ignore the subject-specific nature of teaching. Instruments that help articulate and develop science teachers' PCK could potentially be included in science teacher evaluation systems. However, whereas these instruments have demonstrated clear alignment with improving teacher learning, more research is needed to explore their potential use for assessing teacher quality. Last, current teacher evaluation systems do not articulate differences in expectations between beginning and experienced teachers. Future research on PCK learning progressions (see Chapter 15, Friedrichsen & Berry this volume) will help inform the level of knowledge and skills that should be expected of teachers at different stages of their careers.

Conclusion

In this chapter, we have considered four major policy areas, explored connections between existing PCK research and current policy initiatives, and posited future research to provide future policy implications. Education policies are informed by different values and political structures within unique contexts, and will evolve over time. Yet, it is clear that education policy will continue to be informed by a wide range of stakeholders. If our aim is for research to have meaningful implications for educational practice, it will become increasingly imperative to communicate the implications of PCK research to policymakers.

We also think it is important to acknowledge inherent tensions that can arise between what policymakers advocate and what teachers need for their own professional growth. Shulman (1987) described PCK as "uniquely the province of teachers" and "their own form of professional understanding" (p. 8). Therefore, policies that are top-down and done *to* teachers rather than *with* teachers are at odds with the notion of teachers as professionals. We advocate that policies should not appropriate PCK, but rather afford structures and supports to facilitate teachers' ongoing PCK development. In turn, more cross-sectional and longitudinal research investigating the development of PCK from pre-service teacher education throughout teachers' careers has great potential to provide meaningful implications for future policy decisions. We encourage PCK researchers to investigate the questions we mentioned above, articulate new questions, and report future implications from PCK research for science education policy.

Acknowledgement

This material is based, in part, upon work supported by the National Science Foundation under Grant No. 0928177. Any opinions, findings, and conclusions or recommendations expressed in this material are those of the authors and do not necessarily reflect the views of the National Science Foundation

Note

*Authors contributed equally to the chapter.

References

Abell, S. (2000). *Science teacher education: An international perspective.* Dordrecht, the Netherlands: Kluwer Academic Publishers.

Banilower, E., Smith, P. S., Weiss, I., Malzahn, K., Campbell, K., & Weis, A. (2013). *Report of the 2012 National Survey of Science and Mathematics Education.* Chapel Hill, NC: Horizon Research, Inc.

Barber, M., & Mourshed, M. (2007). *How the world's best education systems come out on top.* London: McKinsey Education.

Bertram, A., & Loughran, J. (2012). Science teachers' views on CoRes and PaP-eRs as a framework for articulating and developing pedagogical content knowledge. *Research in Science Education, 42*(6), 1027–1047.

Beyer, C. J., Delgado, C., Davis, E. A., & Krajcik, J. (2009). Investigating teacher learning supports in high school biology curricular programs to inform the design of educative curriculum materials. *Journal of Research in Science Teaching, 46,* 977–998. doi:10.1002/tea.20293

Brown, P., Friedrichsen, P., & Abell, S. (2013). The development of prospective secondary biology teachers' PCK. *Journal of Science Teacher Education, 24,* 133–155.

Carlson, J., Davis, E. A., & Buxton, C. (2014). *Supporting the implementation of NGSS through research: Curriculum materials.* Retrieved from https://narst.org/ngsspapers/curriculum.cfm (accessed November 14, 2014).

Carlson, J., Gess-Newsome, J., Schneider, R. (2014). *Pedagogical content knowledge: Considering models, methods, and recommendations from the PCK Summit.* Paper presented at the American Educational Research Association Conference, Philadelphia, PA.

Collins, C., & Amrein-Beardsley, A. (2014). Putting growth and value-added models on the map: A national overview. *Teachers College Record, 116*(1), 1–32.

CAEP (Council for the Accreditation of Educator Preparation). (2013). *CAEP glossary.* Retrieved from http://caepnet.org/resources/glossary/ (accessed November 14, 2014).

Daehler, K. R., & Shinohara, M. (2001). A complete circuit is a complete circle: Exploring the potential of case materials and methods to develop teachers' content knowledge and pedagogical content knowledge of science. *Research in Science Education, 31*(2), 1–24.

Darling-Hammond, L., Amrein-Beardsley, A., Haertel, E., & Rothstein, J. (2012). Evaluating teacher evaluation. *Phi Delta Kappan, 93*(6), 8–15.

Danielson, C. (2010). Evaluations that help teachers learn. *Educational Leadership, 68*(4), 35–39.

De Jong, O., Van Driel, J. H., & Verloop, N. (2005). Developing preservice teachers' pedagogical content knowledge of models and modelling. *Journal of Research in Science Teaching, 42,* 947–964.

Donovan, M. S., & Bransford, J. D. (2005). Pulling threads. In M. S. Donovan & J. D. Bransford (Eds.), *How people learn: Science in the classroom* (pp. 569–590). Washington, DC: National Academies Press.

Forbes, C. T., Biggers, M., and Zangori, L. (2013). Investigating essential characteristics of scientific practices in elementary science learning environments: The practices of science observation protocol (P-SOP). *School Science and Mathematics, 113,* 180–190. doi:10.1111/ssm.12014

Gess-Newsome, J., Taylor, J. A., Carlson, J., Gardner, A. L., Stuhlsatz, M., & Wilson, C. D. (2011). *Impact of educative materials and transformative professional development on teachers' pedagogical content knowledge, practice, and student achievement.* Paper presented at the annual meeting of the National Association for Research on Science Teaching, Orlando, FL.

Grossman, P. (1990). *The making of a teacher.* New York, NY: Teachers College Press.

Hill, H. C. (2009). Fixing teacher professional development. *Phi Delta Kappan, 90*(07), 470–477.

Justi, R., & Van Driel, J. H. (2005). A case study on the development of a beginning chemistry teacher's knowledge on models and modelling. *Research in Science Education, 35*(2–3), 197–219.

Kanter, D. E., & Konstantopoulos, S. (2010). The impact of a project-based science curriculum on minority student achievement, attitudes, and careers: The effects of teacher content and pedagogical content knowledge and inquiry-based practices. *Science Education*, *94*, 855–887.

Landes, N. M., & Roth, K. J. (2013). *Pedagogical content knowledge for science professional development leaders*. Paper presented at the annual meeting of the National Association for Research on Science Teaching, Rio Grande, Puerto Rico.

Loucks-Horsley, S., Love, N., Stiles, K. E., Mundry, S., & Hewson, P. W. (2003). *Designing professional development for teachers of science and mathematics* (2nd ed.). Thousand Oaks, CA: Corwin Press.

Loughran, J. J., Berry, A., & Mulhall, P. (2012). *Understanding and developing science teachers' pedagogical content knowledge* (2nd ed.). Rotterdam, the Netherlands: Sense Publishers.

Loughran, J., Mulhall, P., & Berry, A. (2004). In search of pedagogical content knowledge in science: Developing ways of articulating and documenting professional practice. *Journal of Research in Science Teaching*, *41*(4), 370–391.

Marzano, R. J. (2012). The two purposes of teacher evaluation. *Educational Leadership*, *70*(3), 14–19.

Nelson, M. M., & Davis, E. A. (2012). Preservice elementary teachers' evaluations of elementary students' scientific models: An aspect of pedagogical content knowledge for scientific modelling. *International Journal of Science Education*, *34*, 1931–1959.

Nilsson, P. (2014). When teaching makes a difference: Developing science teachers' pedagogical content knowledge through learning study. *International Journal of Science Education*, *36*(11). Published online January 27, 2014. Retrieved from http://www.tandfonline.com/doi/full/10.1080/09500693.2013.879621#.VGXfvIdyY8w (accessed November 14, 2014).

Nilsson, P., & Van Driel, J. H. (2011). How will we understand what we teach? Primary student teachers' perceptions of their development of knowledge and attitudes towards physics. *Research in Science Education*, *41*, 541–560.

Russell, T., & Martin, A. K. (2007). Learning to teach science. In S. K. Abell & N. G. Lederman, (Eds.), *Handbook of research on science education* (pp. 1151–1176). Mahwah, NJ: Lawrence Erlbaum Associates.

Sadler, P. M., Sonnert, G., Coyle, H. P., Cook-Smith, N., & Miller, J. L. (2013). The influence of teachers' knowledge on student learning in middle school physical science classrooms. *American Educational Research Journal*, *50*(5), 1020–1049.

Schneider, R. M., & Krajcik, J. (2002). Supporting science teacher learning: The role of educative curriculum materials. *Journal of Science Teacher Education*, *13*(3), 221–245.

Shulman, L. S. (1987). Knowledge and teaching: Foundations of the new reform. *Harvard Educational Review*, *57*, 1–22.

Sleeter, C. (2014). Toward teacher education research that informs policy. *Educational Researcher*, *43*(3), 146–153.

Van Driel, J. H., & Berry, A. (2010). The teacher education knowledge base: Pedagogical content knowledge. In B. McGraw, P. L. Peterson, & E. Baker, (Eds.), *International encyclopedia of education* (3rd ed.; Vol. 7; pp. 656–661). Oxford: Elsevier.

Weiss, I. R., Pasley, J. D., Smith, P. S. Banilower, E. R., & Heck, D. J. (2003). *Looking inside the classroom*. Chapel Hill, NC: Horizon Research Inc.

Wilson, S. M. (2013). Professional development of science teachers. *Science*, *340*, 310–313.

15
SCIENCE TEACHER PCK LEARNING PROGRESSIONS
Promises and challenges

Patricia Friedrichsen
UNIVERSITY OF MISSOURI, USA

Amanda Berry
LEIDEN UNIVERSITY, THE NETHERLANDS

Introduction

A prevailing issue in educational research is how to bring together knowledge developed through different disciplines and disciplinary traditions to inform and improve future learning. For example, research on teacher education and research on teaching would be strengthened if these two separate fields were connected by a common framework.

> Such a framework would help pinpoint both what is common to all examples of teaching, across grade-levels and subject areas—such as the ability to engage and motivate learners—and what is more specific to both the subject matter and the context.
>
> *(Grossman & McDonald, 2008, p. 185)*

Boyer (1990) referred to this type of work as the scholarship of integration. "By integration, we mean making connections across the disciplines, placing the specialties in larger context, illuminating data in a revealing way, often educating nonspecialists, too" (p. 18). Boyer elaborates, "The scholarship of integration also means interpretation, fitting one's own research—or the research of others—into larger intellectual patterns" (p. 19). Schneider and Plasman (2011) responded to the call for a common framework for teaching and teacher education research by connecting the fields of student science learning progressions (LPs) and pedagogical content knowledge (PCK). Using a learning progression approach, they reviewed and summarized the extant PCK literature, proposing PCK LPs across the continuum from pre-service teacher education to teacher leaders.

Near the end of the PCK Summit, a work session on PCK development was initiated. During this session, participants shared how their own research explored the question of how PCK develops over time. Most of the 90-minute session was spent sharing research and we did not reach any consensus on methods for studying science teacher PCK development. At the end of the session, one of us (Pat) suggested extending our discussion of PCK development by reading and discussing Schneider and Plasman's (2011) work on PCK LPs. From the larger PCK development session, we formed a small group which included Rebecca Schneider (co-author of the original paper), Amanda Berry, Rebecca Cooper, and Patricia Friedrichsen. We are all science teacher educators as well as PCK researchers, working in different international contexts. We met virtually several times over the following year, discussing the paper and exploring the promises and challenges of science teacher PCK LPs. These discussions resulted in multiple conference symposia presentations at the National Association for Research in Science Teaching Conference (Berry, Cooper, Friedrichsen, & Schneider, 2013), the European Science Education Research Association Conference (Friedrichsen, Berry, Schneider, & Cooper, 2013) and the Australasian Science Education Research Association (Berry, Van Driel, & Cooper, 2014).

In this chapter, we attempt to re-capture the essence of our discussions around applying an LPs framework to PCK and document the insights we gained about ways of understanding PCK development through this framework. Initially, we found ourselves as either 'enthusiastic cheerleaders' or 'cautious skeptics' of PCK LPs; however, through the process of elaborating and sharing our thinking via collaborative discussion over time, we began to recognize that at least some of our differences were more related to our various interpretations of terminology, or the different contexts of our work, than the actual concept of applying LPs to thinking about PCK development. In the end, we didn't all agree and, consequently, this chapter is presented as a synthesis of our collective thinking about the promises and challenges of PCK LPs.

We have organized the chapter around the three guiding questions that framed our discussions: (1) If we use PCK LPs as a framework for thinking about teacher learning, how does it influence the way we define or organize PCK?; (2) how does this view of PCK frame our instruction and curriculum for teachers?; and (3) how do PCK LPs frame how we document and research teachers' PCK development? We explore each of these questions through the lens of promises and challenges. To begin this discussion, we present an overview of LPs and provide an example of one of Schneider and Plasman's (2011) PCK LPs.

Science teacher PCK LPs

LPs are defined as "successfully more sophisticated ways of thinking about a topic that can follow and build on one another as children learn about a topic over a broad span of time" (National Research Council, 2007, p. 217). Schneider and Plasman (2011) applied the construct of LPs to science teachers as learners. They reviewed the PCK literature from 1986 to 2010, using 91 research articles to construct a set of science teacher PCK LPs, beginning with the Magnusson, Krajcik, and Borko (1999) PCK model components as an organizer. Within each PCK component (e.g., student thinking about science), they created subcategories for individual progressions (e.g., students' initial science ideas and experiences, development of science ideas, how students express science ideas, challenging science ideas, and appropriate level of understanding). The individual progressions within a PCK category align with Corcoran, Mosher, and Rogat's (2009) definition of progress variables of an LP that "identify the critical dimensions of understanding and skill being developed over time" (p. 15). Although the 91 research studies were topic-specific PCK studies, the PCK LPs generalize across the studies. As an example, the LP for students' initial ideas and experiences is given:

> *Progression.* Students do not have initial ideas or experiences relevant to science except for ideas from school (correct ideas) → Students do have initial ideas or experiences relevant to science, but these are misconceptions (wrong ideas) or simply unknown to the teacher → Students have initial ideas or experiences relevant to science and it is important for teachers to know (some teachers can give examples) or uncover these ideas as a place to start or correct, and students' initial ideas may prompt teachers to reevaluate their own (teachers') ideas → Students have initial ideas or experiences relevant to science and it is important for teachers to look for these by listening to students, reading students' work, or reading the literature on students' ideas (rarely) → Students think and develop their own ideas from multiple experiences in and out of school and these ideas are the basis of learning.
>
> *(Schneider & Plasman, 2011, p. 546)*

Schneider and Plasman (2011) indicated the above LP was constructed using the findings from fifty studies representing the teaching continuum, including nineteen studies of pre-service teachers, nine studies of beginning teachers with 0–3 years' experience, eight studies of teachers with 4–10 years' experience, ten studies of teachers with more than 10 years' experience, and four studies of teacher leaders. This example illustrates one of the better represented LPs in terms of number of studies and the spread of teacher experience levels, which is perhaps not so surprising given the science education research community's longstanding interest in students' prior science ideas and their implications for teaching. In the remainder of the chapter, we elaborate our collective thinking about the promises and challenges of these science teacher PCK LPs from our perspectives as science teacher educators and researchers.

Promises and challenges

Guiding question 1: If we use PCK LPs as a framework for thinking about teacher learning, how does it influence the way we define or organize PCK?

Promises

A potentially useful framework

To date, research on PCK in science education appears piecemeal with a reliance on short-term studies. Many PCK studies have been conducted at the preservice and beginning teacher levels documenting the lack of PCK among this population (Abell, 2007; Schneider & Plasman, 2011). Some researchers have studied experienced science teachers, giving us insight into what is possible in terms of highly developed PCK (e.g., Lankford, 2010; Park & Oliver, 2008). Between these two career continuum endpoints, studies have been scattered, giving us fragmented knowledge of PCK development. The field lacks extended longitudinal studies to give us a clear picture of PCK development. For teacher educators and professional developers, whose work focuses on fostering PCK development, this has been problematic.

Schneider and Plasman (2011), through their synthesis of the PCK literature, help us see what we have collectively learned about PCK development. By organizing their synthesis into LPs, they offer the promise of a useful framework for teacher educators and researchers, outlining possible trajectories of PCK development. This raises the question, in what ways does Schneider and Plasman's (2011) work re-define or help us re-conceptualize PCK? To speculate on this answer, we need to first examine how the Magnusson et al. (1999) PCK model shaped past PCK research.

Representations shape our thinking

The Magnusson et al. PCK model, although probably not intentional, often leads researchers to view each PCK component as a separate knowledge base, what we refer to as the silo approach to PCK. For example, a researcher might ask what a teacher knows about instructional strategies for a given science topic. With teaching experience and reflection, the silo of knowledge of instructional strategies begins to fill. Over time, teachers develop *more* knowledge of instructional strategies but how does their *use* of instructional strategies change over time? Is there a pattern across teachers in how their use of instructional strategies changes over their career? Furthermore, how does knowledge about instructional strategies interact and influence the development of other PCK components? The Magnusson et al. PCK model has, in some ways, created a stumbling block for researchers interested in PCK development because the model does not lend itself to showing development over time. The PCK LPs offer us working hypotheses of science teacher PCK development.

Collectively, we see advantages to Schneider and Plasman's (2011) PCK LPs. While the LPs are based on topic-specific PCK studies, they allow us to step back from specific topics and see the bigger picture of science teacher development. This approach helps us move from understanding a science teacher's knowledge of a specific topic to thinking about science teacher development across topics—an approach that seems more useful for science teacher educators and professional developers. The PCK LPs are explicit about how science teacher expertise develops over time. If we adopt PCK LPs, it means we agree with the underlying premise that science teachers tend to progress along a generalized pathway of development. In the next section, we explore some of the tensions that arose in our discussions that helped us identify challenges to using PCK LPs as a framework.

Challenges

Limiting definition of PCK

An immediate challenge lies in the selection of PCK model used to inform the development of the science teacher LPs. Different PCK models may lead to different LP outcomes, emphasizing different components. Schneider and Plasman (2011) selected Magnussen et al.'s (1999) conceptualization of PCK for science teaching to organize their analysis of the PCK literature. Hence, the LPs derived from their analysis represent one (albeit widely held) representation of PCK. Accepting these LPs as representative of science teachers' PCK, and using them as a basis for future research, may limit how we understand PCK as a construct and may possibly lead to a narrowed definition of PCK. An important question therefore emerges as to how different definitions of PCK can be accommodated within an LP framework?

Loss of topic specificity

Central to the notion of PCK that Shulman proposed is its topic specificity (Shulman, 1986): that is, the knowledge that teachers develop about how their students learn specific subject matter or topics and the difficulties or misconceptions that their students have regarding this specific subject matter related to the variety of representations and activities that teachers know about how to teach this specific subject matter (Abell, 2007; Van Driel, Berry, & Meirink, 2014). Further, research in PCK tells us that it cannot simply be 'imported' from one topic area into another (Loughran, Berry, & Mulhall, 2006), since the kinds of difficulties that students encounter vary across different topics and, consequently, so too the kinds of teaching approaches required to address these difficulties.

Although the PCK LPs have been derived from science topic-specific studies, in their current form they are expressed as generalized descriptions of science teacher development for different categories of science teacher knowledge. This form of organization sits in tension with the notion of PCK as topic specific. By moving away from the level of topic and increasing the PCK 'grain size' to the level of the discipline, (i.e., science), what happens to how we define PCK as a construct? Does it lose its topic-specific nature?

Linear, isolated nature of PCK LPs

A further challenge to current conceptions of PCK presented by the LPs lies in their generalized and linear representation of science teacher development. PCK research to date clearly demonstrates that the ways in which teachers build their PCK is a complex, non-linear process that can be quite different from one teacher to another, according to context, situation, and person (Abell, 2007; Mulholland & Wallace, 2005; Padilla & Van Driel, 2011; Van Driel & Berry, 2012). In contrast, the PCK LPs characterize development as continuous, incremental, and stable for each knowledge component, and generalizable across all teachers. By representing PCK in such a way, does it lose some of its core identifying features?

Moreover, PCK is a form of teacher personal knowledge that involves the transformation and integration of different knowledge types. (We recognize that there is still debate on the issue of PCK as transformative or integrative, or a combination: See Kind (2009), for an overview of this issue.) PCK research with experienced teachers highlights the highly integrated nature of their PCK, with teachers drawing on multiple components as they make instructional decisions (Lankford, 2010; Park & Chen, 2012). Studies of beginning teachers indicate that development in one PCK component is often linked to or sparks development in another component (Friedrichsen et al., 2009). A coherent integration among PCK components appears to be critical to teacher development (Loughran et al., 2006). Given these characteristics of PCK, a tension emerges in terms of the representation of the PCK LPs as linear and isolated. Shavelson and Kurpius (2012) reflected on student LPs and cautioned that LPs may not accurately reflect cognition: "Knowledge comes in pieces that seem to be cobbled together in a particular context that calls for a particular explanation; this cobbled together explanation may or may not align neatly with a learning trajectory" (p. 14).

In our group discussions, Schneider acknowledged that PCK component development does not occur in isolation and pragmatic issues necessitated a synthesis of the PCK literature into isolated, linear PCK LPs (personal communication, October 23, 2012). This representational issue is an important one to sort out, that goes beyond merely representing teacher knowledge and learning but goes to the heart of how we think about learning. Hence, an important challenge lies in how to represent the non-linear pathways of PCK development as well as the complex, dynamic integration among the different PCK LP components as

PCK develops. In the next generation of LPs, we need to explore the potential of learning progression maps that might allow us to show the interconnectivity of LPs.

Guiding question #2: How does this view of PCK frame our instruction and curriculum for teachers?

Promises

Multi-domain science methods courses

The PCK LPs offer a promising tool for science teacher educators teaching in multi-domain science methods courses. At various teacher education institutions around the world, it is common practice to group science pre-service teachers (PSTs) from biology, chemistry, physics, and earth science into the same science pedagogy courses. From a PCK researcher perspective, this design is problematic and raises the following question: What are the most effective ways to help heterogeneous groups of PSTs develop PCK?

In many science teacher education programs, teacher educators engage PSTs in model lessons. For example, at the University of Missouri, Pat teaches a 5E series of lessons on diffusion and osmosis (Friedrichsen & Pallant, 2007). She begins with a diagnostic pre-test to assess PSTs' prior knowledge and to make them aware of common misconceptions. In the exploration phase, the PSTs explore the phenomenon using model cells made from dialysis tubing (Lankford & Friedrichsen, 2012). Next, the PSTs make claims about which materials move across the dialysis membrane, supporting their claims with evidence. For the elaboration phase, PSTs apply their knowledge of osmosis in a new context: chemical de-icer used on icy sidewalks killing grass. Formative assessments are used in each phase and PSTs re-visit the diagnostic test items for the summative assessment.

What do PSTs learn from this particular set of lessons? There is anecdotal evidence that the biology PSTs develop some topic-specific PCK. But what do the physics and chemistry PSTs learn? For example, do they learn to explore the phenomenon first or do they remember struggling with the design of the dialysis tubing investigation? Do they learn to engage students in argumentation or do they just remember holding the poster while their biology peers share their group's claims and evidence? Together, the instructor and PSTs unpack the lessons and extract the 'take home messages,' but the physics and chemistry PSTs face the additional challenge of applying these principles to topics in their domain.

Pat tries to address the needs of heterogeneous groups by varying the science content of the lessons, carefully unpacking the model lessons, and having PSTs design and teach lessons in their domain. Several studies indicate PSTs learn science discipline-level PCK in their heterogeneous science pedagogy courses—for example, they learn they should use student-centered, inquiry-based teaching strategies (Brown, Friedrichsen, & Abell, 2012; Demir & Abell, 2010). Based on alignment of the model lessons to their domain, they may or may not be developing topic-specific PCK.

Given the context of heterogeneous grouping in science pedagogy courses, PCK LPs have the potential to be a useful tool. Because the PCK LPs are at the science discipline level, they offer a road map across topics and domains (e.g., physics, chemistry) for science teacher knowledge development. Teacher educators could use PCK LPs to help PSTs reflect on their own development, and to help make explicit for PSTs what to pay attention to, as they develop their practice. PCK LPs could also be a useful supervision tool during field practice and student teaching/internships. At many institutions, graduate students and retired teachers supervise PSTs in K-12 classrooms. The PCK LPs offer generalized trajectories and a common vocabulary, allowing the course instructor, the supervisor, the host teacher, and the PST to communicate about the PST's development. The provision of a common vocabulary resonates with Cohen and Ball's (2007) call for the improvement of mathematics education through establishing a shared language of practice among educators, content specialists, and researchers.

In this way, PCK LPs offer considerable promise in science teacher education by taking us beyond teaching specific topics, helping both teacher educators and PSTs consider the bigger picture of a pathway of teacher development. And, since LPs represent a trajectory of development rather than discrete events (Heritage, 2008), the role of the science teacher educator may be conceptualized as supporting PSTs to begin their own trajectory, one that is personally relevant, productive, and will continue beyond the formal teacher education program.

Professional development

From a professional development perspective, school-based science teachers need ongoing opportunities to develop their knowledge of science teaching and learning to create effective learning environments for their students. However, much in-service professional development tends to be restricted to short-term, discrete 'events' that provide limited opportunities to support the ongoing development of science teachers' knowledge of practice that is specific to their students and contexts (Borko, 2004). The PCK LPs offer a potentially valuable framework for the design of more effective PD programs, that can be organized according to a coherent trajectory of teacher thinking and that can be developed over time and individualized.

In addition, the PCK LPs offer the potential to be a metacognitive tool to support in-service teachers' reflection on their own professional growth and the vision for a target practice. Windschitl and colleagues are engaged in pioneering work using LPs with teachers. In one project, they developed a model-based inquiry learning progression for teachers (Furtak, Thompson, Braaten,

& Windschitl, 2012). They proposed that teachers can: "(1) locate elements of their own practice within the LP and (2) use the 'next levels' on those continua to image what their practice could become" (p. 414). In a second project, the Daphne Project, Furtak et al. (2012) worked with a group of teachers to design a student learning progression for natural selection. The goal of the project was to use the student LP and formative assessment prompts to help the teachers focus on students' ideas and make appropriate modifications to their instruction. Furtak (2012) noted, "several of the teachers seemed to use [student] learning progressions simply as a catalog of misconceptions to be 'squashed' rather than drawing upon the developmental affordances offered by a learning progression" (p. 1181). If we refer back to the PCK LP for student ideas described earlier in the chapter, these teachers could be located at the second level, "Students do have initial ideas or experiences relevant to science, but these are misconceptions (wrong ideas) or simply unknown to the teacher" (Schneider & Plasman, 2011, p. 546). We see the promise of coupling the student LPs with the PCK LPs as a way for teachers to reflect on their own practice. Using the PCK LPs as a reflective tool, these teachers might gain awareness of their current thinking about student ideas and their use of formative assessment which could act as a catalyst to help them move toward the end target: "Students think and develop their own ideas from multiple experiences in and out of school and these ideas are the basis of learning" (p. 546).

Challenges

While the PCK LPs provide useful information that describes the development of teachers' thinking about students' science learning, various challenges emerge in considering their use in informing instruction and curriculum for teacher education. For example, we do not yet know how teachers shift from one level to the next within a learning progression. Is the role of reflection implicit in the LPs, as a type of feedback loop? Or, what kinds of instructional supports (such as tools or scaffolds) or pedagogical approaches might be useful to stimulate progression in a teacher's thinking along a particular knowledge component pathway? Are there some key or critical experiences that learners need to have in order to progress their thinking along a trajectory of development? Also, we do not know about how teachers learn as they move within a trajectory, or whether there is a timing related to the introduction or sequencing of specific LPs or their sub-categories. Specifying what teacher thinking looks like within particular trajectories also does not take into account research to suggest that there may be different 'types' of PCK based on teachers' concerns and purposes for teaching (e.g., Van Driel, Henze, & Verloop, 2008). This means that in their current form, the PCK LPs are rather limited as a means of framing curriculum and instruction for teacher education. Enhancing their "instructional utility" (Furtak, 2009) for educators will therefore be an urgent next step. A further challenge lies in developing approaches that will support integration of different knowledge components, and how this might be differentiated for teacher learning in different contexts, career stages, or within different science disciplines.

From a learning and assessment perspective, the PCK LPs represent a double-edged sword. On the one hand, the LPs offer descriptions of, and a common vocabulary about, science teacher development that may contribute to a more consistent and focused approach to identifying and evaluating teacher development. On the other hand, because the LPs specify progression at a detailed level, they invite potential misuse, particularly in a standards-based learning environment, to espouse "micro-standards" (Wiggins, 2013) of performance, thereby creating narrow definitions of development that do not take into account the different possible pathways that may be followed toward high levels of specialized expertise.

Guiding question #3: How do PCK LPs frame how we document/research teachers' PCK development?

Promises

The PCK LPs hold the promise of an international collaborative research agenda with a common framework for studying science teacher development. Our current path of small, isolated PCK studies in a variety of topics makes it difficult to see the bigger picture of teacher development. If researchers embrace the PCK LP agenda and work together, the potential exists to make tremendous progress in understanding teacher development. If we reach a consensus research agenda around PCK LPs, we propose potential phases of research including: (1) consensus around a set of common PCK assessment tools and filling in the gaps by researching under-studied groups in the teacher continuum; (2) testing, revising, and validating the PCK LPs; and (3) developing and testing teacher education curriculum to support development along the PCK LPs.

Shavelson (2009) expressed the following concern during his keynote address at the Learning Progressions in Science (LeaPS) Conference: "It's the hypothetical and under-researched nature of learning progressions that causes great fear in me" (p. 3). This warning bears repeating for the proposed PCK LPs. While Schneider and Plasman's (2011) PCK LPs represent a synthesis of 24 years of science teacher PCK research, the proposed LPs are only as solid as the literature upon which they were derived. Schneider and Plasman (2011) noted the unevenness of studies across the teacher career continuum with an abundance of studies on PSTs and a scarcity of research on teacher leaders, as well as unevenness across the PCK components and sub-components. For example, "Research on orientations and student ideas was more frequent and research on what teachers think about science phenomena or assessment was uncommon" (p. 540). Based on the scarcity of research in some areas, the authors were unable to propose LPs for some PCK sub-components, including *science phenomena strategies* and *appropriate level of science understanding*. We suggest the initial phase in a research agenda is to reach agreement on a set of common assessments and use those tools to conduct studies to fill the gaps in the literature (i.e., under-represented teacher career stages and under-researched PCK components and sub-components).

Corcoran et al. (2009) define LPs as "empirically grounded and testable hypotheses" (p. 15). Once we have a complete set of testable hypotheses, the next step is to test, revise, and validate the PCK LPs using data from teacher education programs and professional development programs at multiple sites. Professional science education research organizations could play a role in facilitating a collaborative research agenda around PCK LPs.

Shavelson and Kurpius (2012) describe two roads researchers have taken to develop LPs; the first road is the cognition and instruction road, and the second is the curriculum and instruction road. Many of the PCK studies that both Pat and Mandi have engaged in are of the first type—for Pat, describing beginning teachers' PCK development from teaching experience and for Mandi, describing shifts in experienced teachers' PCK development. As researchers, we need to travel both roads. We need to develop and research science teacher education curriculum to develop *educative* PCK LPs for use by science teacher educators. Furtak (2012) describes *educative* LPs as "a form of curriculum material that scaffolds the development of teacher knowledge and practice" (p. 1183). Furtak (2009) suggests four design criteria for LPs that will help support teacher development: (1) accounting of students' ideas as they develop; (2) formative assessment prompts to elicit student thinking; (3) age-appropriate examples of actual student responses; and (4) suggested feedback strategies to move students between levels. These same design principles should be applied to developing *educative* PCK LPs that provide guidance to science teacher educators and professional developers.

Challenges

The goal of developing a common research agenda around *educative* PCK LPs presents challenges on multiple levels. The most obvious challenge is rallying support for this idea. In the US, we can draw a parallel to the task of getting 50 individual states to adopt the *Next Generation Science Standards* (NGSS; NGSS Lead States, 2013). In exploring the promises and challenges of PCK LPs in this chapter, we hope to begin a fruitful discussion about the potential of a common research agenda. If there is agreement around pursuing this goal, a set of practical challenges must be addressed: How does the group create and maintain an organizational structure that allows researchers at all career stages to have input? How would the leadership team be structured? How would research priorities be determined? How would collaboration be fostered? What structures and technology tools need to be in place to support collaboration and information sharing (e.g., database of PCK studies)? To answer these questions we can draw upon the wisdom gained from large-scale international projects in science, from highly successful ones (e.g., European Organization of Nuclear Research [CERN], the Human Genome Project [HGP]) to ones that were not sustainable (e.g., International Biological Program [IBP]).

If consensus is reached around a science teacher PCK LP research agenda and practical organizational issues are worked through, there are still many more challenges. One challenge relates to reaching consensus on the end targets of the LPs. The earlier stages of the PCK LPs appear to reflect teacher thinking in the absence of interventions while the later stages are more reflective of contemporary reform efforts, with some of the LPs lacking end targets due to lack of teacher leader studies. Should the PCK LPs be more explicitly goal-oriented and what should those goals be? "Currently, what 'counts' as advanced pedagogical practice is underspecified" (Furtak et al., 2012, p. 406). In the US, it makes sense to have PCK LPs oriented toward the teaching knowledge and skills needed to fully implement the NGSS (NGSS Lead States, 2013), but a collaborative international research project cannot be driven by one country's policies. Windschitl, Thompson, Braaten, and Stroupe (2012) call for "the development of a set of research-based core practices for beginning educators that are limited in number and represent broadly applicable instructional strategies known to foster important kinds of student engagement and learning" (p. 879). Using model-based inquiry as a framework, they identified four core high leverage teaching practices within this framework. As we debate the promises and challenges of PCK LPs, we need to closely examine the type and number of current PCK LPs to see if they reflect a core set of teacher practices that are both critical to student learning and attainable by teachers.

Conclusion

It is clear that bringing together the previously separate fields of PCK research and research on LPs offers both considerable promise and substantial challenge. In the past, the piecemeal approach to studying PCK and the limitations of the Magnusson et al. (1999) PCK model have made it difficult to understand PCK development across the teacher career continuum. Thinking about PCK development from an LP perspective helps us to make sense of nearly 25 years of PCK research, to look across topics to see generalized pathways of PCK development. As a result, we see utilitarian promise in this grain size for science teacher educators and professional developers.

Yet, we should be cautiously optimistic in proceeding with this work. We have explored a potential research agenda with suggested phases—using common PCK assessments to fill in the gaps in the literature, testing and validating the LPs, and developing and testing teacher education curricula to develop educative LPs. While the LPs are helping us map out the so-far uncharted territory of teacher knowledge development, we should be careful that in specifying the details of the map, it does not become a blue-print that ignores important aspects of PCK as personal, contextual, and topic specific. Allied to this is a concern that the more elaborated the LPs become, the greater the possibility that they become attractive to testing agencies and policymakers whose priorities are typically directed more toward the development of convenient, large-scale evaluation measures of teachers' work, rather than supporting the specific needs of individual teachers.

References

Abell, S. K. (2007). Research on science teacher knowledge. In S. Abell & N. G. Lederman (Eds.), *Handbook of research on science education* (pp. 1105–1149). Mahwah, NJ: Lawrence Erlbaum Associates.

Berry, A., Cooper, R, Friedrichsen, P., & Schneider, R. (2013). PCK learning progressions. In J. Gess-Newsome (Chair), *Report on the PCK Summit: Current and future research directions*. Symposium conducted at the meeting of the National Association for Research in Science Teaching Conference, Rio Grande, Puerto Rico.

Berry, A., Van Driel, J., & Cooper, R. (2014). *Are we headed in the right direction? Emerging issues in PCK research*. Presentation at the meeting of the Australasian Science Education Research Association, Melbourne, Australia.

Borko, H. (2004). Professional development and teacher learning: Mapping the terrain. *Educational Researcher, 33*(8), 3–15.

Boyer, E. L. (1990). *Scholarship revisited*. Princeton, NJ: Carnegie Foundation for the Advancement of Teaching.

Brown, P., Friedrichsen, P., & Abell, S. K. (2012). The development of prospective secondary biology teachers' PCK. *Journal of Science Teacher Education, 24*, 133–155. doi:10.1007/s10972-012-9312-1

Cohen, D. K. & Ball, D. L. (2007). Educational innovation and the problem of scale. In B. Schneider and S. K. McDonald (Eds.), *Scale-up in education, Volume 1: Ideas in principle*. Lanham, MD: Rowman & Littlefield.

Corcoran, T., Mosher, F. A., & Rogat, A. (2009). *Learning progressions in science: An evidence-based approach to reform* (Report #RR-63). Philadelphia, PA: Consortium for Policy Research in Education.

Demir, A., & Abell, S. K. (2010). Views of inquiry: Mismatches between views of science education faculty and students of an alternative certification program. *Journal of Research in Science Teaching, 47*, 716–741. doi: 10.1002/tea.20365

Friedrichsen, P., Abell, S., Pareja, E., Brown, P., Lankford, D., & Volkmann, M. (2009). Does teaching experience matter? Examining biology teachers' prior knowledge for teaching in an alternative certification program. *Journal of Research in Science Teaching, 46*, 357–383.

Friedrichsen, P., Berry. A., Schneider, R., & Cooper, R. (2013, September). Science teacher PCK learning progressions: Promises and challenges. In J. Gess-Newsome (Chair), *Reports from the Pedagogical Content Knowledge (PCK) Summit*. Symposium conducted at the meeting of the European Science Education Research Association Conference, Nicosia, Cyprus.

Friedrichsen, P., & Pallant, A. (2007). French fries, dialysis tubing & computer models: Teaching diffusion & osmosis through inquiry and modeling. *American Biology Teacher, 69*, 22–27. Retrieved from http://www.nabt.org/websites/institution/File/pdfs/publications/abt/2007/069-02-0031.pdf (accessed November 14, 2014).

Furtak, E. M. (2009). *Toward learning progressions as teacher development tools*. Paper presented at the Learning Progressions in Science (LeaPS) Conference, Iowa City, IA. Retrieved from http://education.msu.edu/projects/leaps/proceedings/Furtak.pdf (accessed November 14, 2014).

Furtak, E. M. (2012). Linking a learning progression for natural selection to teachers' enactment of formative assessment. *Journal of Research in Science Teaching*, 49, 1181–1210. doi: 10.1002/tea.21054

Furtak, E. M., Thompson, J., Braaten, M., & Windschitl, M. (2012). Learning progressions to support ambitious teaching practices. In A. C. Alonzo & A. W. Gotwals (Eds.), *Learning progressions in science: Current challenges and future directions* (pp. 405–433). Rotterdam, the Netherlands: Sense Publishers.

Grossman, P., & McDonald, M. (2008). Back to the future: Directions for research in teaching and teacher education. *American Education Research Journal*, 45, 184–205.

Heritage, M. (2008). Learning progressions: Supporting instruction and formative assessment. Washington, DC: Council of Chief State School Officers. Retrieved from the Council of Chief State School Officers website http://www.ccsso.org/Documents/2008/Learning_Progressions_Supporting_2008.pdf (accessed November 14, 2014).

Kind, V. (2009). Pedagogical content knowledge in science education: Perspectives and potential for progress, *Studies in Science Education*, 45(2), 169–204.

Lankford, D. (2010). *Examining the pedagogical content knowledge and practice of experienced secondary biology teachers for teaching diffusion and osmosis* (Doctoral dissertation). Retrieved from https://mospace.umsystem.edu/xmlui/handle/10355/8345 (accessed November 14, 2014).

Lankford, D., & Friedrichsen, P. (2012). Red onions, elodea or decalcified chicken eggs: Selecting and sequencing representations for teaching osmosis and diffusion. *American Biology Teacher*, 74, 392–399. doi:10.1525/abt.2012.74.6.7

Loughran, J. J., Berry, A., & Mulhall, P. (2006). *Understanding and developing science teachers' pedagogical content knowledge*. Rotterdam, the Netherlands: Sense Publishers.

Magnusson, S., Krajcik, J., & Borko, H. (1999). Nature, sources, and development of pedagogical content knowledge for science teaching. In J. Gess-Newsome & N. G. Lederman (Eds.), *Examining pedagogical content knowledge: The construct and its implications for science education* (pp. 95–132). Dordrecht, the Netherlands: Kluwer Academic Publishers.

Mulholland, J., & Wallace, J. (2005). Growing the tree of teacher knowledge: Ten years of learning to teach elementary science. *Journal of Research in Science Teaching*, 42, 767–790.

National Research Council. (2007). *Taking science to school*. Washington, DC: National Academies Press.

NGSS Lead States (2013). *Next generation science standards: For states, by states*. Washington, DC: National Academies Press.

Padilla, K., & Van Driel, J. H. (2011). The relationships between PCK components: The case of quantum chemistry professors. *Chemistry Education Research and Practice*, 12, 367–378.

Park, S., & Chen, Y. C. (2012). Mapping out the integration of the components of pedagogical content knowledge (PCK): Examples from high school biology classroom. *Journal of Research in Science Teaching*, 49, 922–941.

Park, S. & Oliver, J. S. (2008). National Board Certification (NBC) as a catalyst for teachers' learning about teaching: The effects of the NBC process on candidate teachers' PCK development. *Journal of Research in Science Teaching*, 45, 812–834. doi: 10.1002/tea.20234

Schneider, R. M., & Plasman, K. (2011). Science teacher learning progressions: A review of science teachers' pedagogical content knowledge development. *Review of Educational Research, 81*, 530–565. doi: 10.3102/0034654311423382

Shavelson, R. J. (2009). Reflections on learning progressions. Keynote Address presented at the Learning Progressions in Science Conference, Iowa City, IA. Retrieved from http://www.education.msu.edu/projects/leaps/proceedings/Shavelson.pdf (accessed November 14, 2014).

Shavelson, R. J., & Kurpius, A. (2012). Reflections on learning progressions. In A. C. Alonzo & A. W. Gotwals (Eds.), *Learning progressions in science: Current challenges and future directions.* (pp. 13–26). Rotterdam, the Netherlands: Sense Publishers.

Shulman, L. S. (1986). Those who understand: Knowledge growth in teaching. *Educational Researcher, 15*, 4–14.

Van Driel, J. H., & Berry, A. (2012). Professional development of teachers focusing on pedagogical content knowledge. *Educational Researcher, 41*, 26–28.

Van Driel, J. H., Berry, A., & Meirink, J. (2014). Research on science teacher knowledge. In N. Lederman & S. Abell (Eds.), *Handbook of research in science education* (Vol. II, pp. 848–870). New York, NY: Routledge.

Van Driel, J. H., Henze, I., & Verloop, N. (2008). Developing science teachers' pedagogical content knowledge. *Journal of Research in Science Teaching, 35*, 673–695.

Wiggins, G. (2013). Getting students to mastery. *Educational Leadership, 71*(4), 10–16.

Windschitl, M., Thompson, J., Braaten, M., & Stroupe, D. (2012). Proposing a core set of instructional practices and tools for teachers of science. *Science Education, 96*, 878–903. doi: 10.1002/sce.21027

16
GATHERING EVIDENCE FOR THE VALIDITY OF PCK MEASURES

Connecting ideas to analytic approaches

Sophie Kirschner

UNIVERSITY OF GIESSEN, GERMANY

Joseph Taylor

BSCS, COLORADO SPRINGS, USA

Marissa Rollnick

WITS SCHOOL OF EDUCATION, WITS UNIVERSITY, SOUTH AFRICA

Andreas Borowski

UNIVERSITY OF POTSDAM, GERMANY

Elizabeth Mavhunga

WITS SCHOOL OF EDUCATION, WITS UNIVERSITY, SOUTH AFRICA

Introduction

The purpose of this chapter is to explore several ideas about how focused empirical measurement work in science education can provide insight into lingering questions about the structure of PCK. We first summarize leading models for the conceptualization of PCK, highlighting key differences. These differences suggest the merits of a few types of specific analyses of PCK measures, each contributing uniquely to evidence of measurement validity for PCK measures. PCK can be measured in different ways, including written test instruments (open-ended and multiple choice), interviews and videos from the classroom, that are centered on the teacher and the class. Then, as a guiding validity framework, we draw on the work of Messick (1995, 1998) and Thorndike and Thorndike-Christ (2010), focusing on selected types of validity evidence that we assert to be the most salient for PCK research community, which are predictive validity, known groups validity, convergent, structural, and statistical validity.

Theoretical models of PCK

Many researchers, including Kind (2009) and Abell (2007) have argued that there is a lack of consensus about the nature of PCK. This lack of consensus was one of the primary reasons for the Summit and clearly one that needed to be addressed before issues of measurement could be addressed. In the measurement of PCK, it is vital that there is clarity about the meaning of PCK being measured. This does not eliminate the diversity of understanding of the nature of PCK, but it does call on those conducting the measurements to provide clarity on what they are measuring and hence what information the measurements may provide about teaching. Several decisions need to be made prior to carrying out any measurement. The level of specificity of the conception of PCK is critical. The 'C' in PCK implies that the knowledge to be measured has some connection to content knowledge (CK) but the level of generality of that knowledge needs to be defined. Veal and MaKinster (1999) established a taxonomy of PCK that established three levels—general PCK, which was essentially PCK at the level of discipline; domain-specific PCK at the level of sub-discipline, for example physics, chemistry, or biology; and finally topic-specific PCK, which is at the level of topics such as stoichiometry. Mavhunga (2012) argues strongly that PCK differs greatly between topics and hence needs to be measured at the topic-specific level. This view was endorsed at the Summit with the production of the consensus model (see Chapter 3) that defined canonical PCK. Views on more generic approaches could be supported by the definition of personal PCK but by its very nature, personal PCK would be difficult to measure.

Once a level of specificity has been clarified by those doing the measurement, the components of the model need to be defined. Most researchers at this point return to Shulman's (1986) definition which explicitly mentions representations and knowledge of students' learning difficulties as articulated in his much cited quote, "the most useful forms of those representations of those ideas" and "an understanding of what makes the learning of specific topics easy or difficult: the conceptions and preconceptions that students of different ages and backgrounds bring with them" (p. 9). Although there is little disagreement about the necessity of CK as a prerequisite for PCK, there is less agreement about whether it is merely a precursor or a central component.

One of the most widely cited PCK models is that of Magnusson, Krajcik, and Borko (1999) that has been adapted for the purposes of measurement by Park, Jang, Chen, and Jung (2011). Magnusson et al.'s model defines five components of PCK including knowledge of students' understanding of science, science curricula, assessment of science learning, instructional strategies, and orientation to teaching science. CK is not explicitly included, and the way in which Park et al. (2011) have used the model suggests that these authors regard PCK as topic specific. Park et al. also found the model too complex to be used to measure all five components in one study, choosing to focus only on two—knowledge of students' understanding in science and instructional strategies. Borowski et al. (2012) define PCK as a merger between CK and PK (pedagogical knowledge), hence explicitly excluding CK and PK as components of PCK (see Figure 16.1).

Finally Mavhunga's PCK model (Mavhunga, 2012) is drawn from a teacher's ability to transform the content of specific topics into a teachable form. This model is based on Shulman's idea (Shulman, 1987, p. 16) that "comprehended ideas must be transformed in some manner if they are to be taught." Mavhunga's model works with the following five components: (1) students' prior knowledge, including misconceptions; (2) curricular saliency; (3) what makes a topic easy or difficult to understand; (4) representations including analogies; and (5) conceptual teaching strategies. These five components have a content-specific orientation to CK, requiring specific considerations to be made about CK. In this model, topic-specific pedagogical content knowledge (TSPCK) as a theoretical construct is defined as the capacity to transform a specific topic through the five content-specific components. Hence, measurement of PCK using this model implies measuring each of the five components by topic. Figure 16.2 shows how a particular element of CK (topic K) is thought about and reasoned through these content-specific components. Understanding for teaching is generated specific to that topic (K').

The applicability of the various models depends largely on the nature of the construct being measured and particularly on the level of generality of the science content being considered. While Park et al. (2011) worked with two topics—photosynthesis and heredity—Kirschner, Borowski, Fischer, Gess-Newsome, & von Aufschnaiter (2014) and Mavhunga (2012) worked with a single topic, mechanics and chemical equilibrium, respectively. However, the Kirschner et al.

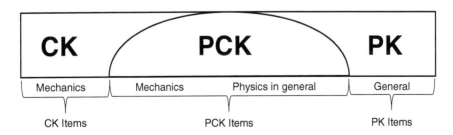

FIGURE 16.1 Model from Kirschner et al. (2014)

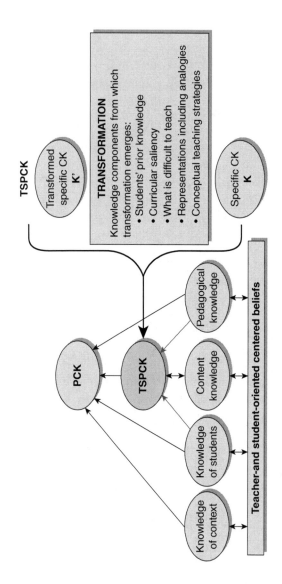

FIGURE 16.2 Mavhunga's (2012) model of TSPCK

instrument measures a whole spectrum of knowledge from pure CK to pure PK, while the Mavhunga et al. model and the Park et al. models measure knowledge and knowledge from teaching practice around specific topics.

Examples of PCK measures

PCK is not only conceptualized in many different ways but it is also assumed that PCK can be measured using metrics of varying formats. Current tools include paper-and-pencil tests with open-ended or multiple-choice questions (e.g., Baumert et al., 2010; Kirschner et al., 2014; Rollnick & Mavhunga, 2014), written tests associated with short (video) vignettes (e.g., Brovelli, Bölsterli, Rehm, & Wilhelm, 2013; Roth, et al., 2011), coding schemes for teachers' written notes about a lesson (e.g., Roth et al., 2011), and interview guides or a coding scheme for a videotaped lesson (e.g., Olszewski, 2010). Other ways to capture PCK are presented in this book. Three measures, constructed by the authors and/or their colleagues, are presented here as examples.

One example of a written test based on video vignettes is the PCK instrument developed for the *Science Teachers Learning from Lesson Analysis* (STeLLA) project (Roth et al., 2011). The STeLLA PCK model suggests that PCK comprises two factors—knowledge of student thinking and knowledge of how to help students construct a coherent content storyline. The PCK instrument used in this project is an innovative video-based lesson analysis task that measures teachers' abilities to analyze teaching practices using PCK related to student thinking and to the science content storyline. Teachers watch between two and four 5–10-minute video clips of science lessons across the target content areas. These video clips are carefully selected from authentic classroom video to focus on specific science content, as well as to include a range of student activity and teacher pedagogical moves. Teachers respond to a prompt to make analytical comments about the science content, the teaching, and/or the students. A rubric is used to code teachers' attention to specific STeLLA strategies and their appropriate use of the strategies, as well as teachers' understanding of more general aspects of PCK (e.g., attention to student thinking, coherence, and content accuracy). The strategies and corresponding rubric elements can be found in Table 16.3. Each line of the rubric is scored 0 (not present), 1 (present but limited understanding or analysis), or 2 (sophisticated analytical understanding).

An alternative measure comes from the physics section of the ProwiN project, where biology, chemistry, and physics teachers' CK, PCK, and PK is analyzed (Borowski et al., 2010). Using the model described above, 17 open-ended, paper-and-pencil PCK items were developed and used with 279 physics teachers (Kirschner et al., 2014). One example of an item is: Why do you need experiments in physics lessons? Expected answers related to the pedagogical/psychological function, the subject related/epistemological function, and the practical function. Answers were coded using a manual with 0, 1, and 2 points, where 1 point was given for partly correct answers or answers from only one category. To get an interval measurement level and to analyze two data sets (from pilot and main study) and coding from two raters together, a partial credit Rasch model (Bond & Fox, 2007; Boone, Staver, & Yale, 2014) was used. Statistical and psychometric indices suggest good instrument function. Different approaches of validation were performed. Besides describing content validity and examining the internal structure with a multidimensional Rasch analysis, criterion validity was analyzed by testing teachers with different school subjects, teachers from different school types, teacher students, and physicists (Kirschner et al., 2014).

In the case of the PCK measures used by Mavhunga (2012), a rubric linking responses to categories (limited, basic, developing, and exemplary) were scored on a scale of 1–4 and also converted to Rasch person measures.

Approaches to thinking about the validity of PCK measures

For the purposes of this chapter, we draw on the validity frameworks of Messick (1998) and Thorndike and Thorndike-Christ (2010) focusing on validity issues most consistent with the state of the field's thinking about PCK. First, one major if not the main theoretical premise behind studying PCK, is that teachers with higher levels of PCK are better able to help students learn (*predictive validity*). In terms of Messick, the extent to which scores from PCK measures are useful in predicting or explaining student achievement is a test of the *external construct validity* of PCK which refers to the extent to which scores from a measure have the expected relationship(s) with other constructs. Thorndike and Thorndike-Christ (2010) refer to this same test as one of *criterion-related validity*. In this same vein, exploring the correlation between scores from multiple instruments that purport to measure the same components of PCK would test their *convergent validity*. Testing whether groups theorized to differ on PCK do indeed have significantly different scores on the PCK measure would test "*known groups*" *construct validity* (Thorndike & Thorndike-Christ, 2010). We highlight the latter as an important use of PCK measures—to distinguish between teachers who have well-developed PCK and those who do not, or to detect growth in PCK over time. Finally, the variability in the theoretical models described above, in terms of the component knowledge bases of PCK, suggests that the field still has much to learn about internal structural relationships of PCK and whether previous attempts to measure PCK have indeed measured the same or similar constructs. Thus, investigating the factor structure of PCK measures could provide much needed evidence of *structural validity* (Messick, 1998). In order to analyze *statistical validity*, researchers need to cross-reference statistical methods with their intended use and investigate whether the required assumptions are met (Shadish, Cook, & Campbell, 2002). In the following sections, we describe several different types of validity explorations, using as examples PCK instruments studied by the authors.

Predictive validity

The field needs more rigorous testing of the relationship between teacher PCK and student outcome data and we assert here that this should occur in a multivariate, multilevel analytic framework. More specifically, as students' outcomes are influenced by many factors, including control variables in the analyses to account for their confounding effects is critical for confident attribution of student outcomes to teacher PCK levels. Student-level variables whose effect should be controlled in a multivariate analysis include prior achievement, pre-knowledge/competency, interest, attitudes, cognitive abilities, motivation, self-concept, socio-economic status, race/ethnicity, language learner status, sex, special education status, and others as available. In addition to their use as control variables, many of these student-level variables are intended outcomes of interventions and could be modeled as such, including analyses of how each might mediate intervention effects on other outcomes. Further, teacher-level variables (characteristics) that are distinct from PCK should be controlled in the analysis when this information is available. Teacher-level variables to control include teachers' CK and PK, beliefs, self-regulating skills, cognitive abilities, motivation, self-concept, and satisfaction.

Another group of potentially confounding variables includes those related to the teaching and learning context. Contextual factors such as teacher turnover, school culture, and school resources can all influence student outcomes. If these variables cannot be controlled analytically as suggested above, researchers can control for them in the sampling design by only drawing participants from schools that are homogeneous on these variables.

In the following section, we describe the types of data needed for various types of validity evidence. Further, a multilevel analytic approach such as hierarchical linear modeling (Raudenbush & Bryk, 2002) allows for the appropriate handling of hierarchical or 'nested' data. Inferential statistics make the assumption that every observation is independent of the observations that precede and follow it. In situations where students or teachers are members of a larger aggregate or cluster (e.g., classrooms, schools, school districts), this independence assumption is often violated. The results from analysis where this nesting is ignored can be quite inaccurate (Moerbeek, 2004).

Known groups construct validity

Known groups validation is administering the same PCK measure with multiple groups hypothesized to differ in PCK. For example, teachers who never taught physics should, on average, get lower scores on a physics PCK measure than a physics teacher. If the results are instead quite similar, that may suggest that the measure is tapping another construct, possibly cognitive ability or general PK. Different groups that could be used for known groups validation of a PCK test for physics teachers are listed in Table 16.1. Note that hypotheses may differ for different knowledge areas or facets of PCK, for example, chemistry teachers or physicists are expected to have more general knowledge about experiments than knowledge of physics-specific student misconceptions.

Convergent validity

For evidence of convergent validity, scores from different measures of PCK can be used; possibly tests (e.g., Olszewski, 2010), interviews, or classroom videos, and correlations (or other relationships) among the data are examined. Some examples of combinations of measure types are found in Table 16.2. For example, we expect a stronger connection between a written lesson plan and the reflection on the lesson than between the same lesson plan and the coding of the lesson (compare row 1). Clearly, the strength of the expected relationships for convergent validity will vary by the types of measures analyzed.

Structural validity

In this section, we briefly describe an example of a structural validity exploration. We return to our STeLLA (Roth et al., 2011) example and describe a factor analysis that sought to examine whether scored teacher responses to the STeLLA PCK instrument correlated to their hypothesized PCK component (factor) in ways consistent with theory. Recall that the STeLLA PCK model suggests that PCK comprises two factors—knowledge of student thinking (Factor 1) and knowledge of how to help students construct a content storyline (Factor 2). In Table 16.3, we provide statistical output from a principal axis factor analysis with varimax rotation. The PCK data were collected over several time points from the first cohort of STeLLA teachers (n = 77). In this analysis, the number of extracted factors was constrained to two.

TABLE 16.1 Test persons for the known groups validation of a PCK test for physics teachers

Test persons	*Hypotheses and reason*
Expert (for example, mentor teachers) and novice physics teachers	Expert physics teachers will score higher than inexperienced physics teachers, *because PCK can be gained by experience.*
Physicists	Physics teachers will score higher than physicists (while controlling CK), *because PCK is not CK but something connected to teaching.*
Chemistry teachers	Physics teachers will score higher than chemistry teachers, *because PCK is at least domain specific and not the same for all science teachers.*
Math teachers	Physics teachers will score higher than math teachers, *because PCK is at least domain specific and not the same for all STEM teachers.*

TABLE 16.2 Hypothesized relationships among data from different PCK measures

Sets of measures with strong relationships expected	Sets of measures with moderate relationships expected	Sets of measures with weak relationships expected
• written lesson plan • reflection on the same lesson	• multiple-choice test • open-ended questions about the same facet of PCK	• written lesson plan • coding of the same lesson
• open-ended questions • think aloud to the same items • questions about how these items were solved and understand	• vignettes about lessons • reflection about your own lesson with similar questions	• multiple-choice test • coding of a lesson
• two similar tests with the same topic and same underlying model	• two similar tests with different topics (e.g., mechanics and electricity)	• two different tests (item format, underlying model, topic)

Note. Every row shows examples of measure sets for which we might expect strong, moderate, or weak relationships among the data. The columns show three different measure sets for the strength of each expected relationship.

The results of the exploratory factor analysis suggest that scores from most of the rating items tend to correlate more strongly with their theorized factor (i.e., student thinking, content storyline) than with the other possible factor. The result of this analysis provides some evidence of theory confirmation and as such, structural validity. The correlations that are not consistent with theory bring into question elements of the PCK theory, including the notion that there are only two latent factors being measured with this instrument. In fact, when the two factor constraint is lifted for this analysis and one uses eigenvalues greater than 1 as a cutoff for reliable factors, the analysis suggest the possibility of six factors in the inherent structure.

The details of this particular factor analysis are not critical. The point of presenting these results is to provide an example of a way of thinking about PCK measurement that could address the ambiguity that lingers about the structure of PCK and the significant inter-correlations that likely exist between theorized components of PCK. In short, we suggest that the field will benefit from additional empirical work that seeks to clarify the inherent structure of PCK.

Statistical validity

Statistical conclusion validity means that statistical methods are well aligned with their intended use and the assumptions of those statistical tests are met (Shadish et al., 2002). Even the most powerful statistical analysis can be undermined by

TABLE 16.3 Rotated factor matrix

PCK rubric elements	Factor		Consistent with theory?
	1. Student thinking (Elements 1–7)	2. Content storyline (Elements 8–16)	
1. Ask questions to elicit student ideas and predictions	0.422	0.321	Yes
2. Ask questions to probe student ideas and predictions	0.607	0.304	Yes
3. Ask questions to challenge student thinking	0.606	0.129	Yes
4. Engage students in interpreting and reasoning about data and observations	0.060	0.185	No
5. Engage students in using and applying new science ideas in a variety of ways and contexts	0.225	−0.041	Yes
6. Engage students in making connections by synthesizing and summarizing key science ideas	0.298	0.103	Yes
7. Engage students in communicating in scientific ways	0.159	0.121	Yes
8. Identify one main learning goal	0.069	0.550	Yes
9. Set the purpose with a focus question or goal statement	0.134	0.511	Yes
10. Select activities that are matched to the learning goal	0.079	0.516	Yes
11. Select content representations matched to the learning goal and engage students in their use	0.272	0.338	Yes
12. Sequence key science ideas and activities appropriately	0.106	0.103	No
13. Make explicit links between science ideas and activities	0.333	0.496	Yes
14. Link science ideas to other science ideas	0.225	0.369	Yes
15. Highlight key science ideas and focus question throughout	0.063	0.654	Yes
16. Summarize key science ideas	0.117	0.260	Yes

unmet assumptions or invalid measurement. In the examples of PCK measures, we highlighted Rasch analysis as a way to process PCK data. Doing so can have multiple benefits. First, inferential statistics such as multivariate hierarchical linear modeling make the assumption that the dependent variable is measured on an equal interval scale. It would be dubious to proceed as if that were the case if the PCK measure included rating scales or multiple-choice items of differing item difficulty. When PCK dimension-specific raw scores are converted to Rasch person measures of PCK, one now has a standardized uni-dimensional metric for that dimension of PCK that is on an equal interval (logit) scale for use in inferential statistics as well as a way to equate across other measures of that PCK dimension. This latter benefit is especially relevant to bringing coherence to the field as researchers continue to use a variety of measures for PCK, with a variety of inherent dimensions. Besides the benefits of Rasch analysis, we have also provided an example of how factor analysis can provide information about the inherent structure of PCK measures and thus the theory upon which they are based. This includes both the nature and number of reliable factors within a PCK measure.

Another approach that is not described in this chapter in detail but is worth mention and consideration is multilevel factor analysis that would take into account nesting of teacher PCK data within a larger context whose influence could be worth estimating. In addition, latent class analysis is a process that identifies unobservable subgroups within a population (Collins & Lanza, 2010). Such a technique could be used to identify common PCK classes or profiles for teachers. Customized professional development could then be designed to meet the specific learning needs of teachers whose PCK levels align to a given latent class.

Outlook

Our community is currently active in the development of PCK measures. Most researchers are collecting important validity evidence for their measures but neither the process nor focus of these validity studies is standardized. One lingering issue is that the connection between PCK and student outcomes often goes unexplored. A group investigating this issue is the Heller group (see Chapter 2). As scholars, we tend to focus much of our resources on learning how to develop PCK in teachers but much less on its relationship to student outcomes. A second limitation in the state of our work is that construct validation is often conducted by comparing scores from a PCK measure with scores from a variety of other criterion measures (like CK and PK) (e.g., Kirschner et al., 2014) and, across studies, these external criterion are not consistent and their measurement is not standardized. Further, there is little consistency in the types of research participants we compare in known groups validity studies. Finally, an underlying assumption of convergent validity studies is that the measures that are being correlated with the measure of interest also have strong validity characteristics. The usefulness of convergent validity studies will not be known until our community has a fuller set of PCK instruments with sound validity evidence to support them. This will require continued effort and dedicated resources toward the development of PCK measures. Up until now, only a few studies have explored convergent validity.

Despite these challenges, we are optimistic for continued progress in PCK measurement. Our optimism is, in part, based on the existing and newly emerging instruments and analytic approaches that can help PCK researchers address lingering questions about validity.

References

Abell, S. A. (2007). Research on science teacher knowledge. In S. A. Abell & N. G. Lederman (Eds.), *Handbook of research in science education* (pp. 1105–1150). Mahwah, NJ: Lawrence Erlbaum Associates.

Baumert, J., Kunter, M., Blum, W., Brunner, M., Voss, T., Jordan, A., . . . Tsai, Y.-M. (2010). Teachers' mathematical knowledge, cognitive activation in the classroom, and student progress. *American Educational Research Journal*, 47(1), 133–180.

Bond, T., & Fox, C. (2007). *Applying the Rasch model: Fundamental measurement in the human sciences* (2nd ed.). Mahwah, NJ: Lawrence Erlbaum Associates.

Boone, W. J., Staver, J. R., & Yale, M. S (2014). *Rasch analysis in the human sciences*. Dordrecht, the Netherlands: Springer.

Borowski, A., Carlson, J., Fischer, H. E., Henze, I., Gess-Newsome, J., Kirschner, S., & Van Driel, J. (2012). *Different models and methods to measure teachers' pedagogical content knowledge*. Paper presented at the ESERA 2011 Conference – Science learning and Citizenship, Lyon, France.

Borowski, A., Neuhaus, B. J., Tepner, O., Wirth, J., Fischer, H. E., Leutner, D., . . . Sumfleth, E. (2010). Professionswissen von Lehrkräften in den Naturwissenschaften (ProwiN) – Kurzdarstellung des BMBF-Projekts [Professional knowledge of science teachers (ProwiN) – A brief outline of the BMBF project]. *Zeitschrift für Didaktik der Naturwissenschaften*, 16, 341–349.

Brovelli, D., Bölsterli, K., Rehm, M., & Wilhelm, M. (2013). Erfassen professioneller Kompetenzen für den naturwissenschaftlichen Unterricht: Ein Vignettentest mit authentisch komplexen Unterrichtssituationen und offenem Antwortformat [Assessing professional competencies for science teaching: A vignette test using authentically complex teaching contexts and an open-ended answer format]. *Unterrichtswissenschaft*, 41(4), 306–329.

Collins, L. M., & Lanza, S. T. (2010). *Latent class and latent transition analysis: With applications in the social, behavioral, and health sciences*. Hoboken, NJ: John Wiley & Sons, Inc.

Kind, V. (2009). Pedagogical content knowledge in science education: Perspectives and potential for progress. *Studies in Science Education*, 45(2), 169–204.

Kirschner, S., Borowski, A., Fischer, H. E., Gess-Newsome, J., & von Aufschnaiter, C. (2014). Assessing physics teachers' pedagogical content knowledge with a paper and pencil test. Manuscript in preparation.

Magnusson, S., Krajcik, J., & Borko, H. (1999). Nature sources and development of pedagogical content knowledge for science teaching. In J. G. Newsome & N. G. Lederman (Eds.), *Examining pedagogical content knowledge: The construct and its implications for science education* (pp. 95–132). Dordrecht, the Netherlands: Kluwer Academic Publishers.

Mavhunga, E. (2012). *Explicit inclusion of topic specific knowledge for teaching and the development of PCK in pre-service science teachers* (PhD thesis). University of the Witwatersrand, Johannesburg.

Messick, S. (1995). Validity of psychological assessment: Validation of inferences from persons' responses and performances as scientific inquiry into score meaning. *American Psychologist, 50*(9), 741–749.

Messick, S. (1998). Test validity: A matter of consequence. *Social Indicators Research, 45*, 35–44.

Moerbeek, M. (2004). The consequence of ignoring a level of nesting in multilevel analysis. *Multivariate Behavioral Research, 39*(1), 129–149.

Olszewski, J. (2010). *The impact of physics teachers' pedagogical content knowledge on teacher action and student outcomes*. Berlin: Logos.

Park, S., Jang, J.-Y., Chen, Y.-C., & Jung, J. (2011). Is pedagogical content knowledge (PCK) necessary for reformed science teaching? Evidence from an empirical study. *Research in Science Education, 41*, 245–260.

Raudenbush, S. W., & Bryk, A. S. (2002). *Heirarchical linear models: Applications and data analysis methods* (2nd ed.). Thousand Oaks, CA: Sage Publications, Inc.

Rollnick, M., & Mavhunga, E. (2014). PCK of teaching electrochemistry in chemistry teachers: A case in Johannesburg, Gauteng Province, South Africa. *Educación Química, 25*(3), 354–362.

Roth, K. J., Garnier, H., Chen, C., Lemmens, M., Schwille, K., & Wickler, N. I. Z. (2011). Videobased lesson analysis: Effective science PD for teacher and student learning. *Journal of Research in Science Teaching, 48*(2), 117–148.

Shadish, W. R., Cook, T. D., & Campbell, D. T. (2002). *Experimental and quasi-experimental designs for generalized causal inference*. Boston, MA: Houghton Mifflin.

Shulman, L. S. (1986). Those who understand: Knowledge growth in teaching. *Educational Researcher, 15*(2), 4–14.

Shulman, L. S. (1987). Knowledge and teaching: Foundations of the new reform. *Harvard Educational Review, 57*(1), 1–22.

Thorndike, R. M., & Thorndike-Christ, T. (2010). *Measurement and evaluation in psychology and education* (8th ed.). Boston, MA: Prentice Hall.

Veal, W., & MaKinster, J. (1999). Pedagogical content knowledge taxonomies. *Electronic Journal of Science Education, 3*(4).

PART IV
Provocations and closing thoughts

17

RE-EXAMINING PCK

A personal commentary

Richard F. Gunstone

MONASH UNIVERSITY

Introduction: A little context

In the latter 1990s, when I was involved in the very early work that led to CoRes and PaP-eRs (e.g., Cooper, Loughran, & Berry Chapter 5, this volume; Loughran, Berry & Mulhall, 2012; Loughran, Milroy, Berry, Gunstone, & Mulhall, 2001), I described PCK as a "seductive" construct. This was a label I chose very carefully as it reflected what was for me, an old science teacher and long-term science teacher educator, the very powerful and intriguingly innate attraction of the construct.

The complete definition of 'seductive' in the Shorter Oxford English Dictionary (5th edition, p. 2736) is surprisingly succinct: "Tending to seduce a person; alluring, enticing," and PCK was all of these for me. Even the very most superficial inspection of the literature of the last 25 years makes it abundantly clear that the 'personal seducing,' 'alluring,' and 'enticing' nature of PCK is seen by very many researchers, from very many and widely varied perspectives, in very many and widely varied contexts, and with very many and widely varied motivations/hopes/concerns/expectations. And it is not surprising that within such a huge range of so many variables there has been considerable variation in understanding of the most fundamental matters, such as: What do I mean when I say 'PCK'? What do I hear/see that I can validly interpret as representing PCK? And other such questions. This has at times been compounded by writing that has not clarified the particular personal understanding of the writer. It has been a variation of sufficient breadth and depth as to lead me to quite some confusion and frustration at times over the last decade and a half. Friedrichsen (Chapter 11, this volume) makes the point succinctly and powerfully: "We cannot make progress in a field that lacks a common conceptualization of the construct being studied." For such reasons, and others that I hope emerge below, I find the essential notion of the Summit and the structure adopted for it both wonderful and potentially remarkably powerful.

In my reading that underpins the following set of personal musings about the idea and actuality of the Summit, the chapters in this book and the post-Summit website, I have been struck by many things. Below I raise some of these—some that I am utterly delighted to find raised in these ways in such work, some that I react less well to, and a couple that I believe ought to have been raised and are not. I make no claim that what follows is somehow comprehensive or systematic or seeking to embed in some broader literature; my choice of 'musings' to describe what follows is very deliberate.

My musings have been focused very much by the second and third of the intended major outcomes of the Summit:

- Conceptual advancement of a consensus model that reflected the perspectives of multiple research approaches. This model would be the result of iterative conversations among participants about the benefits and challenges a unified model may present to individual researchers and to their field.
- "Identification of specific next steps that would move the field forward" (Carlson, Stokes, Helms, Gess-Newsome, & Gardner, Chapter 2, this volume).

The first of these two points, and my expressions of my intermittent confusion and frustration above regarding what some researchers might or might not mean when they use the term PCK and how to recognize PCK in the forms of data we have all at times sought, led me to a beginning thought about the evolution of meaning of new constructs, of emerging ideas. Part of this is the rather obvious point that there is nothing automatic in that evolution being either in a time frame we hope for or toward greater precision.

The development of ideas: Two very different examples

I value a great deal lessons that might be learned from the past to help us understand the dilemmas and problems of the present and future. When it comes to history, I am most certainly not of the Henry Ford school.[1] I lean more toward the notion that "Those who cannot remember the past are condemned to repeat it,"[2] although that is in some contexts just a little too strong for my taste. One of the examples of the development of ideas I now give is from the more distant past, the other is part of the current experience and recent past of all science educators. One is from science itself, the other from science education.

Energy

The ideas embraced by the construct we now ubiquitously label and understand as 'energy' were the overwhelming focus of many of the very best physical scientists on the planet through most of the nineteenth century (e.g., Elkana, 1974). Whether the label used was 'living force' or 'caloric' or 'heat' or 'vis viva' or . . . , clearly there was for very many scientists in this field of inquiry a very broad and very deep and very 'seductive' construct. Some of the intellectual grapplings that have been recorded by scientists of the era are powerfully revealing. For example, the person so central to the development of the idea that we honor him by naming our unit of measurement of energy for him, at times wrote in very oddly anthropomorphic ways. For a period he also wrote internally quite inconsistent 'explanations' for latent heat, and used the term 'living force' in ways sometimes consistent with our current notions of kinetic energy and sometimes to describe some form of impetus property (Joule, 1847/1963). This is in absolutely no way to diminish Joule, it is only to emphasize that the development of this idea took a very long time and involved very many tentative and ill-formed and part formed and re-formed ideas.

What do I see as the relevance of this for this present commentary? First, time is a necessary (and not sufficient) part of the processes of moving toward greater precision in our shared understanding and description of powerful and complex ideas. Second, part of the evolution toward greater precision in the idea has been increasing concern with precision in the use of language around the construct of energy. And third, aspects of the construct are amenable to empirical investigation—that is, part of the development of the construct of 'energy' did involve experimental work, such as the many quantitative studies by Joule on what we came to term the mechanical equivalent of heat. This is in sharp epistemological and ontological contrast with what is plausible to consider in the evolution of meaning for constructs such as PCK.[3]

Scientific literacy

When this idea first emerged in the literature of the latter part of the twentieth century it too was for many science educators highly 'seductive.' It is also clearly much nearer in epistemological and ontological nature to PCK. While definitions have been advanced, and even relatively widely accepted within some countries by some people (e.g., the NSES or OECD/PISA definitions), it is also very clear that in many science curriculum documents around the world and in some research studies reported in the science education literature 'scientific literacy' is being used so broadly it is functionally a synonym for 'science education.'

What do I see as the relevance of this for this present commentary? First, the seductiveness of an idea can lead to such varied forms of meaning/usage that the idea just loses its potential and is sharply diminished in value. Second, the passing of time as new ideas are considered and worked with and reconsidered can lead to divergence of meaning rather than convergence—there is no automaticity in evolution toward greater precision, it can be evolution to greater variation (even chaos).

The ongoing development of the idea of PCK

In seeking to foster the ongoing development of PCK, to generate a 'common conceptualization,' I see issues of significance in my comments above about the relevance of the examples of energy and scientific literacy. In brief these are: Time is needed; time alone is not sufficient (there is no automatic process of convergence of thinking, divergence can and does happen); a 'definition' can often be an unreasonable expectation, a widely accepted 'description' or 'model' is often a more appropriate goal; and part of evolution toward convergence of thinking requires increased common understanding and precision in the use of language around the construct of PCK (I return to this in the next section).

Gess-Newsome (Chapter 3, this volume), early in her extremely valuable account of the "Results of the thinking from the PCK Summit," notes that "Early in our conversations, it became apparent that too many ideas were packed into the construct of PCK." This resonates strongly with me and the ways I interpret the development of (better, lack of development of!) the construct of 'scientific literacy.' At least a significant part of the move away from greater refinement and precision in any commonly agreed conceptualization of scientific literacy has been the extent to which the inherent seductiveness of the idea has resulted in it becoming all things to far too many people (and hence often used as just a synonym for 'science education'). The potential parallels with PCK are clear I think—PCK too has over the last 25 years at times been a victim of its seductiveness, and has for some researchers and policymakers become all things rather than specific and clear things. The Gess-Newsome statement ("Early in our conversations, it became apparent that too many ideas were packed into the construct of PCK"), and a number of closely related points in her chapter, deserve to be writ large in the minds of those who seek to refine our shared understandings of PCK.

Issues of language and ideas in this volume

In a number of the chapters in this volume I see problems with the use of language around the construct of PCK. Friedrichsen and Berry (Chapter 15, this volume) note early in their chapter, in the specific context of Summit discussions around Learning Progressions [LPs] and PCK, that:

> through the process of elaborating and sharing our thinking via collaborative discussion over time, we began to recognize that at least some of our differences were more related to our various interpretations of terminology, or the different contexts of our work, than the actual concept of applying LPs to thinking about PCK development.

I see the problem as much broader than just LP considerations; I see language use as obscuring meaning (and hence reader understanding) in many aspects of the considerations of PCK here. I now give two examples of language use that confused me, the second perhaps quite minor but certainly a fair example of the extent of impact of the point I am making, and the first something I find a major problem.

The use of the term 'measurement'

I find the notion of 'measuring' PCK a genuinely disturbing one—or, perhaps, when this term is used in this book the writers do not really mean 'measure' with the meaning it usually has. While it is the case that I have long ago and very happily abandoned some of the basic tenets of conventional 'educational measurement' as I was taught these over 40 years ago, this abandonment has only been when these tenets clearly offended data and/or logic. A good personal example of such abandonment is the ways in which my professional experience with setting and analyzing system-wide school physics examinations caused me to abandon the notion that reliability is a necessary but not sufficient condition for validity (a very common tenet of conventional Educational Measurement courses and texts). Quite the opposite I came to realize—a focus on high reliability often diminishes validity because it leads to a focus on examining only those things that are easier to reliably measure and so results in ignoring program aims that are much more problematic to assess.

But I cannot see a reason to abandon the very common and very widely accepted meaning for 'measurement'—a quantitatively driven process, the seeking of numerical features to describe some property. This is in contrast with 'assessment,' a label to describe the collection of data (not necessarily quantitative) about some property. I interpret the first paragraph of Gess-Newsome's chapter (Chapter 3, this volume) as reinforcing my point here (although I must emphasize she is writing about something completely unrelated to my point!):

> Educational researchers are interested in how teaching is related to student outcomes. It seems obvious that what a teacher knows should influence how they teach and what students learn. Unfortunately, when examining the relationship between *measures* [emphasis added] of teacher content knowledge (i.e., grade-point average, courses taken, standardized test scores), only weak relationships to student outcomes are found, accounting for less than 1 percent of the variation.

This is not surprising, not for me at least. 'Measures' of teacher content knowledge in the normative form needed to explore quantitative relationships with student outcomes do tend to lead to such simple and gross data forms; it is harder to quantitatively conceive of the subtlety and fine distinction and fine discrimination between differing forms of teacher knowledge that one might hypothesize would lead to differences of substance in student outcomes.

To be blunt, I am not confident I understand what a writer means when they write of 'measuring' PCK. 'Assessment' of PCK I understand, or the weaker 'identification and description,' but both these do not *require* quantitative data (measurement). Data-based judgments of 'better'/'poorer' PCK and suchlike, data-based categorizations of PCK on single or multiple dimensions (something certainly quite adequate for exploring relationships) do not require quantitative data.

My second example of language and the need for precision

This is both quite minor and by itself not an issue. It is an issue for me because of the ongoing consequences of the not uncommon lack of precision in language use around PCK across time which exists well beyond this book. At the end of the first paragraph of the Carlson et al. chapter (Chapter 2, this volume) they write of "a willingness to consider whether or not it was possible to agree to a consensus model for studying PCK." Because of the lack of precision in language elsewhere (across time in writings about PCK as well as other chapters in this volume), and given the intended outcomes of the Summit, I am confused as to whether they mean 'consensus model for studying PCK' or 'consensus model for PCK'—potentially quite different things.

Issues of context and ideas in this volume

I bring a particular perspective to issues of context, for this current task or any other I am undertaking. That is that: (1) Those of us who have backgrounds in science can bring from that discipline notions of it being valuable to generate context-independent knowledge claims; however, (2) it is almost ubiquitously the case that context in science education is a causally determining variable rather than something we should seek to factor out of our thinking. And this perspective no doubt influences my musings in this section.

The impact of the context of the broad professional work of the teacher

I was struck by an almost passing reference in the Cooper et al. chapter (Chapter 5, this volume) to Cooper's doctoral study and that the science teacher educators who were the subjects of her research[4] generated more PK (professional knowledge) than PCK. I now think (and did not at the time I was interviewed) that this is very likely a function of the powerful context that is the professional focus of these teacher educators, the prime purposes they hold for their teaching (or, in the circumstances of these reflections, it is more honest to say "the prime purposes I hold for my teaching").

In my first career as a science teacher, my prime purposes in teaching involved student engagement with and learning of science; even when in my latter years of real and active participation with school science teaching I was beginning to play with metacognitive objectives in my classes, these were at heart about seeking better student learning of science and more engagement with science (e.g., Northfield & Gunstone, 1985). On the other hand, when I taught pre-service science teachers, my primary purposes were about many matters concerned with the development of learner-teachers, and even my metacognitive plans and intentions played out rather differently (e.g., Gunstone & Northfield, 1994). While I often taught science per se with my pre-service students, this was not my primary responsibility toward them nor my primary objective with them. Here in this strong contextual difference I see a plausible explanation for Cooper's finding.

Categories and boundaries and modes of analysis and interactions with what PCK is asserted to be revealed by those modes

This is something I had not thought about for many years, but which has been regenerated in my mind by these chapters. In my work with Loughran and Berry on PCK last century we were (collectively as I recall) rather engrossed with what we termed the 'boundary' issue (I think the only point at which we wrote anything about this was in Loughran, Gunstone, Berry, Milroy and Mulhall (2000)). Working as we were at that time with Shulman's initial seven categories of teacher knowledge we obviously had concern with discriminating between the seven categories. However, the central concern in what we labeled the 'boundary' issue was not this, it was that (in succinct terms) if we 'moved' the boundary between two categories, then all boundaries between all categories were perturbed. The general issue I see from this and in some chapters of this volume, a point about which I am just now starting to think again, is that there is a likelihood that the modes of analysis adopted for the data that seek to reveal PCK themselves impact on the fundamental nature of the PCK asserted to be revealed by these modes of analysis.

The model that evolved through the Summit (Gess-Newsome, this volume, Figure 3.1 and explanatory text)

This model is clearly a significant step forward. Gess-Newsome has written persuasively, succinctly and with great clarity about the model and significant points from the Summit that shaped it. It will have real impact on the further evolution of our shared understanding of PCK.

I have already pointed to the great importance I see in the comment early in the Gess-Newsome chapter about recognition that "too many ideas were packed into the construct of PCK" and the need to avoid the fate I see of 'scientific literacy.' Here I make comment on just a further few issues that particularly struck me as I read this account of the model. These are now listed as they occur in the chapter, and introduced via a relevant quote from the chapter.

"The importance here is not that an exhaustive set of knowledge bases be named, but that we recognize and define the kind of knowledge that falls into this category." At the risk of boring and repetitive overemphasis, here I was struck again by the clear recognition that the value of the construct of PCK lies in its potential to represent powerful ideas not otherwise represented in our lexicon of teacher knowledge and expertise; the construct has little value if it is seen as all things relevant to teacher knowledge and expertise.

'TSPK [topic specific professional knowledge] is clearly recognized as codified by experts and is available for study and use by teachers." As I write this I am still uncertain about some of the set of issues raised in the rich and most valuably intriguing page or so that begins with this quote. The West, Fensham, & Garrard (1985) distinction between public and private knowledge (see also Pines & West, 1986) is one that has had considerable impact on my considerations of learning (particularly science learning and my early work on alternative conceptions and conceptual change) since West first aired this thinking at an ASERA (Australasian Science Education Research Association) conference at Monash University in 1984.

The fundamental point here of seeking to separate 'public' and 'private' teacher knowledge in this PCK context has great appeal to me (yes, I see it as quite 'seductive')—this and the relevant detail advanced in the model may eventually be seen as a real turning point in the development of a cohesive model of PCK and a research field about PCK. The uncertainty I currently have after first reading this (and the other) chapters is powerful testament to the ways in which I have been provoked by this aspect of the model to re-think some fundamental things about my personal view of PCK.

My current uncertainty is about whether or not aspects of the 'public' knowledge laid out in the model are in fact 'public' in the context-free and genuine shared-by-the-whole-field sense that was at the heart of the West et al. thinking, and which is at the heart of the value of the idea in considering PCK. In particular, I am currently still struggling with topic-specific professional knowledge as completely 'public' and so as context free. Of course it is clear that the processes involved in the development of ideas have individual private knowledges that gradually coalesce and over time form public knowledge. It is also clear that this public knowledge is also dynamic. These matters were at the heart of West et al.'s use of the idea of public/private to consider conceptual change. It is also clearly one powerful way of describing the development of the construct of energy that I briefly considered at the beginning of this chapter; in the evolution of complex scientific ideas there always remains a dynamic form of interaction between the developing private knowledge of individual researchers seeking to advance knowledge and the developing public knowledge that is the accepted consensus emerging from the researchers' endeavors.

What I am particularly still grappling with then is, in effect, how valid is the placing of 'topic-specific professional knowledge' in the basket of 'public' and 'context-free' knowledge, and to what extent does this category of knowledge actually represent part of PCK—is there something seriously recursive here?

The beginnings of the later section in Gess-Newsome's chapter titled "Classroom practice: the interaction of personal PCK and the classroom context" raises this issue for me in slightly different ways; in particular:

1. Can a distinction be so clearly drawn between "TPKB [teacher professional knowledge bases] and TSPK [topic specific professional knowledge] . . . as context free, relatively static, visible, and clearly identified as a knowledge base" and the dynamic classroom and the uses of knowledges by the teacher in making decisions?; and, clearly related,
2. What of the dynamic and two-way influences of topic-specific professional knowledge and personal PCK&S on each other?

I suspect there is a major research agenda here.

"Teachers also have a personal knowledge base that might act as an amplifier or filter." Perhaps a quite trivial point, but I was very surprised to find the word "might" here—rather than "might" I would argue this is 'very likely to' for most teachers. For example (one of many), in her thesis research Mulhall (Mulhall & Gunstone, 2012) found very strong filters in the personal knowledge base of physics teachers; in simple terms, teachers seeing physics as unproblematic meant they saw learning physics as unproblematic (and had views of learning that matched this simplicity), while teachers who recognized abstraction and complexity in physics concepts saw learning these ideas as hard (and had essentially constructivist views of learning).

"PCK research has been in progress for the last 30 years." Again at the risk of being boringly repetitive, this concluding section of the elaboration of the model gives a form of context (PCK)-specific account of what I argued earlier about the development of ideas. What I can see the Summit and this model doing is giving new zest to attempts to converge rather than diverge in the ongoing development of the construct of PCK.

Postscript

There are a number of comments made in chapters here about the great value of the Summit as opposed to a standard conference. I want to briefly reinforce this and the very positive consequences of focus (a broadly singular task over the time of the gathering), preparation (everyone thinks and writes beforehand), and giving (in perhaps twee terms this is experiencing the social construction of knowledge through genuine sharing, not writing about it in ways that can sometimes seem to be about protecting one's knowledge). The Monash science education group has generated a number of edited research collections in the same ways—specifically, authors writing draft chapters beforehand, gathering together for an intensive workshop (not talkfest) to discuss and link and seek common themes, and then subsequent rewriting. The first of these was a workshop in 1992 (Fensham, Gunstone, & White, 1994) and there has been an ongoing series this century. The workshops have always been positively described, and some participants have been moved to describe their participation as "the most powerful professional development I have ever experienced." I am a completely unabashed supporter of the approach used in the Summit, and I have absolutely no doubt that such collaborative and focused approaches have much greater benefit for the development of complex ideas than any formal conference can ever achieve.

Notes

1 Yes, it is certain that he did say "History is bunk," along with many other related epithets on the subject.
2 Probably from George Santayana in the early twentieth century, maybe from Edmund Burke in the eighteenth century.
3 There is for me a fourth very relevant point here—that even with the evolution toward great precision etc. with this powerful idea, in my view energy is still not able to be acceptably defined (the standard statement by my fellow physicists that it is 'the capacity to do work' [with work narrowly defined in terms of force and distance] is fine only for mechanical energy, and that is a circular argument anyway); energy is more appropriately thought of in terms of a 'widely accepted description,' but, in the precise meaning of the word, in my view not able to be 'defined.' (You should know too that I have been publically castigated on a number of occasions by other physicists for arguing this position.)
4 I was one of the subjects.

References

Elkana, Y. (1974). *The discovery of the conservation of energy*. London: Hutchinson.
Fensham, P. J., Gunstone, R. F., & White, R. T. (Eds.). (1994). *The content of science*. London: Falmer.
Gunstone, R. F., & Northfield, J. R. (1994). Metacognition and learning to teach. *International Journal of Science Education, 16*, 523–537.
Joule, J. P. (1847/1963). On matter, living force and heat. Reprinted in H. M. Jones & I. B. Cohen (Eds.), *A treasury of scientific prose* (pp.173–187). Boston, MA: Little, Brown & Co.
Loughran, J. J., Berry, A., & Mulhall, P. (2012). *Understanding and developing science teachers' pedagogical content knowledge* (2nd ed.). Rotterdam, the Netherlands: Sense Publishers.
Loughran, J., Gunstone, R., Berry, A., Milroy, P. & Mulhall, P. (2000). *Science cases in action: Developing an understanding of science teachers' pedagogical content knowledge*. Paper presented at the meeting of the American Educational Research Association, New Orleans, LA.

Loughran, J., Milroy, P., Berry, A., Gunstone, R. & Mulhall, P. (2001). Science cases in action: Documenting science teachers' pedagogical content knowledge. *Research in Science Education*, *31*, 289–307.

Mulhall, P., & Gunstone, R. (2012). Views about learning physics held by physics teachers with differing approaches to teaching physics. *Journal of Science Teacher Education*, *23*, 429–449.

Northfield, J. R., & Gunstone, R. F. (1985). Understanding learning at the classroom level. *Research in Science Education*, *15*, 18–27.

Pines, A. L., & West, L. H. T. (1986). Conceptual understanding and science learning: An interpretation of research within a sources-of-knowledge framework. *Science Education*, *70*, 583–604.

ABOUT THE CONTRIBUTORS

Eric R. Banilower is a senior researcher at Horizon Research, Inc. (HRI) in Chapel Hill, NC, and has worked in education for over 20 years. His career started as a high school physics and physical science teacher. During this time he participated in the California Scope, Sequence, and Coordination project developing curriculum and assessment materials for the California science reform project. Currently, he is principal investigator of Assessing the Impact of the MSPs (AIM).

Amanda Berry is an associate professor at ICLON Graduate School of Teaching, Leiden University, in the Netherlands. As a former high school biology teacher, Amanda's research interests are specialist knowledge and practices of science teachers and teacher educators and how they are articulated, shared, and developed to facilitate high-quality student learning. Amanda is associate editor of *Research in Science Education* (RISE) and editor of *Studying Teacher Education*.

Andreas Borowski is a professor of physics education. On completion of his doctoral thesis at the University of Dortmund, Germany he worked as a secondary teacher. His post-doctoral research was with the research group Teaching and Learning of Science at the University of Duisburg-Essen, Germany. He is currently the chair of physics education at the University of Potsdam, Germany. His research interests are based around the connections between the knowledge of teachers, their quality of instruction, and student outcomes.

Janet Carlson began her career as a middle and high school science teacher. She is currently an associate professor (Research) and executive director of the Center to Support Excellence in Teaching (CSET) in the Graduate School of Education at Stanford University following a 23-year history at BSCS (Biological Sciences

Curriculum Study), including serving as the organization's first female executive director. Her research interests include studying educative curriculum materials and transformative professional development.

Rebecca Cooper is a science educator in the Faculty of Education, Monash University, Australia. She works with pre-service and in-service science teachers and her research interests include: considering how science teachers and science teacher educators develop pedagogical knowledge throughout their career; improving the quality of science teaching to increase student engagement; and working with teachers on promoting values in their science teaching in an effort to better understand the development of scientific literacy with students.

Kirsten R. Daehler began her work in science education as a high school chemistry and physics teacher before joining WestEd where she served as the lead teacher in the development of the National Board for Professional Teaching Standards portfolio assessment. Kirsten currently directs the Making Sense of SCIENCE (MSS) project at WestEd. Her research has focused on the dimensions of expert teacher knowledge and the interplay between teacher practice and student learning.

Hans Ernst Fischer[‡] is professor for physics education at the Faculty of Physics at the University Duisburg-Essen and head of the Centre of Teacher Education. His main research focus is on teaching and learning physics from primary to university level and professional knowledge and professional development of pre- and in-service teachers.

Patricia Friedrichsen is an associate professor at the University of Missouri. Pat was a secondary school biology teacher for 13 years before completing her PhD at Penn State. Pat researches secondary science teachers' PCK development with a particular interest in science teaching orientations. She has conducted studies from recruitment of pre-service teachers to beginning teachers to experienced teacher leaders. She is currently a member of the Executive Board for the National Association for Research in Science Teaching (NARST).

April Gardner has spent the last 13 years as a science educator at BSCS following 12 years as a university instructor. Her work has included co-directing a project on the impact of curriculum-based professional development on biology teachers' development of PCK; editing the most recent edition of the BSCS publication. *The Biology Teachers Handbook*; and providing professional development for AP biology teacher leaders. Her interests include increasing the interest and participation of girls in science-related careers.

Andoni Garritz is a professor at the School of Chemistry, National University of Mexico (UNAM). His research focuses on pedagogical chemistry knowledge. Recent publications have centered on amount of substance, stoichiometry, condensed matter bonding, and inquiry. He is part of the National System of Researchers in Mexico, at the highest level and has received four National Prizes from chemistry and engineering associations. He has been a consultant of UNESCO, coordinating chemistry education projects in Latin America.

Julie Gess-Newsome is a professor in science education and the associate dean of Human Health and Wellness at Oregon State University-Cascades. Her career has centered on the preparation and support of teachers and she has received recognition from the National Association for Research in Science Teaching, the Association for Science Teacher Education, and the American Education Research Association for her work. Most recently, she was the dean of the Graduate School of Education at Willamette University in Salem, Oregon.

Richard F. Gunstone[*] is emeritus professor of science and technology education in the Education Faculty, Monash University. He was a high school teacher of physics, science, and mathematics for 12 years. He is editor of the first *Encyclopedia of Science Education* (Springer), a Fellow of the Academy of the Social Sciences in Australia, and a Life Member of the Science Teachers Association of Victoria. He was a recipient of the 2014 NARST Distinguished Contributions to Science Education Through Research Award.

Joan I. Heller is an educational psychologist who specializes in analyzing school-based learning and thinking. Post PhD she directed projects at the University of California, Berkeley then joined the Center for Performance Assessment at Educational Testing Service. She currently directs Heller Research Associates, an educational research firm based in Oakland, California conducting studies that have evaluated publicly and privately funded projects in mathematics, science, data science, and the visual and performing arts.

Jenifer Helms was an assistant professor of science education at the University of Colorado in Boulder and taught high school science in California before becoming an educational consultant and researcher with Inverness Research—specializing in studying improvements in STEM-related formal and informal education programs. She has been the director of education at two nationally recognized informal learning institutions—The Tech Museum of Innovation in San Jose, California and Ocean Journey in Denver, Colorado.

Ineke Henze is a qualitative researcher interested in science teacher professional knowledge and beliefs. Currently, she is an instructor at Delft University of Technology teaching courses on methodology of science teaching focusing on pre-service science teachers' PCK development during school internship. Prior to completing her PhD, she obtained a Master's in chemistry and a Master's in education and child studies from Leiden University. For about two decades she taught chemistry in secondary education.

Heather C. Hill[†] is a professor in education at the Harvard Graduate School of Education. Her primary work focuses on teacher and teaching quality and the effects of policies aimed at improving both. She is also known for developing instruments for measuring teachers' mathematical knowledge for teaching (MKT) and the mathematical quality of instruction (MQI) within classrooms.

Vanessa Kind is reader in education in the School of Education, Durham University, UK. She is currently exploring how differences in teachers' science knowledge, their beliefs and viewpoints about science and personal factors such as self-confidence and attitudes impact on teaching and student learning. She has also been the director of Durham University's Science Learning Centre and has been a teacher and a principal of an international school in Norway.

Sophie Kirschner is a physicist whose main interest is physics education with a particular focus on teacher knowledge and learning. She received her diploma in physics in 2009 at the Goethe University Frankfurt. In 2013 she earned her PhD. at the University of Duisburg-Essen with the dissertation *Modeling and Analysing Physics Teachers' Professional Knowledge*. Since 2013, she has been a postdoctoral researcher at the Justus Liebig University Giessen.

John Lannin[†] is an associate professor of mathematics education following a decade as a mathematics teacher in middle and secondary schools in the state of Nebraska, USA. He is currently the division executive director of Learning, Teaching, & Curriculum and Special Education at the University of Missouri. His research interests are the professional knowledge of teachers and the generalizations that students develop as well as their mathematics justifications.

John Loughran is the foundation chair in curriculum and pedagogy and dean of the Faculty of Education, Monash University. John was a science teacher for ten years before moving into teacher education. John was the co-founding editor of *Studying Teacher Education* and is an executive editor for *Teachers and Teaching: Theory and Practice* and on the international editorial advisory board for a number of other journals.

Elizabeth Mavhunga is a senior lecturer in chemistry education at the University of Witwatersrand, South Africa. Elizabeth initially worked in the chemical industry as a research officer before joining the national initiative for improving science education in South African schools. She has contributed to the development of the Revised National Curriculum Statements in physical science and technology learning. She currently heads a nested research team in TSPCK across science and technology pre-service education.

Kira Padilla has a Master's degree in physical chemistry and a PhD from the University of Valencia, Spain. Her doctoral thesis was about chemistry teachers' thinking related to amount of substance, after which she completed her postdoctoral research on the PCK of quantum chemistry professors at the University of Leiden, the Netherlands. She is currently an associate professor in the Faculty of Chemistry at UNAM, Mexico. Her research interests focus on science teachers' PCK and how this is translated in their practice.

Soonhye Park is an associate professor and program coordinator of science education at the College of Education at the University of Iowa. Park's research interests include teachers' PCK, teacher change, and professional development. She has been leading a number of federal, state, and internally-funded grant projects on teacher development that explicitly seek ways to advance knowledge and skills of teachers and achievement levels of students.

Marissa Rollnick completed her BSc and teaching diploma at Wits University, after which she taught at high school level. She obtained her MSc in chemical education at the University of East Anglia and her PhD at Wits University. She is currently the director and chair of science education at the Marang Centre at the Wits School of Education. Her research interests include language in science and learning of chemistry at the foundation level and subject matter for teaching (PCK).

Rebecca M. Schneider is a professor of science education and director of secondary teacher education at The Judith Herb College of Education at The University of Toledo. She was named the 2012 Outstanding Science Teacher Educator of the Year by the Association for Science Teacher Education. She is one of the lead designers of the Licensure and Master's Program (LAMP), which was selected for the 2014 Outstanding Field Experience Program Award by The Ohio Association of Teacher Educators for an exemplary field experience program.

John Settlage[†] earned his PhD at the University of Missouri after four years as a high school science teacher. He is co-author with Sherry Southerland of the science teaching textbook *Teaching Science to Every Child: Using Culture as a Starting Point*. With Adam Johnston he developed the ongoing conference series *Science Education at the Crossroads*.

Lee S. Shulman is president emeritus of The Carnegie Foundation for the Advancement of Teaching. His work has devoted special attention to the role of PCK, the scholarship of teaching and learning, and on the role of 'signature pedagogies' in education, in the professions, and in doctoral education. He is the Charles E. Ducommun Professor of Education Emeritus and Professor of Psychology Emeritus (by courtesy) at Stanford University.

Aaron J. Sickel is a lecturer in secondary science curriculum at the University of Western Sydney, Australia. A former secondary science teacher, he earned a BSEd and MSEd from Northwest Missouri State University, and a PhD in science education from the University of Missouri (USA). He studies how beginning teachers develop knowledge, beliefs, and practice for teaching science; the affordances and constraints of beginning teacher development; and the interactions between education policy initiatives and science teacher learning.

P. Sean Smith was a high school chemistry and physics teacher and is now a senior researcher at Horizon Research, Inc. (HRI). He led the external evaluations of numerous NSF-funded projects, was the principal investigator of ATLAST (Assessing Teacher Learning About Science Teaching) and is currently the co-principal investigator for the 2012 National Survey of Science and Mathematics Education, a nationally representative survey focusing on the status of the K-12 education system.

Laura Stokes has worked with Inverness Research since 1993, directing studies for a variety projects focusing on teacher leadership, professional development, and systemic reform in literacy and science education. Before joining Inverness Research, she was director of the UC Davis site of the National Writing Project, director of the Composition Program at UC Davis, and Assistant Director of the California Subject Matter Projects at the University of California Office of the President.

Jee Kyung Suh is a PhD candidate in science education at the University of Iowa. She earned her MA in educational measurement and statistics at the University of Iowa and MS in science education at Ewha Womans University in Korea. Her dissertation examined the relationship between teachers' epistemic orientations toward teaching science and their instructional practices, which has had important implications for teacher education and improving the teaching of science.

Joseph Taylor was a high school physics and mathematics teacher before completing a doctoral degree in science education at Penn State University. He has been directing research efforts at BSCS since 2006 and has been a principal investigator on eight federally-funded studies, including funding from the National Science Foundation, US Dept. of Education, and National Institutes of Health. He has expertise in research design, statistics, and measurement.

Jan H. Van Driel is a professor of science education at ICLON, Leiden University Graduate School of Teaching, the Netherlands. Over the last 15 years, his research has focused on the knowledge base of science teachers with studies on PCK of pre-service science teachers about models and modeling coming to the fore. He has published extensively and is currently the associate editor of the *International Journal of Science Education*.

Nicole Wong* is a former school teacher but is now an educational researcher who studies science and mathematics teaching and learning. She is currently a senior research associate at Heller Research Associates providing expertise in qualitative research, including the design, implementation, and analysis of user tests of educational software, cognitive interviews of adults and children, open-ended written assessments, and classroom observations with video documentation.

Note

All contributors are chapter authors and PCK Summit participants unless otherwise noted.
† denotes PCK Summit participant only
* denotes chapter author only

INDEX

Abd El-Khalick, F. 190
Abell, S. K. 67–8, 92
action 10
action research 124–5
activities 90; hands-on 54–5
adaptive expertise 165
affect 9–10, 34–5; chemistry professors' beliefs 75–87
Alant, B. 136
alternative certification project 149–58; challenges 156–8; methodology 150–1; selected PCK development studies 151–6; theoretical framework 149–50
amplifiers and filters: student 31, 38; teacher 30, 31, 34–5
apartheid 135
articulated PCK 127, 130–1
assessment: National Board for Teaching 7–8; of PCK *see* measurement of PCK; of students 85, 122–3, 128, 154, 182–3, 185; of teaching performance 208, 209–10
assessment knowledge 32

Ball, D. 9, 98–9
Bandura, A. 77
Banilower and Smith model 182, 185, 186
Banks, F. 190
Barendsen, E. 127–31
Barnett, C. S. 50

Barnett-Clarke, C. 46
beginning teachers *see* new teachers
beliefs: alternative certification project 151–5; and assessment of PCK 95, 99; university professors' 75–87
Berliner, D. C. 69
Berry, A. 60, 68, 137, 200
Big Ideas 62, 63
Biological Science Curriculum Study (BSCS) 4, 18, 166
biology 4
Borko, H. 148; Magnusson, Krajcik and Borko PCK model *see* Magnusson, Krajcik and Borko PCK model
boundary issue 251
Boyer, E. L. 214
Braaten, M. 221–2
Bromme, R. 180
Brown, P. 152
Bruner, J. 164

canonical PCK 90, 91, 100, 141, 179
canonical science 109–10
Carlsen, B. 7
Carter, G. 77
case discussions 48–52
case studies: alternative certification project 150–1; classroom teaching and PCK development 127–31
categories 251

check of students' understanding 128, 129
chemistry professors' beliefs 75–87
chemistry teacher case study 127–31
Chen, Y. 108
Cheyenne Mountain Resort 21
classroom connections 56
classroom practice: consensus model 31, 36–8, 253; PCK development 125–31; transfer of learned TSPCK to 142–3
clinical diagnosis 5
Cochran, K. F. 189–90
Cochran-Smith, M. 32, 37–8
collaborative learning 57
collective PCK 100–1
Collins, A. 8
common vocabulary 221
community: professional 26, 57, 206, 208; sense of 20
computer-based measurement 116
concept advancement 26
concept mapping 132
conceptual change 154–5, 190
conceptual learning goals 54–5
conceptual understanding 57, 63
conceptualization of PCK 107–10, 114, 118
conferences 14; PCK Summit *see* PCK Summit
consensus PCK model 28–42, 137, 141, 143, 230, 250; classroom practice 31, 36–8, 253; implications for research and professional development 39–40; issues of context and ideas 251–3; PCK Summit 23–4, 26, 29–30; pinning down elusive qualities of PCK 192–3; student amplifiers and filters 31, 38; student outcomes 28, 31, 38–9; teacher amplifiers and filters 30, 31, 34–5; teacher professional knowledge bases 30, 31–2, 34; topic-specific professional knowledge 30, 31, 32–4, 39, 40, 141, 252–3
construct validity 234, 235–6, 239
constructivism 189–90
contemporary learning theory 109–10
content knowledge *see* subject matter knowledge (SMK)
Content Representations *see* CoRes
content-specific strategies 89–90, 93–7

context 10; classroom practice 31, 36–8; issues of 250–3
context specificity 115
contextualization 7–8, 84
continuity principle 164
control of choices 128, 129, 130
convergent validity 234, 236, 237, 239–40
Cook-Smith, N. 209
Cooper, R. 64–7
CoRes (Content Representations) 33, 62, 63–4, 71–2, 98, 127, 210; South Africa 137–8
Council for Accreditation of Educator Preparation (CAEP) 202
Coyle, H. P. 209
criterion-related validity 234
culture 10
curricular knowledge 32, 182–3, 184
curricular saliency 139, 140, 142, 143, 190
curriculum 169, 170, 171, 173
curriculum reform 203–5

Daehler et al. model 183, 190
Daphne Project 222
data collection problems 156
Davidowitz, B. 137, 138
Davis, E. A. 201
decision-making 82; frameworks 126, 131
deductive teaching model 34
Dewey, J. 164
diagnosis, clinical 5
dialogue 158
discourse 169, 170
divergence: in the field 16–17; in PCK research 16
documenting PCK development 223–5
domain definition 8–9
domain specificity 5, 7–8, 11–12, 191
double layer of knowledge 68
Duschl, R. A. 46
Dyer, E. 92–3

education system 207
educative curriculum materials 203–5
educative learning progressions 224
electric circuits 48–50, 52
eliciting PCK 98
emotion 9–10
empty space, concept of 73–4

enacted PCK 45, 58
enactment: measurement of PCK 107, 112–13, 113–14; problem of 126, 132
energy 246–7; flow of matter and energy in living systems 93–7
epistemological beliefs 75–87
Examining pedagogical content knowledge: The construct and its implications for science education (Gess-Newsome and Lederman) 147, 148, 159
expanded papers (EPs) 19–20
experience 64, 138, 147–61
experienced teacher PCK 155–6, 157–8
expert pedagogue 69
external construct validity 234

facets of PCK 89–90, 99, 122, 123; teacher educator's perspective 168–9, 170, 171, 173
facilitation 24–5
Fenstermacher, G. D. 104–5
Fernández-Balboa, J.-M. 189–90
filters *see* amplifiers and filters
fixity of content 84
flow of matter and energy in living systems 93–7
focus, shifts in 67
force and motion 93–7
frameworks: decision-making 126, 131; for science teaching 169, 170, 171, 174
Furtak, E. M. 221–2, 224

Gage, N. 10
Gagnon, M. J. 67–8
Garritz, A. 75–6
general PCK 191
generative topics 167–8
generic teaching strategies 35
Gess-Newsome, J. 16–17, 136–7, 147, 148, 159, 185–6
goals: conceptual learning goals 54–5; knowledge about objectives and 122–3, 128
Gordon, A. 50–1
Grossman, P. 7, 149, 181, 184, 214
Guzey, S. S. 142

hands-on activity 54–5
Hanuscin, D. L. 67–8

Hashweh, M. 7
Heck, D. 92–3
Heller, J. I. 50–1
Henze, I. 122, 127–31
high leverage topics 167–8
Hill, H. C. 98–9, 193
Hodson, D. 122
Horizon Research 18, 92–3

ideas: Big 62, 63; development of 246–8; development of the idea of PCK 248; issues of context and 250–3; issues of language and 248–50; sequencing of 89
identity, professional 12
ideological claim 11, 29
idiosyncratic PCK 109, 117–18
indispensable PCK 109–10; measuring 110–18
inductive teaching model 34
inquiry 169, 170
Institute for Research on Teaching (IRT) 5–6
instructional methods 128, 129, 130
instructional strategies 108, 111, 178–80; PCK development 122–3, 128; teacher educator's perspective 169, 170, 171, 174
integrative PCK 157–8, 185–6, 187–9, 214, 219–20
interactive cognitions 132
international research collaboration 225
interview prompts 62, 63, 101

Jackson, P. 9
Jones, M. G. 77
Joule, J. 247
journal writing 64

Kanter, D. E. 209
Keeley, P. 33
Kennedy, M. 37
Kirschner, Borowski and Fischer model 183, 190, 231–3
knowing–doing gap 126
knowledge domains 149, 189–90
known groups construct validity 234, 235–6, 239
Koballa, T. R. 190
Konstantopoulos, S. 209

Krajcik, J. 148; Magnusson, Krajcik and Borko PCK model *see* Magnusson, Krajcik and Borko PCK model
Kurpius, A. 219, 224

Lampert, M. 9
language, issues of 248–50
Lankford, D. 155
learning: conceptual learning goals 54–5; contemporary learning theory and indispensable PCK 109–10; coupling science learning and science teaching 56–7; professors' beliefs about 79, 84; relationship to teaching 104–5
learning difficulties, students' 89, 178–80
Learning Mathematics for Teaching model 98–9, 193
learning progressions 190–1, 214–28, 248; defining and organizing PCK 217–20; documenting/researching PCK development 223–5; science teacher education 220–3; teacher educator's perspective 163–5, 166
Learning Science for Teaching (LSFT) series 52–5
Lederman 147, 148, 159
Lee, M. H. 67–8
lesson content 128, 129, 130
Licensure and Master's Program (LAMP) 169–72, 173–4, 175
literacy investigations 56
Looking at Student Work intervention 53–5, 56
Loughran, J. J. 33, 60, 137, 200
Lytle, S. 32, 37–8

Magnusson, S. 148
Magnusson, Krajcik and Borko PCK model 28–9, 137, 149–50, 153–4, 217–18, 230–1; challenges relating to use in research 157–8; facets of PCK 89–90, 122, 123; models based on presented at PCK Summit 181–6
main principles of teaching 82–3
Making Sense of SCIENCE (MSS) model 46, 47, 55–7
MaKinster, J. G. 157, 191, 230
Malcolm, C. 136
Marks, R. 187

Marzano, R. J. 208
Math Case Methods (MCM) project 50–1
mathematical knowledge for teaching model 98–9, 193
Mavhunga, E. 142, 143, 183, 230; TSPCK model 139–40, 189–90, 231, 232
McDonald, M. 214
meaning-making 54–5
measurement of PCK 88–119, 202, 229–41; administration, analysis and validation 113–14; conceptual framework and procedures 107–10; design 110–13; emerging dilemmas 114–16; examples 233–4; language issues 249–50; multiple-choice approach 93–7, 99–100; PCK Summit 100–1; rationale for 92–3; research directions 116–18; rubric-type measures 110–11, 112–13, 113–14, 115, 233; shift from PCK portrayal to measurement 104–7; South Africa 139–40; survey-type measure 110–12, 113, 114–15; theoretical stance on PCK 89–92; validity 116–17, 234–40, 249
mentor teachers 153, 155–6
Messick, S. 234
Metacognitive Analysis intervention 53–4
methods courses 201, 220–1
Miller, J. L. 209
misconceptions 94–5
Models of the Solar System and the Universe topic 122–3
modes of analysis 251
moral dimensions 9–10
motion, force and 93–7
Mulhall, P. 60, 137, 200
multi-domain science methods courses 220–1
multilevel factor analysis 239
multiple-choice assessment 93–7, 99–100

National Board for Teaching 7–8, 11
necessity criterion 96
Nelson, M. M. 201
Nespor, J. 77
Netherlands, the 122
new teachers: knowledge and beliefs 152–5; PCK in planning 172, 173–4; well-started beginner 191

Next Generation Science Standards (NGSS) 33, 34, 203, 225
Nilsson, P. 201
non-linearity 219
nothing, concept of 73–4

observation: chemistry teacher case study 127–31; cycle 151; peer 64, 65
observation-based measures 115, 116
Oliver, J. S. 77, 107
open-ended teacher tasks 93–4, 98, 101
orientations *see* teaching orientations
osmosis 220
outcomes: of PCK Summit 25–6; student outcomes *see* student outcomes
outcomes-based curriculum 138

Padilla, K. 75–6
PaP-eRs *see* Pedagogical and Professional-experience Repertoires
paper-and-pencil tests 233–4
Pareja, E. 154
Park, S. 77, 107, 108, 182, 186, 231
particle theory 71–4
passivity, student 83
PCK cases 48–52
PCK development 120–34; classroom teaching 125–31; documenting and researching 223–5; learning progressions and 215, 223–5; research implications 132–3; self-reports 122–5
PCK measures *see* measurement of PCK
PCK models 178–95, 230–3; based on alternative theoretical perspectives 189–91; consensus model *see* consensus PCK model; Kirschner, Borowski and Fischer model 183, 190, 231–3; limitations of Shulman's model 178–80; Magnusson, Krajcik and Borko model *see* Magnusson, Krajcik and Borko PCK model; pentagon model 107–8, 186; presented at the PCK Summit 180–6, 189–91; teacher educator's perspective 168–9, 170, 171, 172, 173–4
PCK and skill (PCK&S) 36–7
PCK Summit 14–27, 29–30, 158; agenda design and structure 21–2; and conceptualization of PCK 109–10; consensus model 23–4, 26, 29–30; effect on South Africa 141–3; factors contributing to success 24–5; intended major outcomes 15, 246; measurement of PCK 100–1; outcomes 25–6; PCK models presented 180–6, 189–91; preparation tasks 19–20; presentation on beliefs 76; primary work during 22–4; rationale for and focus of 15–17; selection of participants 18; selection of setting 20–1; value of the approach 253–4; website 24
pedagogical complexity 51
pedagogical content knowledge (PCK) 3–13; challenges of domain definition 8–9; conceptualization 107–10, 114, 118; domain specificity 5, 7–8, 11–12, 191; evolution of 7–8; facets of *see* facets of PCK; lack of consensus on 98–9, 114; learning progressions and defining and organizing 217–20; limitations of the original formulation 9–10; limiting definition 218; origins 3–6; personal vs canonical 90, 91, 100, 141; policy claim 11, 29; re-examination of 245–55; taxonomy of 157, 191, 230; theoretical stance on 89–92; typologies of 122–3, 124
pedagogical knowledge 32, 66
Pedagogical and Professional-experience Repertoires (PaP-eRs) 62, 63–4, 73–4, 98, 210
pedagogical reasoning 50–1
peer observation 64, 65
pentagon PCK model 107–8, 186
person specificity 115
personal PCK 90, 91, 100, 141; consensus model 35, 36–8, 253
personal views, professors' 78, 79, 80–2
photosynthesis 110–11
physicians 5
planning 82; teacher educator's perspective 169–72, 173–4
Plasman, K. 214, 216, 217, 218, 223–4
plate tectonics 93–7
policy claim 11, 29
policy issues 199–213; curriculum reform 203–5; professional development 206–8; teacher education 200–2; teacher evaluation 208–10

policy trends 200–1, 203, 206, 208
portfolio-based assessment 8
portraying/capturing-mode PCK research 105, 106
Prawat, R. S. 77, 79
precision 250
predictive validity 234, 235
preparation for PCK Summit 19–20
pre-service teachers 172, 173–4; *see also* teacher education
prior knowledge 151–2
priorities of university professors 84
private knowledge 252–3
process–product research approach 6, 126
professional community 26, 57
professional development: consensus model 35, 39–40; learning progressions 221–2; PCK development in the context of a professional development program 124–5; policy issues 206–8
professional development models 45–59; LSFT series 52–5; MSS model 46, 47, 55–7; PCK cases 48–52
professional identity 12
professional knowledge 120–1
professional learning communities (PLCs) 206, 208
program design 169–72, 173–4
prompts 62, 63, 101
ProwiN project 233–4
psychological barriers 126, 131
public knowledge 252–3
Public Understanding of Science syllabus 122–3

quality teaching 104–5
questionnaire on epistemological beliefs 77–80
questions 90; PCK Summit preparation 19–20

reflection 64–5; in action 36–7; on action 36
reliability 249
repertory grid technique 132
replicability 118
representations 90; learning progressions 217–18

research base, thinness of 98–9
research directions 159; capturing PCK in its complexity 132–3; consensus model 39–40; learning progressions and PCK development 223–5; PCK measures 116–18; PCK Summit 26; policy issues 202, 205, 208, 210; professional development 58; teacher educators' PCK 67–8
Resource Folios 63
respect 82–3, 83
Richardson, V. 104–5
Roehrig, G. H. 142
Rogers, M. A. P. 67–8
role, professors' view of 80–1
Rollnick, M. 137, 138, 142, 143, 183, 189–90
rubric-type measures 110–11, 112–13, 113–14, 115, 233

SAARMSTE 136
Sadler, P. M. 100, 209
scaffolding 64, 68
Schilling, S. G. 98–9
Schneider, R. M. 183, 190–1, 214, 216, 217, 218, 219, 223–4
Schwab, J. 4
Schweingruber, H. A. 46
science investigations 55
Science Teachers Learning from Lesson Analysis (STeLLA) project 233, 236–7, 238
science teachers' PCK 60–74; CoRes 33, 62, 63–4, 71–2, 98, 127, 137–8, 210; PaP-eRs 62, 63–4, 73–4, 98, 210
scientific literacy 247, 248
scientific thinking skills 84
scorers 116
self-efficacy 77, 82, 85
self-reports 114–15, 122–5
semantic complexity 51
sense-making, by students 204–5
sequencing of ideas 89
Settlage, J. 166
Shavelson, R. J. 219, 223, 224
shifts in focus 67
Shouse, A. W. 46

Shulman, L. S. 21, 28, 45, 69, 75, 136, 137, 156, 211, 230; address to the PCK Summit 3–13, 22–3, 29, 148, 166; limitations of the Shulman PCK model 178–80
signature pedagogies 11–12, 166
small group discussions 22, 23
small group work 57
Smith, D. C. 67
Smith, S. 92–3
social justice 9–10
Sonnert, G. 209
South Africa 135–46; development of PCK research 136–40; effect of PCK Summit 141–3; influential literature 136–7; science education research climate 136
Spaull, N. 135
spiral curriculum 164
statistical validity 234, 237–9
status problem 17
Stiehl, J. 189–90
stimulated recall 132
Stodolsky, S. 6
strategic knowledge 9
strengths of university professors 81
structural validity 234, 236–7, 238
student amplifiers and filters 31, 38
student outcomes 10, 249; consensus model 28, 31, 38–9
student understanding 108, 111; measurement of PCK 89, 93–7; PCK development 122–3, 128, 129
students: assessment of 85, 122–3, 128, 154, 182–3, 185; learning difficulties 89, 178–80; perceptions of teachers/ professors 82, 132–3; professors' beliefs about 79, 83; teacher evaluation and student learning 208, 209, 210; teachers' knowledge of 32; thinking of 96, 97, 169, 170, 171, 174, 204–5
subject matter knowledge (SMK) (content knowledge) 32, 40; alternative certification project 149–50, 156–7; curriculum reform 204; difficulty in qualitatively assessing 156–7; measurement of PCK and 93–7, 99, 117; origins of PCK 4–6; PCK models 181, 182–3, 187–9; teacher education 201–2; university professors' beliefs 79, 80, 84

subject specialization 138
subject-specific PCK strategies 191
sufficiency criterion 96
Suh, J. 182, 186
survey-type measure 110–12, 113, 114–15
Sykes, G. 7

tacit knowledge 61
Taking science to school: Learning and teaching science in grades K–8 46
Tamir, P. 68, 185
taxonomy of PCK 157, 191, 230
Taylor, M. 92–3
teacher amplifiers and filters 30, 31, 34–5
teacher beliefs *see* beliefs
teacher candidate selection 202
teacher education 250–1; learning progressions and 220–3; policy issues 200–2; program design informed by PCK 169–72, 173–4; progressing 172–5
teacher educators' PCK 64–8
teacher educator's perspective 162–77; framing 163–6; view on PCK 166–8; working model of PCK 168–9, 170, 171, 172, 173–4
teacher evaluation 208–10
teacher experience 64, 138, 147–61; *see also* experienced teacher PCK
Teacher Knowledge Project 7
teacher performance, assessment of 208, 209–10
teacher professional knowledge bases (TPKB) 30, 31–2, 34
teacher professional knowledge and skill (TPK&S) model *see* consensus PCK model
teachers' concerns 124–5
teachers' personal views 78, 79, 80–2
teachers' understanding 107, 111–12, 113
Teaching Cases intervention 53–5, 56
teaching investigations 55
teaching–learning relationship 56–7, 104–5
teaching orientations 152–3; PCK models 181–4; teacher educator's perspective 169, 170, 171, 173; university professors' beliefs 79, 82–3
team-teaching 65–6

think-aloud interviews 112
thinking 10; skills 84; student 96, 97, 169, 170, 171, 174, 204–5; teacher educators 165–6
Thompson, J. 221–2
Thorndike, R. M. 234
Thorndike-Christ, T. 234
topic-specific PCK (TSPCK) 115, 141–3, 231, 232; learning progressions and loss of topic specificity 218–19; transfer across chemistry topics 141–2; transfer to classroom practices 142–3
topic-specific professional knowledge (TSPK) 30, 31, 32–4, 39, 40, 141, 252–3
trajectories 164, 165
transferability of PCK 141–3
transformative PCK 185–6, 187–9
typologies of PCK 122–3, 124

understanding: conceptual 57, 63; students' *see* student understanding; teachers' *see* teachers' understanding
unified model *see* consensus PCK model
university professors' beliefs 75–87

validity of PCK measures 116–17, 234–40, 249
Van Driel, J. H. 68, 76, 201
Veal, W. R. 157, 191, 230
video vignettes 233

Walter, E. 155–6
weaknesses of university professors 81–2
well-started beginner 191
West, L. H. T. 252
WestEd 18
Windschitl, M. 221–2
Wongsopawiro, D. 124–5

eBooks
from Taylor & Francis

Helping you to choose the right eBooks for your Library

Add to your library's digital collection today with Taylor & Francis eBooks. We have over 50,000 eBooks in the Humanities, Social Sciences, Behavioural Sciences, Built Environment and Law, from leading imprints, including Routledge, Focal Press and Psychology Press.

Choose from a range of subject packages or create your own!

Benefits for you
- Free MARC records
- COUNTER-compliant usage statistics
- Flexible purchase and pricing options
- 70% approx of our eBooks are now DRM-free.

Benefits for your user
- Off-site, anytime access via Athens or referring URL
- Print or copy pages or chapters
- Full content search
- Bookmark, highlight and annotate text
- Access to thousands of pages of quality research at the click of a button.

Free Trials Available

We offer free trials to qualifying academic, corporate and government customers.

eCollections

Choose from 20 different subject eCollections, including:

- Asian Studies
- Economics
- Health Studies
- Law
- Middle East Studies

eFocus

We have 16 cutting-edge interdisciplinary collections, including:

- Development Studies
- The Environment
- Islam
- Korea
- Urban Studies

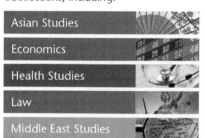

For more information, pricing enquiries or to order a free trial, please contact your local sales team:

UK/Rest of World: **online.sales@tandf.co.uk**
USA/Canada/Latin America: **e-reference@taylorandfrancis.com**
East/Southeast Asia: **martin.jack@tandf.com.sg**
India: **journalsales@tandfindia.com**

www.tandfebooks.com

An environmentally friendly book printed and bound in England by www.printondemand-worldwide.com

This book is made entirely of sustainable materials; FSC paper for the cover and PEFC paper for the text pages.

#0141 - 030915 - C0 - 229/152/15 [17] - CB - 9781138832992